Advance Praise for

ALLIES ACROSS THE BORDER
Mexico's "Authentic Labor Front" and Global Solidarity

"Globalization requires that we develop new ways to organize. Mexico's Frente Auténtico del Trabajo brings trade unionists, members of cooperatives and credit unions, and rural workers together with women's organizations and those fighting for housing rights, all in one organization. The trade union movement and activists everywhere have much to learn from the people Dale Hathaway profiles in this book. Real international solidarity is the best answer to corporate-controlled globalization."

— Bob Clark, General Secretary-Treasurer
United Electrical Workers (UE)

"Dale Hathaway's history of the FAT is essential reading for anyone interested in unions and labor solidarity in Mexico. Organizing in face of massive employer and government opposition and repression, the Authentic Labor Front represents an important development for workers and democratic forces within Mexico. Now, at last, there is a history of the political and philosophical origins of this remarkable insurgent worker and community movement."

—Elaine Bernard, Harvard University
Trade Union Program

"Allies Across the Border is a riveting history of visionary Mexican workers at the forefront of the struggle for a democratic labor movement. Struggling against government repression, corporate power and 'charro' unions, the FAT is an important example for 21st century labor organizing."

—Tom Hansen, Mexico Solidarity Network

Allies Across the Border

Allies Across the Border

Mexico's "Authentic Labor Front" and Global Solidarity

Dale Hathaway

South End Press
Cambridge, MA

Library of Congress Cataloging-in-Publication Data

Hathaway, Dale A., 1951–
Allies across the border : Mexico's "Authentic Labor Front" and global solidarity / by Dale Hathaway.
 p. cm.
Includes bibliographical references.
ISBN 0-89608-633-X (HC) — ISBN 0-89608-632-1 (PB)
1.   Frente Auténtico del Trabajo (Mexico) 2. International labor activities—Mexico. 3. Labor unions—Mexico—Political activity. 4. Mexico—Foreign economic relations. I. Title.

HD8112.F74 H37 2000
322'.2'0972—dc21   00–057343

South End Press, 7 Brookline Street, #1, Cambridge, MA 02139

www.southendpress.org
05 04 03 02 01 00 1 2 3 4 5 6

PRINTED IN CANADA

Table of Contents

Preface

The Mexican *corrido* sings of pain and of pride, of great love, great courage, of great betrayals and heartaches. And in its determination to tell the history of common people who laugh through their tears, the corrido is a testimony to a people's determination that what is most important—their dreams, their dignity—will survive. The corrido's rhythmic structure allows for the most basic of guitar accompaniment. And its simple melody allows people to easily catch the words and to sing along, as though the history were their very own.

David García Hernandez of Leon insisted that I have a copy of one of his corridos celebrating the history of the FAT. It never seemed to fit into the structure of this book's historical narrative, but it captures much of the spirit of what this book has been about for me. It sings of "fighting with honor to defend the rights of workers." It sings of the "terrible austerity tormenting the people" and the determination to fight on "under the torch of insurgency." Though the lyrics may sound awkward to those of us raised on US pop music, when I heard it, it sounded mighty fine. I could join in with it as though its history were a part of my own.

I thought of this song as I wrote this book and as I followed the reports of the anti-WTO demonstrations in Seattle in 1999. "The Battle in Seattle" put the issue of working peoples' rights in the global economy at the top of the news. What the media did a bad job of portraying was why so many people were in the streets. They portrayed the involvement of organized labor groups as simply an effort to save US jobs. What they didn't get was that US workers had begun to identify with the life stories of workers in Mexico and Indonesia, South Africa and China, in a way that made their stories part of the same song. What is exciting is that the FAT, despite its relatively small size, has been doing a great job of spreading that song throughout the Americas.

The goal of this book is to help readers, through a combination of history, economics, political analysis, and lots of stories of the lives of Mexican workers, to see that workers everywhere are caught up in the same global economic system, even if it sounds different in different countries. Its goal is never to inspire pity for "those poor oppressed people," but to offer a new understanding and familiarity, which is the basis of real solidarity.

I was fortunate to have a sabbatical that allowed me to spend major portions of 1996 and 1997 in Mexico getting to know the people of the FAT, their struggles and their visions. Two grants from Butler University allowed me to journey to Mexico since then, to stay in touch and to expand my research. I have to thank Robin Alexander of the United Electrical Radio and Machine Workers of America (UE) for getting me started on this project. I thank all the FAT activists throughout Mexico who opened up their archives, their memories, their homes, and often their hearts to me. Their assistance, as well as that of other Mexican labor activists and Mexican academics, allowed me to gain firsthand knowledge of the histories recorded here. While I have tried to cite all secondary sources I have used in developing this record, readers will find many uncited quotations. These remarks come from direct interviews or from direct observations I have made.

It is important to note that while I am indebted to the FAT and the UE for making my work possible, all judgments made in this book are ultimately mine and should not be taken to represent the thinking of the FAT or the UE unless explicitly stated.

Finally I need to give special acknowledgment and warm *abrazos* to both Benedicto and Jorge, who have become important parts of my own song; to note my fatherly pride in Forest, whose growing involvement with Mexico has made it natural that he see his fellow workers in fast food establishments not as illegals but as friends; and to recognize my deepest gratitude to my beloved Dot, without whose encouragement, support, and love this book would not have been possible.

Principal Acronyms

ANAD   Asociacion Nacional de Abogados Democraticos
National Association of Democratic Lawyers

CEFOCEM   Centro de Formación del Estado de Morelos
Workers Training Center of the State of Morelos

CDP   Popular Defense Committee
Comite de Defensa Popular

CETLAC   Centro de Estudios y Taller Laboral, Asociacion Civil
Study Center and Labor Workshop, Non-Profit Organization

CIPM   Coordinadora Intersindical Primero de Mayo
May First Inter-Union Coordinator

CISC   Confederación Internacional de Sindicatos Cristianos
International Confederation of Christian Unions

CJM   Coalition for Justice in the Maquiladoras

CLASC   Confederación Latino Americano de Sindicalistas Cristianos
Latin American Confederation of Christian Unionists

CLAT   Congreso Latino Americano del Trabajo
Latin American Labor Congress

CMT   Confederación Mundial de Trabajadores
World Federation of Labor

CNTE   Coordinadora Nacional de Trabajadores de Educacion
National Coordinator of Education Workers

CODIM   Centro de Organizacion y Desarollo Integral de Mujeres
Women's Center for Integral Development and
     Organization

COR   Confederacion de Obreros Revolucionarios
Revolutionary Workers Confederation

CRISA   Congeladora del Rio
River Freezer-Plant, Inc.

CROC	Confederacion Revolucionario de Obreros y Campesinos Revolutionary Federation of Workers and Peasants
CROM	Confederacion Regional de Obreros Mexicanos Regional Confederation of Mexican Workers
CSN	Confederation Syndicale National National Union Confederation (of Canada)
CT	Congreso del Trabajo Congress of Labor
CTM	Confederacion de Trabajadores Mexicanos Federation of Mexican Workers
EZLN	Ejercito Zapatista de Liberacion Nacional Zapatista Army of National Liberation
FAT	Frente Autentico del Trabajo Authentic Labor Front
FDN	Frente Democratico Nacional National Democratic Front
FESEBS	Federacion de Sindicatos de Bienes y Servicios Federation of Goods and Services Unions
FOCEP	Frente de Obreros, Campesinos, y Estudiantes Popular Popular Workers', Peasants', and Students' Front
Foro	Foro: El Sindicalismo Ante la Nacion Forum: Unions Facing the Nation
ILO	International Labor Organization
IMF	International Monetary Fund
IMSS	Instituto Mexicano de Seguro Social Mexican Institute of Social Security
INFONAVIT	Instituto de Fomento Nacional de Viviendas para Trabajadores National Worker Housing Institute
JOC	Juventud Obrera Catolica Catholic Working-Class Youth
MSF	Movimiento Sindical Ferrocarrilero Railworkers Union Movement
NAFTA	North American Free Trade Agreement
NAO	National Administrative Office (created by NAFTA)
PAN	Partido de Accion Nacional National Action Party

PCM   Partido Comunista Mexicano
             Mexican Communist Party

PRD   Partido Revolucionario Democratico
             Democratic Revolutionary Party

PRI   Partido Revolucionario Institucional
             Institutional Revolutionary Party

PRM   Partido Revolucionario Mexicano
             Mexican Revolutionary Party

PROVISA   Union de Productores de Vidrio Plano, S.A
             Union of Producers of Plate Glass of the State of Mexico,
                  Incorporated

PT   Partido del Trabajo
             Labor Party

RMALC   Red Mexicana de Accion Frente al Libre Comercio
             Mexican Action Network Confronting Free Trade

SME   Sindicato Mexicano Electricista
             Mexican Electrical Union

SNTE   Sindicato Nacional de Trabajadores de Educacion
             National Educational Workers Union

SNTIHA   Sindicato Nacional de Trabajadores de la Industria Hierro y
                  Acero
             National Union of Iron and Steel Workers
                  (part of FAT)

SNTSS   Sindicato Nacional de Trabajadores del Seguro
                  Social
             National Union of Social Security (Health Care) Workers

SSM   Secretariado Social Mexicano
             Mexican Social Secretariat

STERM   Sindicato de Trabajadores Electricistas de la Republica
                  Mexicana
             Union of Electrical Workers of the Mexican
                  Republic

STFRM   Sindicato de Trabajadores Ferrocarrileros de la Republica
                  Mexicana
             Railroad Workers Union of the Mexican Republic

STIMAHCS	Sindicato de Trabajadores de la Industria Metal-Mecanica, Acero, Hierro, Conexos y Similares Union of Metal-Mechanic, Steel, Iron, and Related or Similar Industries Workers (part of FAT)
STRM	Sindicato de Telefonistas de la Republica Mexicana Telephone Workers Union of the Mexican Republic
STUNAM	Sindicato de Trabajadores de la Universidad Nacional Autonoma de Mexico Union of Workers of the Autonomous National University of Mexico
SUTERM	Sindicato Unitario de Trabajadores Electricistas de la Republica Mexicana Union of Electrical Workers of the Mexican Republic
SUTIN	Sindicato Unitario de Trabajadores de la Industria Nuclear Nuclear Workers Union
SUTSP	Sindicato Unico de Trabajadores de la Secretaria de Pesca Union of the Workers of the Secretary of Fisheries
TD	Tendencia Democratica Democratic Tendency
TLC	Tratado de Libre Comercio Free Trade Treaty (NAFTA)
UE	United Electrical, Radio and Machine Workers of America
UNAM	Universidad Nacional Autonoma de Mexico National Autonomous University of Mexico
UNT	Union Nacional de Trabajadores National Workers Union
UOI	Unidad Obrera Independiente Independent Worker Unit
WTO	World Trade Organization

Chronology

1521	Cortez defeats last Aztec emperor, Cuauhtemoc, and claims Mexico for Spain and the Catholic church.
1821	Mexican Independence proclaimed by conservative Iturbide; he declares himself emperor in 1822.
1836	Texas becomes independent from Mexico.
1846-48	U.S. wages war; gains New Mexico, Colorado, Arizona, Utah, Nevada, and California.
1861	Benito Juarez becomes first indigenous president; liberal reforms erode Church and landowner elites.
1862-67	Conservatives invite French domination; Archduke Maximillian of Austria reigns as emperor.
1867	Republic restored under Juarez; anti-clerical laws, liberal economic policies spur some development and end communal lands.
1876-1911	Dictatorship of Porfirio Diaz; economic development by and for foreign elites under advice of the científicos.
1906	Strike at Cananea copper mine crushed by U.S. and Mexican troops.
1907	Bloody repression of Rio Blanco textile strike.
1910-24	Mexican Revolution ends Porfirian era.
1917	Mexican Constitution adopted, guarantees ejido and land reform; right to organize unions, to strike, and to receive adequate wage for an 8-hour day; Catholic church barred from politics and education; subsoil minerals declared patrimony of the nation. Agri-biz magnate Caranza becomes President.
1919	Carranza has peasant leader Emiliano Zapata ambushed and killed.
1924	Plutarcho Elias Calles peacefully elected president.
1926-29	Cristero rebellion.

1929	President Calles constructs the National Revolutionary Party (later PRI) which controls government until 2000.
1934-40	Lazaro Cardenas, president; conducts aggressive land reform, assures constitutional minimum wage, protects right to strike, nationalizes oil, incorporates unions and peasant organizations into the ruling party.
1958-64	Adolfo Lopez Mateos, president.
1958-59	Railworkers movement to resist government domination of their union ended by armed repression.
1958	Founding of Catholic Working-Class Youth (Juventud Obrera Catolica - JOC,) and Promoción Obrera (Workers' Promotion).
1960	Oct. 18, founding of the Authentic Labor Front (FAT).
1962	FAT organizes its first unions in Guanjuato state: shoes in Leon, textiles in Irapuato.
1963	FAT organizes its first unions in Chihuahua.
1964-70	Gustavo Diaz Ordaz, president.
1968	Massacre at Tlatelolco kills hundreds of students; Olympics held; FAT unions in Chihuahua and Leon face repression.
1970-76	Luis Echeveria Alvarez, president.
1970-76	Insurgencia Obrera – Workers' Insurgency.
1973	U.S. workers average hourly wage reaches peak, decline begins.
1974	FAT leads or advises strikes at Cinsa-Cifunsa in Saltillo, Aceros de Chihuahua, Alumex glass plant, Rivetex in Cuernavaca. Union at HILSA in Leon becomes independent of CTM and joins FAT.
1975	121-day strike at Spicer.
1976	Mexican minimum wage reaches peak, decline begins.
1976-82	Jose Lopez Portillo, president.
1982-88	Miguel de la Madrid, president.
1982	Mexico accepts International Monetary Fund plan as basis of its economy; governmental prioritizes exports over domestic economy.
1984	FAT-affiliated union PROVISA opens as plate glass cooperative.
1986	Mexico joins GATT.
1988-94	Carlos Salinas de Gotari, president; his defeat of the PRD's Cuauhtemoc Cardenas is widely regarded as fraudulent.
1990	Salinas proposes NAFTA.

1991	FAT helps found anti-NAFTA coalition RMALC; FAT-UE Strategic Alliance begins.
1994	Jan.1, NAFTA comes into effect and Zapatista rebellion begins in Chiapas.
1994-2000	Ernesto Zedillo, president.
1995	Economic collapse, peso loses half its value; Salinas flees country; official May Day labor march canceled.
1997	PRI loses control of lower house of Congress and government of Mexico City; death of Fidel Velasquez, leader of CTM since 1936; UNT formed.
2000	Vicente Fox Quesada of the PAN is elected president; FAT wins recognition of new unions in service sector and transportation.

1.

Encounters in the Global Economy

"This is what democracy looks like!" shouted the demonstrators as they marched through the streets of Seattle protesting the week-long 1999 World Trade Organization (WTO) meeting. Television viewers and newspaper readers worldwide saw daily coverage of marches festooned with giant puppets, environmentalists dressed like turtles marching side-by-side with thousands of union members, and religious activists and black-clad anarchists chanting "Whose streets? Our streets!" Long-shoremen joined in by shutting down ports from Alaska to San Diego. Protestors who blockaded intersections met a fierce assault from police using tear gas, rubber bullets, and clubs.

The thousands of insistent world citizens gathered in Seattle for teach-ins, marches, and civil disobedience demanded that their vision for an egalitarian global economy be recognized as more democratic than the track record of the WTO. The World Trade Organization, virtually unknown to most people before the Seattle protests, has coordinated and enforced global trade policies since 1995. In its short existence it has earned a reputation for running roughshod over labor and environmental rights as well as national sovereignty. Congressman David Bonior told the demonstrators: "Business domination through the WTO looks to the people like an effort to take away their power of decision making. People see it as a threat to democracy."

The WTO's opening ceremonies, including speeches by Secretary of State Madeleine Albright and UN Secretary-General Kofi Annan, had to be canceled when only 500 of the 3,000 WTO delegates could get through the blockade. After the first few days of protests, President

Clinton shocked official delegates by abandoning his earlier suggestion of a mere "working group" to study the effect of trade on labor, replacing it with a call to include core labor rights enforceable by sanctions in future trade agreements. While some of his staff rushed to clarify that that was not what he really meant, and many within the labor movement doubted his sincerity, it was clear that decision-makers worldwide were hearing the protesters' message.

The WTO adjourned in chaos. Efforts to force a face-saving agreement failed when delegates from Third World nations—left out of the meetings of "important" countries and emboldened by the demonstrators' calls for more democratic trade relations—refused to accept decisions they had not influenced. In the meeting rooms as well as the streets, democracy was breaking out all over.

Reflecting on labor's contribution to the Seattle protests, John Sweeney, president of the AFL-CIO, said that the meeting's breakdown was a "breakthrough in the public debate over globalization." The broad coalition in Seattle had insisted that "the global economy must be fundamentally changed to respect people and the environment, and not just the interests of multinational corporations. That new international coalition will redouble its efforts ... to generate broadly shared prosperity and foster democratic and equitable development around the world."[1]

The new international coalition of which Sweeney spoke had been ignored in most media coverage. It had been most evident not in the street demonstrations but in the dozens of forums held around Seattle, often in local churches that saw their mission as one of spreading social justice. Panels on biotechnology, indigenous rights, human rights, farming, labor organizing, and intellectual property featured an international array of experts and activists. They had the information to concretize an alternative to the unquestioned corporatization of the planet. Though the media paid them scant attention, preferring to focus on window-breakers they condemned as thoughtless Luddites,[2] these hundreds of alternative world leaders proceeded in their work of informing and organizing those interested in a vision greater than generating profits. These sophisticated leaders did not reject a global economy; rather, they pointed out the need to build an environmentally sustainable global society in which human rights and human dignity were preconditions for progress. They condemned the sort of "progress" that had spread devastation in their communities.

"What is good for a Ford worker in Detroit must also be good for a worker in South Africa. And it must also be good for a Ford worker in Hermosillo, Mexico," a representative from the South African Labor Network told the crowd at one of the many rallies.[3] Testifying to the Mexican opposition to the WTO, Manuel Mondragon told how transnational corporations close plants in the United States and Canada, then routinely deny workers in their new Mexican factories the right to form meaningful labor unions; dump toxins into waterways; and expose workers to debilitating chemicals that cause birth defects in their children.

David Foster of the United Steel Workers commended the protestors and spelled out a new tactic for US labor: "We are proving that the mobilization of the people can change history.... Our objective is to raise the standard of living of workers in every part of the world; we aren't just interested in protecting the US market."[4]

Jeff Crosby, president of the United Electrical Workers Local 201, went to Seattle with 15 members of the Massachusetts North Shore Labor Council. Reflecting on the events, Crosby wrote, "Trade unionists in the U.S. don't exist in a vacuum, and we see ourselves more clearly when we see ourselves in relationship to others." He recalled that economists had predicted that global trade would result in the loss of low-skilled manufacturing jobs. Now he was seeing *skilled* assembly and engineering jobs in the aircraft engine business go abroad to Mexico, Russia, China, and Brazil. But he added, "We've come a long way from thinking that the answer is just to 'Buy American.' "[5]

Citizens of the World

The "Battle in Seattle" was not an isolated event. Although it was the first time the media had actually been forced to cover the burgeoning movement to democratize the global economy, the most progressive unions in Canada, Mexico, and the United States have been working together for years. The 1993 fight over NAFTA (the North American Free Trade Agreement) brought together labor, environmentalists, peace activists, and faith-based movements for economic justice. By 1997, it had already claimed a victory in blocking the secret move for a Multilateral

Agreement on Investment (MAI) that then WTO head Renato Ruggiero had called "the constitution of a single global economy."[6] The trouble with this constitution was that only the rights of corporations were to be protected. Although the coalition had not been strong enough to block or meaningfully influence the shape of NAFTA, it had managed to block the president's ability to extend it or other such treaties with fast-track authority.

Fast-track authority would allow the president and his appointees to negotiate new trade agreements and bring them to Congress for an up or down vote without amendments. In the past this meant that trade ministers consulted regularly with corporate lobbyists but refused to even meet with labor, environmental, or human rights organizations. Treaties such as NAFTA, born of a clearly anti-democratic process, reflected only the interests that had shaped them. However, beginning with the anti-NAFTA fights, the coalition of the excluded had been growing. Networks throughout Canada, the United States, and Mexico developed. Over time they connected with their counterparts throughout the Americas and beyond, building on preexisting networks of labor unions, environmentalists, women's organizations, human rights groups, and religious organizations. They had stopped cold President Clinton's 1994 pledge to extend NAFTA from the Bering Straight to Tierra del Fuego. Now, drawing on resources throughout the world, they were in a position to insist that the WTO could no longer exist without broader public participation.

Cai Chong Guo, an exiled Chinese labor organizer, explained to Seattle activists that part of China's rapid economic growth was based on preventing the formation of unions not controlled by the government. Independent organizers there routinely face long jail sentences. Disappointed by the recent decision of the US government to promote China's entry into the WTO with no discussion of human rights, he told listeners, "We had hoped to count on your political leaders, but now we know our base of solidarity and support is you, the working people of the USA." At another gathering, retired Longshoreman Howard Key Cook seemed to echo Cai Chong Guo's perspective, "For the first time, large numbers of workers are thinking globally. We can't solve our problems nationally anymore—we need international solidarity and support."[7]

Many international politicians rejected the protesters' involvement. Claiming to speak for the citizens of their countries, they appealed to the word, "democracy," using it to bolster claims that according to the laws and procedures of their countries, they could legitimately speak for their citizens. They had been legally elected or appointed. Mexican commerce secretary Hermino Blanco Mendozo insisted, "We cannot let those interests contaminate the agenda of the WTO with labor and environmental themes."[8] Egyptian trade minister Youssef Boutros-Gali distrusted all the talk of international solidarity. "The question is, Why all of a sudden, when Third World labor has proven to be competitive, why do industrial countries start feeling concerned about our workers? When all of a sudden there is concern about the welfare of our workers, it is suspicious."[9]

The question is a pointed one. Why should a US worker care about a worker from Egypt, or China, or Mexico? Is the stated concern of US labor for their international cohorts sincere? One might equally well ask, do the governments of those countries care about workers? Activists in Seattle understood that governments are often more responsive to global corporations than to their own citizens. They, as citizens of the world, were in turn organizing to have a voice in the structures that were emerging to govern much of life throughout the planet. Annie Decker, blockading one of Seattle's intersections, spoke for many when she explained her realization, "Trade and the power of corporations are affecting us in so many areas that we can all make connections and see common elements behind the problems we share."[10]

Activists, with great awareness of the power of money and repression to influence elections, appointments, and policies, preferred to speak of democracy in terms of policies that reflected the interests of the majority of the people. In every country this majority of the people consists of workers, farmers, and students, who often suffer from the results of their government's policies—policies that seem to be increasingly influenced by forces operating at the level of the global economy.

Representatives of these majorities were in the streets and in the public forums of Seattle, not behind the closed doors of the WTO. When they shouted, "This is what democracy looks like!" they spoke on behalf of the majorities of the world who had been excluded. By exchanging information and building new alliances, they sought to build the basis of a more democratic global society.

Economic Realities

Seattle was a battle over economic changes of tremendous historic import. As with previous changes—from village society to feudal society, from feudal society to the rise of industrial nation-states—the strong attempted to seize the lead and force others to follow. While global trade has existed for thousands of years, the WTO is part of an effort to build a corporate-dominated global society that is shifting power from nation-states to the new corporate lords of a global society. This shift began to take shape in the 1970s.

The post-World War II economy that had been dominated by the United States became steadily more competitive in the 1960s as both Western Europe and Japan recovered from war-time devastation. In countries as different as the United States and Mexico workers' wages had risen steadily through the '50s and '60s. Yet economies throughout the world got shaky in the 1970s as oil-producing countries formed the Organization of Petroleum Exporting Countries (OPEC) and drastically raised the price of oil in 1973 and again in 1979.

In the United States, corporations that had grown powerful but complacent in their decades of dominance now faced stiff energy bills; competition from abroad, especially in the market for efficient cars; and a wave of consumer regulation stirred by the expansion of activist participatory politics in the 1960s. They organized to retake the political establishment of the country through a vast increase in political contributions, lobbying, and public propaganda.[11]

In 1972, A.W. Clausen, CEO of Bank of America, on his way to becoming head of the World Bank, wrote:

> The business world has been watching with great interest the development of international economic institutions such as the International Monetary Fund, World Bank, International Finance Corporation, General Agreement on Tariffs and Trade, international private banks, and multinational corporations ... [that] demonstrate a growing substitution ... for what once had been virtually total dependence on political institutions.[12]

Soon after this article appeared, the first experiment in rebuilding a country to fit the new global economy took place in Chile. Until the early 1970s Chile had the longest tradition of democratic politics in all of Latin America. It was a democracy at least in the minimal sense that for over a hundred years elections, not military coups, determined who would rule. The country was not wealthy, but economically it was one of the more advanced Latin American nations. As education and communication increased in the country, a higher percentage of people got involved in politics. In that sense it was becoming more democratic.

Workers organized labor unions, and they became more involved in a variety of parties on the left. To prevent an outbreak of "too much" democracy, the US government worked through the CIA to influence the elections of 1958 and 1964 to assure that the socialist candidate, Salvador Allende, would not win. They tried to do the same in 1970, but the Chileans prevailed and elected him anyhow.[12] As Allende instituted economic reforms favored by his working-class supporters, US corporations and the US government did what they could to bring him down. In September 1973, they helped provoke a military coup that resulted in the immediate death of Allende and 3,000 other Chileans and established the dictatorship of Augusto Pinochet that lasted 16 years.

Pinochet had many eager advisers in his efforts to reorient the Chilean economy. Chile became the laboratory for the "Chicago Boys," protégées of right-wing University of Chicago economist Milton Friedman, who believed that the primary definition of freedom was market freedom.[13] Regarded by many as simplistic, the Chicago Boys believed people with money should be allowed to buy, sell, and invest with no interference from government and that anything that got in the way, such as government efforts to reduce poverty or to direct investment, should be done away with.

Pinochet found their theory consistent with his own instincts. He had built his career within a military that had close ties to the country's wealthy elites. These ties were only strengthened by his Cold War training, which identified hungry people organizing for change, not as fellow citizens but as agents of a global communist conspiracy. Pinochet acted quickly to eliminate unions and eviscerate labor protections. He sold off all state-owned enterprises to the highest bidder and did whatever he could to make Chile attractive to those with money to invest, mostly foreigners. In the meantime many Chileans starved. Malnutrition soared.

Chile became an economic "miracle." With wages and regulations sliced to the bone, investment skyrocketed, as did exports. Chile became the model for how to make an economy grow—regardless of the consequences its workers suffered. Chile even led the world in doing away with its system of social security and replacing it with private investment accounts. Since 1981 Chilean workers have been required to invest 10% of their monthly earnings in the privately managed investment fund of their choice. The government waives taxes on these accounts, but eventually it will have no other responsibility to the worker's retirement. Employers have none. The funds have had the direct effect of strengthening Chile's investment capital resources.[15] Businesses have already won. While it is still to early to judge how workers will fare under this market-based system, initial studies show that much of the funds' good rates of return have been gobbled up by expense fees, that women will do far worse than men under the new system, and that many will qualify only for the minimum required benefit, about three quarters of the minimum wage, hardly enough to live on.[16]

Most of the world condemned the dictatorship of Pinochet and the barbaric freedoms championed by the Chicago Boys. In the 1950s and '60s countries such as Vietnam, Angola, and Zimbabwe had fought to throw off the rule of colonial powers. In the 1970s, governments representing the majority of the earth's population—those living in nations referred to as the South or the Third World—were demanding something they called a New International Economic Order. From Indonesia to India, from Nigeria to Nicaragua, they wanted the rich nations of the North—those that had been the first to industrialize and that had used their industrial advantages to colonize the rest of the planet—to give something back. They used their majority voice in the United Nations to argue for a democratization of the world's economy. They wanted investment from the North to serve the peoples of the South. They wanted better prices for their goods and a more stable supply of food. Several European nations, energized by former German chancellor Willy Brandt, joined in calling for global reforms. So did progressive voices in the United States.[17]

In 1981 Brandt urged leading nations of both the North and the South to meet at the plush resort town of Cancun, Mexico. Encouraged by the presence of Socialist Party leader François Mitterand, the newly elected president of France, Brandt proposed to establish mechanisms for charting the New International Economic Order through the United Nations. The recently elected US president, Ronald Reagan, would have none of it. And he did not care if his manner was upsetting to others. After publicly joking about Latin Americans being late for everything, he arrived 15 minutes late for the formal start of the meetings. He proceeded to say that the only hope for developing economies was to make themselves more attractive for international investors. He would consent to further discussions not through the United Nations General Assembly, which was dominated by the poorer nations of the world, but through the World Bank and the International Monetary Fund (IMF), which were dominated by the United States.

Many world leaders treated Reagan with embarrassed tolerance, as a cowboy, as an actor, not as a politician. Surely he couldn't be serious. But the tide was turning in Reagan's favor. Mitterand's initial pro-worker reforms in France were cut short by a massive flight of capital that did not return until he demonstrated his willingness to administer a capitalist economy under pro-capitalist rules. In 1982 Mexico agreed to abandon its nominally populist economic policies for a pro-corporate investor policy. This was not due to a coup, as in Chile, but was conditioned by the IMF and administered by a staff of Mexican economists educated in US schools teaching the erstwhile radicalism of the Chicago Boys as the new orthodoxy.

The world had taken a new course. In the United States both Presidents Carter and Reagan allowed the Federal Reserve to fight inflation by cutting workers' real wages. An economy that had seen nearly three decades of rising wages, declining poverty, and declining income inequality now saw poverty rise, workers' real wages fall, and the gap between the rich and the poor widen. The worldwide democratic and economic development that had characterized the post-War and Vietnam eras had given way to elite greed and government austerity.

The same story held true in Mexico. Average incomes had risen until the mid-1970s when they spent a few years fluctuating before heading down as a result of government policy to set wage increases based on expected inflation rather than actual inflation. When inflation regularly exceeded government estimates by 20 to 25%, the purchasing power of workers' wages steadily fell. This was not seen as a problem by US-educated government economists, nor by advisers at the IMF and World Bank, as lower wages should make international investment more likely. International investment, especially in export-oriented industries, was seen as essential to pay off the foreign debt, payments which often exceeded half of all earnings from the export sector. As countries like Mexico were driven to increase exports, countries like the United States saw employment in manufacturing steadily shrink.

The bottom line for workers is that the mid-1970s marked a significant turnaround. In the United States, the average hourly worker's wage in the private sector, $12.77 in 1998, could buy 10% less than what that wage bought in 1973. In Mexico the minimum wage is the most broadly applicable indication of workers incomes since many wages are tied directly to it. In 1998 it was worth $3(US) a day. It could buy only a quarter of what the minimum bought at its peak in 1976.

Forces operating in the international economy stimulated changes in both developed and developing economies that tended to lower workers' wages in all countries while strengthening the power of international finance and transnational corporations. This was all justified as efficiency by a new economic orthodoxy, known to many as neoliberalism, that focused on business earnings over human needs, on individual investors over societies.

Measured in terms of Gross Domestic Product, many countries that adopted these new ideas saw economic growth take off after an initial period referred to by the economists as "shock treatment." Yet many other countries, like Mexico, have seen an unsteady mixture of years of growth and years of decline since adopting the new measures. In all cases, however, it is clear that any growth generated was absorbed by those in upper-income sectors and by foreign lenders. For many workers, even the "good" years were years in which their incomes continued to decline.

To bring about these changes, labor unions have been attacked in nearly every country. This is why workers from throughout the world gathered in Seattle to demand a voice within the WTO. All these years of following policies supposedly aimed at helping economies grow had been accompanied with fine words and increasing hardships. Out of necessity, workers began to organize internationally to confront their common problems and to try to exercise some of that glorious democracy of which their politicians loved to speak.

Hector Arellano, head of the building trades council in El Paso, Texas, claims that "the goal of NAFTA and other trade deals is to make it possible to step on workers of all countries with equal ease." He has been spending more time in recent years talking with labor activists from south of the border. He says, "We've been working together long enough that now we aren't just unionists but friends. And friends will do a lot for each other."[18]

Global corporations long ago declared that nations were obsolete. More recently workers have begun to find allies around the world. This history of Mexico's Authentic Labor Front, known by its Spanish initials, FAT (rhymes with "hot," not "cat"), is offered to help that process along. The FAT has been at the center of coalitions formed throughout North America and beyond since at least the early 1990s. Understanding its story will help the rest of us understand what is happening throughout the world. We are all in this together. In North America, it is time that working people come to understand our common situation.

The FAT has been in existence since 1960. Since that time, it has been struggling to increase the wages and improve the working conditions of Mexican workers and to help them achieve a sense of dignity and control over their own lives. In order to do that it has had to wage a constant battle against the government-controlled labor system. When the US and Canadian governments and corporations agreed to NAFTA, they agreed to accept that oppressive system. Many of the corporate executives who have since set up plants in Mexico with government-backed unions see several advantages to such a system. In the long run, they may hope to borrow some of its features for use at home. After all, if they are to continue increasing corporate profits faster than workers' wages, they may need some way to limit the power of workers back home in their "democracies." The goal of this book is just the opposite: to add energy and ideas to those who would make a world with greater democracy and more broadly shared prosperity.

Organizing International Labor Solidarity

Tom Lewandowski is from Fort Wayne, Indiana. He spent years working in a General Electric plant there and became involved in his union. In 1990, as the Cold War was falling apart, Fort Wayne decided to form a sister city relationship with Plotz, Poland. Due to his family heritage and his labor ties, the city council asked him to go to Plotz, establish connections, and report back about the Solidarity labor movement that had challenged the Communist Party for power. It was an interesting era. While the federal government and business leaders were busy breaking unions throughout the United States, they were happy to support a labor union in Poland that might bring down part of "the Evil Empire."[19]

Lewandowski did go, and when he came back he arranged for seven Polish workers to come to Fort Wayne, to work in a factory, and to see how labor unions in the United States did their work. He also found the media were very interested in this story and became adept at getting workers to tell their own stories. This, he found, was the best way to break down stereotypes and develop concerns that crossed borders.

In 1993, as the battle for NAFTA geared up, Lewandowski was disturbed by the xenophobia he heard directed at Mexican workers. Mexicans were described as lazy, dirty, stupid, and hopelessly inept workers. Yet these same Mexicans were somehow going to steal all the jobs that people in the United States counted on. It didn't make sense. He decided it was time to meet some Mexican workers.

Through a bit of investigation he got in touch with the FAT. He had them send an organizer, Ezekiel Garcia, to Indiana for a visit. Tom Lewandowski drove Garcia to union halls around the state and let him tell his story of what life was really like for Mexican workers. Lewandowski saw how Garcia's direct contact and real information transformed suspicious workers into solid allies. Lewandowski made sure the press got the story, too. As workers around the state were informed about how NAFTA was not likely to help workers in either country, they contacted their congressional representatives, and they made a difference. Eight of Indiana's ten representatives voted against NAFTA.

In 1994 Fort Wayne was part of the national trend in congressional elections, replacing its Democratic representative with a new conservative Republican, Mark Souder. Yet Lewandowski won his ear and now swears that he has as much influence over Souder as anyone on international trade issues.

In 1997 with a vote on fast-track authorization approaching, Lewandowski suggested to Souder that he actually go to Mexico and see what conditions were like. Eventually he convinced him and 15 other Republicans to consider going and passed the trip details on to the AFL-CIO. As Lewandowski tells it, the AFL-CIO was so unused to dealing with Republicans that the trip never came to pass, but that did not matter. Lewandowski and Souder had moved the 15 far enough that House Speaker Newt Gingrich knew he could not count on their support in what promised to be—at best—a close vote. The vote was never held that year.

Lewandowski, now the head of the North East Indiana Central Labor Council, was able to organize a group of local workers for a "Visit Your Jobs" tour of the Mexican border area near Reynosa and Matamoros, just south of McAllen and Brownsville, Texas. He brought along a TV crew from the only unionized station in Fort Wayne. Their half-hour program showed the *maquiladoras*, the gleaming new multinational factories that were absorbing jobs from back home, the foul chemical stews oozing out of these factories into open waterways, some of the many children born with birth defects associated with environmental poisons, and the squalid living conditions of highly productive workers earning $5 a day. Response to the program was so strong that they have rebroadcast it several times.[20]

Matamoros: Disabled Babies on the Border

Matamoros is an industrial city of nearly 350,000.[21] Its industrial parks have wide, well-lit streets paved with concrete. The discharge flowing out of many of its factories carries foul smells. The young men and women who work in the maquiladoras (maquilas for short) live in tiny houses, some made almost entirely of cardboard and shipping palettes. The maquilas are 98% foreign-owned and produce almost entirely for export.

Until recently Matias Pecero worked in the Autotrim plant, making leather covers for steering wheels. He and his wife, Cristina, are convinced that the toxic glues and solvents he worked with are responsible for the sudden death of their apparently healthy child on its second day of life. Doctors offered no explanation. Matias and Cristina say they know twelve other couples who have either lost children or had them born with severe defects such as anencephalia or spinabifida. At least one of the parents of each of these infants worked with toxic chemicals on the job. Matias says the union at the plant knows about the problem but does nothing to help. Like most unions in Mexico, it is part of the largest labor federation, the CTM, which is affiliated with the ruling political party. Rather than representing the needs of the workers as a democratic union would do, the CTM makes sure that workers cooperate with the government's economic policies.

Noe Monañes worked at the same plant. While he was working at Autotrim he had an anencephalic child who lived only six months. When he asked his supervisor for time off and a small loan to cover the costs of a two-hour trip to a doctor in Reynosa, he was told there was nothing the company could do. When he mentioned that others in the plant had had problems, he was told to stop making trouble. Later he and other parents of children with disabilities, along with those who had complained of carpal tunnel syndrome, were fired as a "reduction in force"—60 of them at once. Many of those workers found themselves unable to get work in other maquilas in town because they were either blacklisted as troublemakers or labeled as "scrap."

Just blocks away from Noe lives Marybel. She worked for four years at the Mechanical Components plant cleaning steering wheels all day long with toxic solvents. She was never given any instruction in the hazards of the chemicals she used, nor was she given any safety equipment. She did this work all the way through her pregnancy with her son Eric. Eric was eight years old in the summer of 1999. He is a friendly boy with a glint in his one good eye. He has normal intelligence, but his head is overgrown, misshapen, and severely discolored. He has glaucoma and epilepsy. When it became clear that she would have to take a day off every two weeks to take him to doctors, the company told her they could not keep her on.

It is nearly impossible to scientifically establish that these children's problems were caused by chemicals on the job, but the incidence of birth defects here is well above the norm. What is very clear, though, is that each of these workers earns less than one tenth the wage that was paid to workers in the United States or Canada who previously did their jobs. Despite this the companies are unwilling to spend extra money for adequate ventilation, safety equipment, or worker education, all of which they previously provided in the North and all of which are required by Mexican laws—laws that are routinely ignored. No wonder Timothy Peter Joseph, head of the Dominican order worldwide, declared during a 1999 visit to Mexico, "Neoliberalism has deepened racism and the disdain of dominant groups towards indigenous cultures."[21] He was talking about the Mayan Indians of southern Mexico, but the treatment of factory workers in the northern maquilas also indicates an economic system that treats workers as less than human.

Manuel Mondragon, a former General Motors worker, is a young man who heads the work of the Pastorate for Working Class Youth (PJO) in Matamoros. When young Autotrim workers in his parish began to share similar complaints about reproductive problems and repetitive-motion injuries, he wondered what he could do. He talked to Martha Ojeda of the San Antonio-based Coalition for Justice in the Maquiladoras (CJM). The coalition includes Mexican groups like the FAT and the PJO as well as a variety of US and Canadian organizations. Martha found that the plant was owned by a Canadian corporation and put Manuel in touch with the United Steelworkers of Local 1090 in Waterloo, Ontario. Workers there were very interested because their plant was being phased out due to work being transferred to Mexico. The Canadians also informed the Autotrim workers that the parent company, Custom Trim Ltd., had three other plants in the same state as Matamoros. Martha also put Manuel in touch with occupational health specialists from California who could educate him and several of the workers on the dangers in their workplace.

The information the PJO received from California let the workers know they were justified in many of their worst fears about the toxics they worked with—contrary to the assurances given them by their employers and their union. The information from Canada led to the formation of an alliance of workers at the related Mexican plants. Conditions were just as bad at the other plants, but the pay was even worse. In April 1997, the contract for workers at the Custom Trim plant in Valle Hermoso—about an hour outside of Matamoros—was due for renegotiation. Based on the information they now had, several workers insisted that they be allowed to participate in the negotiations rather than leaving them to union insiders, as had always been the case in the past. They demanded a wage increase, but they put a major emphasis on health and safety issues.

In May, faced with the company's refusal to negotiate, workers walked out. The union signed a new contract without them. Dejected about the betrayal and fearful of reprisals, the workers reentered the plant only after the company signed an agreement pledging no reprisals against any of the striking workers. Days later the company fired 28 workers who had played active roles in the strike or on the negotiating team. The Canadians invited one of those workers, Salvador Bruno, on a speaking tour. When he returned home his wife and daughter were threatened with death if he didn't keep his mouth shut. Over the next months Manuel Mondragon, who had coordinated much of the strike activity and the international support, had his house broken into four times. Neighbors report that the last break-in lasted for a day and a half. If he had not been in the hospital for a stomach ulcer, he fears he would have been killed.

With financial support from the Steelworkers, the fired workers filed for reinstatement. The labor board eventually ruled that Custom Trim must take them back, and pay all lost wages. However, in the meantime, Custom Trim had been bought by Florida-based Breed Technologies, which moved the work to a new, nearby factory. On March 11, 1999, a labor board official summoned the workers and accompanied them to the Custom Trim plant. Finding it vacant, he said, "It appears Custom Trim will not be able to reinstate you." When the workers insisted that the labor board was well aware of the plant's sale to Breed, they were told that if they could produce a Mexican government document authenticating the sale they could proceed to file a new claim against Breed. Since the corporate takeover was accomplished in the United States and Canada there is no reason to believe that such a document ever existed.

Tijuana: A Phantom Union at Han Young

Matamoros is as far east as one can go on the Mexican border. Tijuana is at the western extreme. Life in the maquilas, though, is much the same. When workers at the Korean-owned Han Young plant decided that conditions were unsafe and wages were too low they decided to form a brand-new union.[23] The events that followed would be incredibly funny—the stuff of a ridiculous farce—if they were not all too tragically true.

The workers had no trouble organizing themselves. The fifty to sixty workers at the maquilas included many skilled welders who had seen their wages fall from as much as $200 a week before NAFTA took effect to about $50 for a 48-hour week in 1997. Some workers were earning as little as $20 per week. Their job was to assemble the chassis of piggy-back shipping containers that were purchased by the Hyundai Corporation. As they worked, their electric welding cables often dragged through puddles of water as steel frames capable of crushing whole groups of workers dangled overhead.

On June 2, 1997, workers refused to enter the plant until management responded to a list of 10 complaints ranging from failure to pay legally mandated profit-sharing to providing new gloves and lenses for the welders. They were surprised, at this point, by the appearance of a representative from the government-affiliated CROC labor union, who insisted he was their representative and would solve everything for them according to the company contract. The workers had never seen this man before, nor were they aware of any contract. The union had never held a meeting or an election. It was what is called a "phantom union," one that exists on paper but is unknown to the workers. Phantom unions administer "protection contracts," protecting the company from the workers by usurping the workers' right to organize themselves and taking money to keep the workers compliant with company demands.

Knowing they did not want to be represented by the CROC union, workers chose to affiliate with the Metalworkers' Union of the FAT. They filed the requisite legal forms to choose their own union, only to face a series of delays. In the meantime Han Young fired many of the apparent leaders and routinely threatened the rest.

When the labor board finally did schedule an election for October 6, 1997, national representatives of the CROC met with the state's governor and insisted that he fire the head of the labor board. If the labor board president would actually allow an election to be held for an independent union, how could he be counted on to prevent the union from winning the election? On October 3, the governor did his job, and labor board president Antonio Ortiz resigned.

The election was held as scheduled on October 6. In an attempt to prevent fraud or violence from being committed, the workers' attorney, Jose Peñaflor, had invited international observers. The workers lined up, and though they were intimidated by threats from hired goons, and though they had to vote out loud in front of their boss, who had promised to fire them if they voted for the independent union, they all voted for

STIMAHCS, the FAT union. One person who was not a worker jumped into the end of the line and voted for the CROC—with no protest from the labor board officials, who then declared the election closed.

However, at that point, a busload of Han Young managers, secretaries, assorted CROC representatives, 14 people just hired by the plant, and even the plant nurse showed up and demanded the right to vote. Labor board officials at first stuck to the law and refused. Then, in response to entreaties by a former labor board president who had recently been retained by Han Young, the board relented and let them all vote. Nonetheless, it was obvious that the workers had won as the board declared the vote tally to be 54 for STIMAHCS to 34 for the CROC, pending resolution of any protested votes and final certification. The board then simply refused to certify the election, at one point making the absurd contention that a vote was not a sufficient indicator of the workers' preference.

Meanwhile, back in Washington, DC, President Clinton asked Congress to give him fast-track authority to negotiate more treaties like NAFTA. A blow-by-blow description of the events at Han Young, provided on the floor by Representative David Bonior (D-Michigan), helped convince a majority that NAFTA failed to protect the interests of workers on either side of the border. In an effort to forestall this defeat, Clinton reportedly asked Mexican President Zedillo to clear up the embarrassing situation. Labor activists around the United States and Canada began picketing Hyundai dealerships. The Korean autoworkers' union protested to Hyundai at home. Three Han Young workers went on a hunger strike for 26 days. Faced with this pressure, the government still did not recognize the workers' election victory. Instead, they ordered a new election be held on December 16, provided that the workers withdraw the complaint they had filed under the NAFTA provisions.

The new election was even more fraudulent than the first, but the workers managed to win again by a slight margin. Within a month the workers' union was recognized as legitimate. The workers had won the honor of having the only independent union legally recognized in a maquila anywhere along the border. From that point on, the company simply refused to negotiate with them, as required by law, and the labor board refused to intervene on the workers' behalf, as required by law.

In the summer of 1998, faced with the refusal of Han Young to negotiate a new contract, the workers went on strike. The local labor board declared their strike illegal and police tore down their strike banners, insisting on the company's right to bring in strike-breakers if the workers did not return to work. The workers received impressive international support, with regular pickets at 25 Hyundai dealerships around the United States and Canada. In Portland, Oregon, the Cross-Border Labor Organizing Committee shut down Hyundai's docks for 24 hours, declaring, "If corporations can cross international borders to exploit workers, labor and human rights organizations can and must rally across borders to protect workers."[24]

Federal and local Mexican officials, backed by supportive media, repeatedly declared such support from unions in other countries was simply aimed at discouraging foreign investment and thus depriving Mexicans of their jobs. For good measure the government informed Mary Tong, director of the San Diego-based Support Committee for Maquiladora Workers, that she would be deported if she tried to attend any public activity involving Han Young workers.

Since that time Mexican federal courts have ruled that the strike is legal. Local authorities have ignored that ruling and repeatedly driven the workers away from the Han Young factory. They have insisted on even more fraudulent elections, although they have lost each of them. At one point thugs were videotaped threatening the workers with AK-47s. The National Administrative Office (NAO) in Washington, DC, created by NAFTA to investigate labor law complaints, ruled in April 1998 that in the Han Young case, the Mexican government has repeatedly violated its own labor, health, and safety laws. As a result, it recommended consultations with the Mexican government. On July 1, 1999, just days after a meeting of state and national officials had gotten both Han Young management and the union to declare a "truce," police moved in again and forced the workers to abandon the strike barriers they had legally erected in front of Han Young. Nothing had changed.

The workers of Han Young have managed to get the first legally recognized independent union in a maquiladora, and are waging the first legally recognized (at least from time to time) strike by an independent union in a maquila. The state labor board also gave the union an unexpected present. In addition to recognizing them as a local branch of the nationwide STIMAHCS, the board gave them a registry for a statewide union that could organize in any industry. The board's goal—to break the local union loose from the FAT—eventually succeeded. The govern-ment, employers, and official unions seem determined to use whatever measures necessary to deny Han Young workers the rights to which they are entitled under Mexican labor law, under the Mexican constitution, and under NAFTA. It appears the law is irrelevant. Only the will of these Mexican workers, with whatever international support they can muster, will determine if their rights are respected or not.

Organizing Worldwide: Worker-to-Worker

Labor solidarity is not limited to working along the US-Mexican border, nor is it limited to industrial workplaces. The advantages of rapid travel and instant communication that have led to global commerce are also now facilitating a variety of forms of cross-border labor solidarity. Here are a few creative examples.

The Transnationals Information Exchange (TIE) was created in the late '70s to encourage communication among workers employed by the same transnational corporation but living in different countries.[25] Even-tually TIE found that they were succeeding in overcoming the barriers of nationalistic antagonisms embodied in the "Buy American!" campaigns but were inadvertently creating new company loyalties — "Buy Ford!" They now organize workers around common problems. In all cases they invite rank-and-file workers, not union executives, with the hope that they can build pressure for real change from within the unions.

TIE has brought together workers in public-sector unions from Af-rica, England, and the Caribbean to discuss common problems brought about by the push to privatize public services. In Mexico, they are hold-ing meetings of independent labor activists, with union members from Brazil, Russia, Spain, France, and Canada coming to share their experi-ences of working to overthrow corrupt, government-affiliated unions like Mexico's CTM or CROC. They sponsored a conference of autoworkers from Brazil, the United States, Canada, and Germany to plan strategies to confront the newly merged Daimler-Chrysler Corpora-tion, which is locating its new Mercedes plants in the southern United States and the Curitiba region of Brazil to escape the strong unions it has in its existing factories in Germany.

In response to the Ethiopian famines of the early 1980s, some Canadian Steelworkers began pressuring their union for a way to help alleviate suffering in other countries. By 1985 they had won language in their contracts to set aside one cent out of each worker's hourly wage to fund the Steelworkers Humanity Fund. Canadian Autoworkers and the Energy and Paperworkers union also started similar funds. What began as international charity soon led to contacts with NGOs around the world and a better understanding of shared interests. Their strategic solidarity promotes development in other countries, with half of the money going to health, housing, and education and the other half supporting workers involved in building stronger labor unions, like those of Matamoros discussed above. This work has led to a feeling of connectedness with other workers as the issues of the global economy have become far more immediate to workers. Gerry Barr, director of the Steelworkers fund, explains: "Like it or not we are involved globally. Being able to be involved, person-to-person, in the lives of fellow workers is seen as a real strength by our members."[26]

As early as 1991, in response to the proposed NAFTA agreement, Mexico's FAT sent representatives to Washington, DC, to seek allies among US labor unions. What they initially found was a protectionist, nationalistic climate that cast Mexican workers as enemies and a policy of the AFL-CIO to deal only with the Mexican government-approved CTM. Later that year they met the leadership of the United Electrical, Radio and Machine Workers of America (UE) and began developing an alliance of mutual respect and support. They have since supported each other in organizing drives, conducted worker-exchange visits, and helped each other to understand the context of labor relations in each country. Their alliance has helped inspire other unions to overcome their nationalistic blind spots and find allies across the border.

Washington Apples as a Global Industry

Washington State not only supplies apples throughout the United States, it also ships millions of cases around the world each year, with Mexico being its largest export market. The industry employs over 45,000 workers to pick and pack the fruit. Half of them come from Mexico. Just as international ownership has led workers to organize across borders, this international labor force within the United States is beginning to inspire cross-border organizing. In the fall of 1997 Jorge Robles of the FAT traveled to Washington to join a union organizing drive being held by the Teamsters, who hoped to win a contract for workers in many of the packing houses.

The elections were lost due to the employers' threats to call the Immigration and Naturalization Service (INS) and their firing of many workers who were identified as union supporters—illegal but effective measures. Robles says the Teamsters lack the experience of organizing in secret as the FAT must do in Mexico's repressive labor climate. His overall assessment of the low-wage industry, with its abysmal safety conditions and overt discriminatory practices, is, "What's going on is a veritable 'social dumping' of apples exported to Mexico, with companies tripling their profits by violating workers' rights."[26] "Dumping" is a term that describes selling a good at less than its actual cost of production. The practice is generally prohibited by most international trade agreements. In this case, the apple industry would not be able to produce their product at current prices without the social conditions that allow the exploitation of the pickers and packers.

When he returned home, Robles and the FAT joined the Teamsters, the United Farmworkers, and Mexico's National Workers Union (UNT) in filing a complaint with Mexico's NAFTA-related National Administrative Office. They charged that the United States was failing to enforce its health and safety laws, its labor laws, and the labor principles it had agreed to under the NAFTA side accords.

While the industry and Washington state clearly benefit from the labor of Mexican workers, they fail to provide those workers with basic rights. Workers are routinely exposed to toxic pesticides, yet state and federal agencies have done little to enforce the laws supposedly prohibiting such exposure. If a worker is hurt on the job, state law provides less compensation for a migrant than for a resident worker. Thousands of Mexican workers are employed throughout Washington, but the state has only two Spanish-speaking lawyers enforcing the National Labor Relations Act. Although state and federal labor laws provide little or no protection for agricultural workers regarding minimum wage or the right to organize or bargain collectively, the NAFTA side accords require them all. This case, brought by Mexican unions, may eventually help to win basic rights for all agricultural laborers in the United States.

What This Book Is About

This book is about the evolving shape of societies in the global economy. It is concerned with whether the majority of workers will be better off or worse off. This concern for the well being of the majority means the book is also intimately concerned with questions of democracy, whether we are talking about decisions made in Washington, DC, in a global cabal of corporations, or on the shop floor.

But those are just general concerns—a good book has to tell good stories. While so far we have had short stories from around the world, most of this book's stories will come from Mexico. NAFTA has tied the United States, Canada, and Mexico together more than ever before. No one knows how this continental relationship will evolve. What is certain is that, while only a few elite corporate and government officials planned this merger, all of us are affected by it. If working people are to have any influence on how our societies evolve—and there is plenty of evidence to suggest that they can and will—we have to understand both the issues and what is at stake. We have to learn about Mexico and its people, not just to be better neighbors, but because we are all tied up in the same emerging political and economic system. We cannot understand that system without understanding how it works in Mexico.

The system is both political and economic at the same time. On the economic side it is driven by capitalist enterprises whose goal is first and foremost to maximize profits for their shareholders and managers. Workers are seen as factors of production that should be used as productively as possible at the lowest possible cost. International trade theory suggests that countries should concentrate their production in areas of comparative advantage. In the past those advantages were mainly determined by the availability of natural resources and climate. With today's technology of communication and transportation, as well as the abandonment of trade theory's assumption that capital would not move across national boundaries, the basis for most nations' comparative advantage is more than ever political rather than geophysical. In this environment, international capitalists get political elites of various nations to bid against each other in offering the most favorable conditions for production. These include financial subsidies, low rates of taxation, minimal environmental constraints, and low-cost labor. Since the cost of food and clothing throughout the world has become increasingly determined by world markets, the main factor affecting the cost of basic labor is political: to what extent can the ability of labor to organize itself be constrained when wages are held at or below the cost of subsistence?

Crudely simplified, the new global system works like this in North America. Goods that were once produced in the United States or Canada are now manufactured in Mexico at wages that are not only less than those formerly paid to workers north of the Rio Grande, but less than workers in Mexico used to get. Workers in Mexico are prevented from raising their wages by a brutally anti-democratic legal and political process. The goods are then shipped back across the border to be sold at slightly lower prices but with significantly higher profit margins. One result of falling average wages and increasing corporate profits is increasing economic inequality. Another is increasing political inequality, as part of those profits are invested in buying political influence aimed at extending the same system throughout the world. Over the decades the FAT has fought against that system.

Because the FAT has spent its life engaged in struggles against Mexico's authoritarian system, a nominally democratic system that has also been labeled a "perfect dictatorship," the history of the FAT is a good tool for understanding how that system works, and how it can be defeated. The history of the FAT is presented in the context of the evolving political and economic history of Mexico—a history of government manipulation and of a people striving to take control of the structures and policies that shape their daily lives. The struggle of Mexican workers to gain more democracy and a better living is part of a struggle being waged by workers in less industrialized countries all over the world. And if those workers don't win their struggles, workers in wealthy counties like the United States and Canada will not only see their standards of living threatened, they will see the quality of their democracies further eroded as corporate power establishes itself at a global level beyond the reach of mere nation-states.

The history of the FAT is also worth reading simply because it is the story of humble but courageous people who dared to claim the dignity they deserve as human beings, regardless of the forces arrayed against them. A history of presidents, generals, business leaders, and other "important people" too often teaches ordinary people that they are not important, not the shapers of history. This "people's history of Mexico" is informed by the conviction that what is most important in Mexico has been shaped by the farmers, factory workers, shop owners, secretaries, teachers, children, mothers, fathers, and grandparents who are daily trying to make their lives and the lives of those around them a little bit better. These are the actors who must have a voice in shaping a global society if it is to serve us all well.

What this history of the FAT and the experience of workers worldwide now show is that the goals of these workers can no longer be accomplished within their own local communities or countries. They must find the common elements that allow them to make effective alliances and act globally against businesses and capital that has ever greater mobility and ever less social responsibility. Workers around the world are called to a common struggle to win respect for minimum labor standards based on the notion that no full-time worker or child of a worker should live in poverty, danger, or ill health; that those who produce the world's wealth should be able to enjoy it.

Notes

1 Sweeney, John. 1999. "Statement by AFL-CIO President John J. Sweeney on Collapse of WTO Trade Talks." December 4. http://www.AFLCIO.org/publ/press1999/pr1204.htm.

2 Luddites smashed textile machinery that was destroying their jobs as home-based spinners and weavers in early-19th-century England. The term is now used to suggest mindless opposition to technological progress. Actually, the Luddites favored technical advances; they just hated the factory system that was destroying their autonomy.

3 Reyes, Teófilo. 2000. "Locked-Out Steelworkers, Tree-Hugging Environmentalists, Black-Clad Anarchists, Tibetan Monks, Catholic Nuns, Crusty Punks." *Labor Notes* (Detroit) (January): 7, 9–10.

4 Carson, Jim and David Brooks. 1999. "Desafían Manifestantes el Gran Despliegue Policiaco y Militar." *La Jornada* (Mexico, DF) (December 2). www.nuclecu.unam.mx/~jornada.

5 Crosby, Jeff. 2000. "'The Kids Are All Right' and Other Thoughts from IUE Visitors to Seattle." *Labor Notes* (January) 8–9.

6 Nova, Scott, and Michelle Sforza-Roderick. 1997. "M.I.A. Culpa." *The Nation* (January 13–20): 5–6.

7 Reyes, 7, 9–10.

8 Gonzalez Armador, Roberto, and Rosa Elvira Vargas. 1999. "México y Tres Países Centroamericanos Tendrán Acuerdo." *La Jornada* (December 2). www.nucleu.unam.mx/~jornada.

9 Greenhouse, Steven, and Joseph Kahn. 1999. "U.S. Effort to Add Labor Standards to Agenda Fails." *New York Times* (December 3): 4.

10 Bacon, David. 2000. "In the Midst of Tear Gas, History is Made." *Labor Notes* (January): 11.

11 Vogel, David. 1983. "The Power of Business in America: A Reappraisal." *British Journal of Political Science*, 13: 19–43.

12 Clausen, A.W. 1972. "The Internationalized Corporation." *The Annals of the American Academy of Political and Social Sciences* (September): 108–114.

13 Sigmund, Paul E. 1993. *The United States and Democracy in Chile*, 22, 39–41. Baltimore: Johns Hopkins University Press.

14 Friedman, Milton. 1980. *Free to Choose*. New York: Harcourt, Brace, Jovanovich; Sigmund, 91–94.

15 Bettleheim, Adriel. 1998. "Saving Social Security." *CQ Researcher*, (October 2): 859–67.

16 Mitchell, Olivia S. 1998. "Social Security Reform in Latin America." *Review* (Federal Reserve Bank of Saint Louis), 80 (Mar/Apr): 15. Kritzer, Barbara E. 1996. "Privatizing Social Security: The Chilean Experience." *Social Security Bulletin,* 59 (3): 45-55. Arenas de Mesa, Alberto, and Veronica Montecinos. 1999. "The Privatization of Social Security ad Women's Welfare: Gender Effects of the Chilean Reform." *Latin American Research Review,* 34 (3): 7-47.

17 Commission on International Development. 1969. *Partners in Development.* New York: Praeger.

18 Arellano, Hector. 1999. Discussion in open meeting. IBEW Union Hall, El Paso, Texas. June 18.

19 Lewandowski, Tom. 1999. Telephone interview, Fort Wayne, Indiana. June 6.

20 The 30-minute program, "The Mexico Jobs Rush," produced by NBC-33, is available for $15 from Tom Lewandowski, NE Indiana Central Labor Council, 1520 Profit Drive, Ft. Wayne, IN 46808. E-mail: NEICLC@aol.com.

21 This Matamoros account is based heavily on observations and interviews from author's visit June 13–15, 1999, as well as periodic reports in *Mexican Labor News and Analysis* and the locally produced report *Solidaridad sin Fronteras.* 1999. Matamoros: NYSLRC-Caminos A.C.

22 Balboa, Juan. 1999. "Urge el Superior Dominicano a Alcanzar la Paz en Chiapas." *La Jornada* (July 6).

23 Han Young story is based largely on author's interviews conducted in Tijuana, June 28 to July 1, 1999, and also on the following:
David Bacon. 1998. "Border Bosses Go All Out to Stop Strike at Han Young." *Mexican Labor News and Analysis,* III. (June).
International Labor Rights Fund, et. al. 1997. *The Case of Han Young de Mexico, S.A. de C.V. in Tijuana, Mexico.* Submitted to the United States National Administrative Office (NAO), October 28.
Sam Dillon. 1997. "Union Vote in Mexico Illustrates Abuses," *New York Times* (October 13): A6.

24 Campaign for Labor Rights. 1998. "Han Young Update," Washington, DC, June 26.

25 TIE information based on interview with TIE staffer Teófilo Reyes, June 19, 1999, Ciudad Juarez, Mexico.

26 Gerry Barr. 1999. Telephone inteview, Toronto, Ontario, July 16.

27 International Labor Rights Fund. 1998. "Faulting US Labor Laws, Mexican Unions File 'Broadest' NAFTA Labor Complaint on Washington State Apple Industry." May 27. Www.laborrights.com/e-presrel/prapples.html.

2.

Mexico in the Global Economy
A Revolution Betrayed

For workers north of the Rio Grande, the struggle of workers in Mexico is not only close at hand, it is very closely connected to decisions being made in the continent's capital, Washington, DC. The fate of Mexico's workers will play an important role in shaping the future of workers throughout North America.

Since the early 1980s, when export-oriented, neoliberal economic policy became Mexico's official practice, its citizens have experienced the benefits and, more often, the costs of the global economy. Like the United States, Mexico reduced its inequality in the post-war period until 1980. Of the 96 nations reporting data on income inequality in 1999, only 12 had greater income gaps than Mexico.[1] While seven Mexicans counted within the ranks of the world's top 200 billionaires,[2] well over half the population lived in poverty, subsisting on less than $2 per day. Mexico was the 16th-richest nation in the world in terms of total production, but in gross domestic product *per person,* it ranked 81st.[3]

As employment in the manufacturing sector in the United States and Canada has fallen steadily, Mexico has been building more and more plants. Especially in northern Mexico, one finds the production facilities of most of the world's top corporations, often just a short walk from open sewers and the cardboard shacks inhabited by many of their workers. The largest employer in Mexico's private sector is Delco, the auto-electric parts manufacturer. Close behind come General Motors, General Electric, Phillips Petroleum, Ford, and Daimler-Chrysler, along with Sony, Levi's, Honeywell, Baldwin Piano, and Johnson & Johnson.

For a few Mexicans, the global economy seems to be dragging Mexico out of centuries of backwardness. For them, this momentum must be maintained and even accelerated. But many others feel betrayed. Not only have real wages fallen dramatically as Mexican workers have moved from farms and small businesses into jobs in maquiladoras, but many Mexican-owned manufacturing operations have been driven out of business in the process, destroying nearly as many jobs as have been created by new foreign investors.

For the majority of Mexicans shaken up by this economic chaos, whatever faith they may have had in their nation's leaders has been shattered. Many feel that the nation's sovereignty and its ideals have been sold off to whichever to foreign investors seemed interested. Yet despite this feeling of betrayal, very few Mexican workers have rebelled against the political system that has controlled Mexico for so long. The current political turmoil in Mexico is largely a result of this system of control falling apart and being challenged by increasingly emboldened sectors of the population. Why and how the people of Mexico are challenging their political and economic systems of control are questions best answered by looking first at the past.

The Mexican Revolution

Just as US children have been taught to hate Benedict Arnold as a traitor to the American Revolution against Britain, Mexicans have been taught to hate Porfirio Diaz, dictator from 1876 until 1911. The Porfirian era was marked by a shift in power from feudal landlords and the Catholic Church to capitalists, technicians, and foreign investors. During this time, many indigenous and peasant communities lost their landholdings and laborers experienced violent repression. The Mexican Revolution—like the Russian, Chinese, Vietnamese, and other later social revolutions of the 20th century—was fought mainly by peasants hoping to secure their rights to land and put an end to the oppression they suffered. However, it was led and funded mostly by educated modernizers who had been shut out of power by Diaz and his wealthy foreign allies. Those who came out on top and became the first post-revolutionary presidents made money exporting new crops to Europe even while traditional crops of corn and beans fell to famine levels during the years of fighting.[4]

Emiliano Zapata, also a revolutionary leader, had risen up from a traditional village and fought to restore lands to the people. When the other leaders began consolidating power, he wrote to them: "You have betrayed the agrarian reform.... [The] hopes of the people have been turned to scorn."[5]

Even as the revolution consolidated power in the hands of new elites, it also provided a new, apparently democratic constitution that set limits on foreign ownership and control, promised land reform, and seemed to assure strong rights for industrial workers. The revolution also provided the ideals for the people to live by. Since then, the trick has been to keep peasants and workers loyal to these ideals and to a government that claims to embody them while leaving most of the actual power and resources in the hands of the elites.

Contrary to the traditional vilification of Diaz, some Mexican elites argue that Diaz should be remembered for modernizing Mexico. In 1992 Mexico's President Carlos Salinas de Gotari tried to rewrite the textbooks used in Mexican schools in order to treat Diaz more positively. He argued that Diaz enticed foreign investors to bring new technology to Mexico. In this era Mexico got railroads, a new textile industry, development of petroleum, telegraphs, new roads, new measures for sanitation, and improvements in education. To Salinas, it was an age of progress brought about by a more scientific outlook and an openness to what the global economy had to offer.

Salinas was unable to carry out his textbook reforms because Mexicans began to suspect Salinas was up to the same treasonous tricks carried out by Diaz. The problem with the wonderful progress of Porfirio Diaz was remarkably similar to the problem of Salinas's "progress" 100 years later. It was progress for a favored few within the system. Everyone else lost out.

It is not surprising that Harvard-educated Salinas admired Diaz and the technical planners, the *científicos,* who managed his modernization. Salinas also wanted to modernize Mexico by opening it up to foreign investors. Like Diaz, he knew that he and his friends could make plenty in the process. Like Diaz he was willing to offer investors a cheap and controlled workforce.

Educators—especially those in independent university unions and in the dissident democratic current within the schoolteachers' union—blocked his literary restoration of the Diaz dictatorship. Workers have been less successful in resisting other more concrete echoes of the pre-revolutionary policies.

Constructing Post-revolutionary Mexico

The political problem of the post-revolutionary moment for the revolutionary elite was how to stabilize power in a country with so many military leaders wanting power and so many hungry people expecting an improvement in their economic reality. The answer they devised was the basis of the one-party system that defined Mexican politics throughout the 20th century. Its key ingredients were corruption and co-optation, and when those failed, repression. And of course, since this was to be a modern system, leaders would have to be elected by the people—after they had been carefully chosen by the powerful.

Military leaders were given titles, commands, and salaries. They were also given political positions, lands, and other economic concessions as necessary. But if the system had continued in this vein the country would not have progressed as well as it did. Mexico did not remain like so many Latin American countries, oppressed and retarded by an alliance between large landholders and military men. Modernizers carried the day. Eventually the military leaders were elaborately pensioned off and pruned of any political power.[6]

With the military threat under control, political and economic elites needed a strategy to respond to the demands of peasants and workers who wanted their government to more equally distribute economic resources. Ideological control, bolstered by populist and democratic post-revolutionary rhetoric, was one element of the strategy.

The Constitution of 1917, for instance, has some of the finest pro-worker and pro-peasant promises ever made. Article 27 guaranteed that peasants would gain secure access to land, that large estates would be broken up, and that the rights of communities to control their lands would be guaranteed through the *ejido* system. Ejidos held land in common and through their own local assemblies decided how to use the land. To prevent a reconsolidation of land in the hands of a wealthy few, these ejido lands were not allowed to be sold. Article 123 guaranteed the rights of working people to organize unions, to conduct strikes, and to bargain collectively. It also established a minimum wage, the eight-hour day, overtime pay, and minimum health and safety standards. It protected women and children at work and required that companies share 10% of annual profits with their workers.

Mexico's political leaders have always defended the ideals of the constitution as a means of maintaining their legitimacy. The political party of the rulers has always carried a revolutionary name evocative of these values. Those drafting the new constitution called themselves the National Revolutionary Party (PNR) Cardenas reorganized this party into the Party of the Mexican Revolution (PRM), which was reorganized in 1946 into the Institutional Revolutionary Party (PRI). Even the dissident party of the '90s, the Revolutionary Democratic Party (PRD), has followed this practice, claiming that it upholds the true heritage of the revolution.

The president of the republic was identified in the minds of the majority of the Mexican people as the defender of the revolutionary ideals. In the present age it is still surprising how many people, who can detail both their own miserable conditions and the corruption of the political system, feel that the president is a good man who has been betrayed by those who should be serving him.

Ideological control of the Mexican people has been quite effective. But it has never been sufficient. It has been supplemented by a system of political control known in various times and places as clientelism, political patronage, the machine, the Mafia, feudalism, or corporatism. Political elites control resources. They reward their followers with political appointments or with nominations so they can be elected to office. They also determine major government investment priorities. Their friends can suddenly become very wealthy if the government buys land from them or if it decides to sell them an airline or a television franchise during privatization. The same system of rewards goes on down the line all the way to the street vendor who must agree to vote for the ruling party and to show up at demonstrations, when called, in order to get permission to sell in a given location. Failure to cooperate can cost street vendors their livelihood. Failure of a senator to support the party line would likely end a lucrative political career. The system has worked in Mexico the way Mayor Richard J. Daley's patronage machine so long controlled Chicago, from City Hall votes all the way down to block-by-block decisions on whose garbage would be picked up.

A political system built on handing out rewards to supporters is very effective at co-opting challengers. If a group of workers or peasants should become sufficiently organized to demand the distribution of rewards based on their own needs, one standard response of the system is to compliment the group's leader as very promising, very bright, perfectly deserving of more than what he or she has. Such leaders are offered economic and/or political resources sufficient to get them to buy into the system and betray the needs of their peers.

On a large scale, whole villages, even whole classes of people, are offered rewards if they cooperate with the system. The clearest sign that the system was no longer working was the presidential election of 1988: most Mexicans believe that the PRI used massive fraud to defeat the PRD's Cuauhtemoc Cardenas. When the "victor," President Salinas, needed to shore up support, he created Solidarity, a program that targeted funds to specific groups of potentially disaffected people. While Salinas's overall budget showed reduced spending for many programs that had helped poor working people generally, this new system of targeted spending was politically much more effective. Salinas put his brother Raul in charge, but also hired many left-wing community organizers throughout the country to actually implement it. In many areas, organizations that had supported his rival now competed against each other for PRI-controlled funds. Both those employed and those who benefited were expected to show their appreciation politically.[7]

When co-optation and corruption fail to entice compliance from challengers to the ruling party, a final disincentive is at hand: repression. Threats are commonplace. Beatings are tools of policy used, when necessary, with surprising openness. For instance, in 1990, when workers insisted on the right to nominate their own slate of union officers at the Cuautitlan Ford plant near Mexico City, the government-favored union brought in thugs with clubs and guns. Dozens were injured; one was killed.

Sometimes torture is considered a more effective policy instrument. In 1991 Amnesty International estimated that 80% of all Mexican arrestees are tortured.[8] The torture technique of putting cayenne pepper in a bottle of mineral water, shaking it, and then releasing it up the nose of a victim is so widely known that it has been satirized in newspaper cartoons. When it was reported that former president Salinas was going to be questioned about murders and billion-dollar corruption scandals, the cartoonist El Fisgon imagined government agents preparing Perrier water and fine Hungarian paprika for him.[8] In 1997, when Amnesty's secretary-general, Pierre Sane, traveled to Mexico to discuss what he labeled "the human rights crisis" with President Zedillo, the president found no time for him.[9]

Of course, murder is also an option. Ruben Figueroa, governor of the state of Guerrero, got in some trouble when the massacre of 17 peasants was videotaped. It seems the peasants wanted better access to credit to buy agricultural supplies and were on their way to demonstrate in the state capital. Evidence suggests that the army troops who carried out the ambush were acting in response to the governor's stated desire to avoid demonstrations. Despite the nuisance caused by the videotape, Figueroa has not been punished; in fact, he was politically exonerated by his party. One measure of the scale of political murder is the number of PRD activists that were killed after the PRD almost unseated the PRI in the 1988 elections. Party leaders claim at least 400 of their supporters were murdered in the six years following the first party congress in 1990 and that the rate of killing actually accelerated when President Zedillo took office late in 1994.[10]

Given the pervasiveness and the ruthlessness of the political system, it is somewhat amazing that there is as much opposition as there is in Mexico. But opposition is also a heritage of the revolution. The uprising of Mayan peasants under the name of the Zapatista Army for National Liberation at the dawn of NAFTA in January 1994 is just one example. Industrial workers, too, have done battle for the rights promised them by their revolutionary constitution.

How Workers Have Fared

This corrupt system of carrot and stick has kept ruling elites in power since the time of the revolution, partly because it has been able to sell itself as democratic. The claims of the system to be democratic are formally justified by periodic elections that, until recently, have all been either won or successfully stolen by the PRI. Some of the policies of the PRI also appear democratic. The people have been given enough goodies from time to time—a new school, a new clinic, cheaper tortillas—to cause them to see the government as a source of support. This system of winning popular support by helping the people just enough has been undermined in recent years by the campaign to modernize the economy, by reducing the role of government, and by increasing the role of markets. Let's look at how people in Mexico have fared since the revolution.

When Lazaro Cardenas became president in 1934 he was eager to consolidate his power despite opposition from much more conservative factions of the official party. To do this he relied extensively on the political and military support of peasants and industrial workers. Since these groups had previously been taken advantage of, Cardenas had to deliver tangible benefits to secure their support. He began to actually fulfill the promises made in the Mexican constitution. For five years Cardenas distributed close to 45 million acres of agricultural land to peasants. In one region the incomes of peasants rose by more than 400% during the first three years after receiving land. Industrial workers saw their constitutional right to strike recognized and protected by the government. Minimum wages were established. Incomes rose.[12]

After Cardenas, a period of conservative control returned, with the goal being to minimize workers' power while maintaining their support. Real wages fell steadily until the early 1950s, and workers lost nearly 70% of their purchasing power. However, from 1951 to 1976, the Mexican economy grew at an average rate of 6.5%. That was 3% faster than the rapid rate of population growth, meaning that in this 25-year period the value of the economy for each man, woman, and child more than doubled. During this time the value of the minimum wage, after inflation, quadrupled. Clearly workers were getting some tangible benefits from the system. Health care and education were expanded. This time of great progress was known around the world as "the Mexican miracle."

One report explains this period of relatively good times:

> At prevailing average monthly income and yearly average retail prices in Mexico City in 1964, any skilled or semi-skilled worker could support a family of five through his own labor. Those workers in the Federal District who received the minimum wage found it necessary to scrimp and scrounge in order to furnish the minimal needs for their families, but for the first time in the history of the country an unskilled worker could earn sufficient income to support a family and thus leave the children free to attend school. However, half of the population lived in housing averaging five people to a room; only one of three had

running water in [the] building; only one of four had [an] indoor bath-
room with running water; two-thirds used wood or charcoal for cooking and heating.[11]

Wages continued to rise for the next 10 years, but in 1976 this pattern of economic growth with working-class accommodation was abandoned. Until that year Mexico had pursued an import-substitution model
of economic growth. Domestic manufactured goods were protected
from competition, and the domestic market grew. Growing wages were
funneled back into purchases in the expanding Mexican economy. A
sharp economic crisis in 1976 convinced many that it was time for a policy change. But the discovery of vast oil reserves in 1977 allowed the
crisis to be papered over. The growth rate that had slowed to 1.7% in
1976, surged to an amazing 7.3% in 1978. Borrowing heavily on new oil
reserves and high oil prices, Mexico invested lavishly in its industries,
many of them government-owned. But in a time of rapid inflation,
wages did not keep up. For many, the promise of a brighter future was
made to substitute for bread.

In 1982 the world price of oil collapsed and interest rates soared.
The peso, which had been selling at 25 to the dollar in 1981, crashed to
200 per dollar in less than two years.[12] Wealthy Mexicans rushed to send
their money abroad. Outgoing President Lopez Portillo nationalized the
banks in a desperate attempt to stop the hemorrhaging. Mexico was
forced to turn to the United States and the International Monetary Fund
(IMF) for debt relief. With Ronald Reagan in the White House, this
meant that Mexico could no longer even pretend to put obstacles in the
way of global business. To obtain needed financing, Mexico had to implement the structural adjustment program recommended by the IMF.
The restructuring of 1982 was followed by Mexico's entry into the General Agreement on Trade and Tariffs (GATT) in 1986 and NAFTA in 1994.

Mexico's economic strategy since 1982 has been to attract international investment with low-priced natural resources and low-priced labor. Barriers to imports have been eliminated, as have restrictions on
ownership of lands or businesses by foreigners. Just as the age of
Porfirio Diaz had been guided by the *científicos*, the new era would be
governed by the *técnicos,* such as Carlos Salinas and Ernesto Zedillo.

In the midst of this change in economic policy one Mexican scholar
observed:

> [F]or the first time in the history of Mexico there appeared a govern-
> ment, that of Miguel de la Madrid (1982-88), that completely gave in
> to the pressures from the United States and decided to instrument a
> policy of austerity designed by international banking institutions.
> Also for the first time Mexican workers suffered the deterioration
> caused by the economic policy of savage austerity: unemployment,
> alarming shrinkage of the standard of living and of the internal market,
> loss of ten years of economic growth ... all with the point of "curing"
> the economy, reducing economic disequilibriums, and developing a
> capacity to pay the debt.... The punishment imposed on workers
> served for nothing. The hoped for macroeconomic corrections never
> occurred, on the contrary, things got worse. To the economic coloni-
> zation based on exploitation of resources was added political coloni-
> zation which is much more harmful for a nation as it strikes directly
> against its national sovereignty.[15]

In 1991, marveling at the way Mexico had been able to manage this
turnaround of economic policy, Nicholas Scheele, head of Ford Motor
Company in Mexico, exuded, "But is there any other country in the
world where the working class ... took a hit in their purchasing power in
excess of 50% over an eight-year period and you didn't have a social
revolution?"[16]

Just as Lazaro Cardenas had needed support from workers and
peasants and delivered resources to secure their votes and their bodies,
other Mexican presidents were able to purchase worker loyalty from the
early 1950s to the mid-1970s. In that regard a crude approximation of
democracy was accomplished. From the early 1980s on, it became more
important to satisfy foreign capitalists than Mexican workers or farmers.
Even small and mid-size Mexican capitalists lost out. This meant that
the political system had to find new ways to maintain stability. It has,
thus far, found those ways, but the strains on the system are showing. As
the market has taken on an ever larger role in determining the quality of
people's lives, the political system has lost a major means of maintaining its control.

How Workers Have Been Controlled

One of the greatest ironies of Mexican history is that the man who did
the most to deliver concrete gains to workers and peasants, President
Lazaro Cardenas, is also the man who devised the system for keeping

them politically subjugated. In addition to distributing vast amounts of productive land to peasants, Cardenas also made the right to strike, embodied in the Constitution of 1917, a reality, and warned capitalists to go along with the rulings of government arbitration boards "for the good of the nation"—or face expropriation. Government should "intervene in the class struggle on the side of labor, which was the weaker party,"[17] Cardenas explained. He also solidified the nationalist, anti-imperialist side of Mexican political life by expropriating the oil holdings of British and US corporations.

Yet it is essential to put these seemingly revolutionary moves into perspective. In the 1930s governments everywhere altered policy to cope with the Great Depression. In Sweden, the Labor Party came into power and built the modern welfare state. In Germany and Italy, fascist forces came to power with pro-worker programs. And in the United States, Franklin Roosevelt created Social Security and passed the National Labor Relations Act, thus securing the political loyalties of the labor movement.

While Cardenas rewarded workers and peasants as no one had before, he also sought to gain control of their political power. To manage labor disputes, he established arbitration boards composed of representatives of labor, management, and the government. In a clear dispute, the government representative would cast the tie-breaking, controlling vote. (In the pages that follow, we will see plenty of examples of these boards at work.) Cardenas encouraged both rural peasants and urban workers to form national organizations—the National Peasant Confederation (CNC) and the Mexican Workers Confederation (CTM). When he created the new official party, the Party of the Mexican Revolution (PRM), he created four official sectors within the party: workers, peasants, military, and popular. The military sector was later eliminated, but the other three sectors were preserved when the PMR became the PRI. When Cardenas moved to expand the role of government in the economy he created the Federation of Unions of Workers at the Service of the State (FSTSE), which was entirely separate from the CTM. With each sector came benefits, distributed according to the directives of that sector's leadership and contingent on that sector's support for the government in rallies, demonstrations, and elections. The divisions created between the rural, industrial, and public-sector workers meant that the interest of the government would only with great difficulty be challenged by a *united* working class.

The CTM came into existence under the leadership of a charismatic Marxist labor organizer, Vicente Lombardo Toledano. It grew with the encouragement of President Cardenas. Labor leaders were now able to win contracts for their workers. Within the party apparatus, many of them were also able to secure political appointments and exercise direct influence on the implementation of government projects. When more conservative presidents followed Cardenas, the CTM faced a choice between opposition and accommodation. Fidel Velazquez, born in 1900 and first elected secretary-general of the CTM in 1940, chose the course of accommodation. It served him well. He maintained leadership of the CTM and dominance over nearly the entire labor movement until his death in 1997.

While wages declined steadily through the 1940s, political positions for union leaders remained secure. In 1942 the government created the Mexican social security system, which included national healthcare as well as pension benefits and was managed by appointees from business, labor, and government. Workers who had signed on under the Marxist influence of Toledano were now managing bureaucracies jointly with capitalists.

In the early years of the Cold War, Mexico, much like the United States, moved to rid its unions of Communists. Anyone accused of being a Communist could now be purged, and Velazquez used the excuse to eliminate potential rivals. In 1948, miners', railworkers', and oil workers' unions withdrew from the CTM and formed their own federation. Railworkers went out on strike for back pay and wage increases. The government acted swiftly and forcefully. Using both police and military troops, they forced the workers to name a new secretary-general of their union, Jesus Diaz de Leon.

This incident shows the fundamental nature of government control of the labor movement through the leaders of its official unions. It also gives rise to a term that is central to understanding Mexican labor relations. The term is *charro* (cowboy) or sometimes, *charrismo*. Jesus Diaz de Leon enjoyed dressing in the elegant charro clothes of the Mexican horseman, or *caballero*, which were clearly distinguished from the clothes of the *peones,* who lacked horses and had to walk. This taste for dandified class distinction, while having nothing to do with the working-class solidarity one might hope for from union leaders, has everything to do with the corrupt, politically servile leaders of most official unions since that time. To this day corrupt union leaders are known as charros.

In 1968, students all over the world were in revolt. Many protested the Vietnam War and what they perceived to be imperialism. Others reacted against the oppressiveness of industrial capitalism. In May a sudden alliance of workers and students throughout France almost toppled the government of Charles de Gaulle. Mexico was at that time preparing to host the Olympics. While the government spent hundreds of millions of dollars to impress the world that Mexico had finally arrived as an advanced industrialized nation, students sought to join with peasants and workers to denounce the fraud. They felt the money could be better spent on food, education, healthcare, and housing. In October, the government put an end to this movement by massacring hundreds at a peaceful demonstration in Tlatelolco Square in Mexico City. Before he carried out this repression, the interior minister, Luis Echeverria, secured the support of CTM leader Fidel Velazquez. Unions joined in denouncing the students and in supporting the official denial that a massacre even occurred. As a payoff for this essential political support, in 1972 President Echeverria created the National Worker Housing Institute (INFONAVIT).[16] Not only did workers benefit from the subsidized housing, but CTM got to allocate most of the housing units to reward workers who were behaving "properly." Again we see that the power of the PRI and CTM was predicated on repressing challengers while rewarding and controlling collaborators.

The labor arbitration boards first set up by Lazaro Cardenas are crucial to controlling workers on the job. The boards exist at both the national and local levels, and the national government directly controls disputes involving what it considers "strategic" industries. The federal and local labor boards each have three members, one representing business, one representing labor, and one representing government. We know that since the IMF refinancing package was approved in 1982, government policy has not been able to even pretend to oppose the general interests of big business. Labor representatives are generally charros, members of the CTM, and dependent on the government for much of their power. Thus we find few fundamental disagreements among members of labor boards (and little support for workers).

The PRI used to be concerned about preserving workers' favor while it also assured a profitable environment for investors, especially Mexican ones. The shift from this policy to one favoring foreign investors and debt repayment began in the mid-1970s and was solidified with NAFTA in the mid-1990s, and is generally known as the shift to neoliberalism.

Liberalism and Neoliberalism

The seeds of the anti-nationalist (and anti-indigenous) neoliberalism of the late 20th century were ironically sown a century earlier by one of Mexico's greatest nationalist leaders, Benito Juarez, the first and only full-blooded indigenous Mexican to become president.

Juarez is associated with progress, law, and justice. He brought liberalism to Mexico as its president—often in exile—from 1857 to 1872. The key principles of liberalism—the rule of law, the end of communal landholdings, the right to private property, and the separation of church and state—were designed to foster progress. They also redistributed power away from the Church and away from traditional conservative landholders.

Liberalism is an ideology that was created to challenge European feudalism. In the society justified by feudal ideology each person played a specific role in God's universe. People had obligations but also could expect to be supported by society in times of hardship. Obviously, those with the power to interpret God's will for the ordering of society—church leaders and their allies in the nobility—had tremendous advantages. They defined themselves as God's chosen leaders and urged the poor to patiently accept their lot.

The emerging new capitalist class championed liberalism in the 17th, 18th, and 19th centuries. When Adam Smith argued that selfishness was good rather than evil, he not only stood morality on its head, but also provided ammunition for those seeking to promote the rights of the individual over those of the community. As these ideas were accepted, power shifted from old feudal elites to new capitalist elites, sanctified now not by the divine Creator, but by "Progress" resulting from individual initiative and rewarded by private property. Property was to be protected by a government of laws and coordinated by markets. This new ideology opened the way for the industrial revolution and global capitalism. It favored those who got rich, regardless of their birth, and it assured that government would be their ally. It also helped eliminate old obligations to worry about the welfare of others.

Juarez ushered these values into Mexico with the sincere belief they would help end the poverty and ignorance of the majority. With less concern for the majority's liberty, Porfirio Diaz presided over the full-blown implementation of Liberalism by the start of the 20th century. Lands previously held by the Church were now owned by capitalists, who increased the exploitation of those working on them. Many Indian villages found they did not have clear title in the new system of private property. Industry was developed despite wage workers' complaints that they were little more than slaves. Those who complained too loudly were seen to be threatening property rights. Many who complained were sent as prisoners to labor in the henequen plantations of the Yucatan, building the global fortunes of sisal exporters.

This new liberal society eventually provoked the Mexican Revolution, a rebellion of workers and peasants led by other would-be capitalists who were not getting their share of the benefits. Post-revolutionary Mexico put some restraints on liberal capitalism by enshrining certain rights of workers, peasants, and indigenous peoples, and by gradually creating new social obligations to provide education, healthcare, decent housing, and security in old age. Similar social obligations were created in most capitalist countries in the wake of the Great Depression of the 1930s, which showed the need for government to do more than protect property if society were to survive in any meaningful sense.

Mexico, like most other nations, failed to completely fulfill these new obligations to its citizens, but their existence made it easier for citizens to demand more land, more housing, better healthcare, etc. The rejection of liberalism's limited role for government and at least the rhetorical championing of the ideals of social welfare made a real difference in people's lives. As we have seen, the incomes and the quality of life of Mexican workers improved steadily through the 1950s, '60s, and parts of the '70s, as they did in countries around the world.

By the mid-1970s, though, new troubling economic realities—especially the rise of the oil cartel OPEC, the rise of environmental regulations, and the new chaos of competition caused by the blooming of international trade—threatened to erode government's ability to provide for its citizens and business's ability to make profits. Bankers, industrialists, and their allies in governments agreed that in this complex global economy, government should promote growth by shifting its assistance from consumers and voters to corporate employers and donors. How could business elites justify this self-serving power grab? By reviving the ideology of classical liberalism and by promising that, if they got their way, the economy would grow and the benefits would "trickle down" to all sectors of society. Thus was born neoliberalism.

In the 1980s, neoliberalism became a force throughout the world. When Mexico had to refinance its debts in 1982, it was forced to adopt the neoliberal model mandating government austerity, privatization of national resources and industries, and export-oriented manufacturing and agriculture. Thus, the neoliberal ideology that had been widely ridiculed by leaders of most nations as late as 1981 rapidly became official policy in Mexico and in all countries dependent on IMF assistance.

Much to the delight of those benefiting from the adoption of neoliberal ideology, the PRI chose Carlos Salinas de Gotari to be their presidential candidate in the 1988 election. Salinas, as secretary of budget and planning under the previous administration, had managed the IMF plan for Mexico. In campaign speeches Salinas reaffirmed the promise of neoliberalism, which he called "modernization." A favorite word of Porfirio Diaz, modernization would bring growth, Salinas promised. "Without growth, there is no possibility of justice." He did not stop at praising modernization, but also tried to cut himself loose from social commitments enshrined in the rhetoric of the Mexican Revolution. "Most of the reforms of our revolution have run their course and no longer guarantee the fulfillment of Mexico's needs."[19]

Reeling from the economic crisis of the 1980s, the majority of Mexican voters apparently had another idea. At least until the government's computers "broke down" in the process of tallying the election results, it seemed that a majority had chosen Cuauhtemoc Cardenas to lead them. The candidate's name symbolically communicated his platform. Cuauhtemoc was the last leader of the Aztecs in their resistance to Spanish invasion. The former president and workers' hero, Lazaro Cardenas, was the candidate's father. Cuauhtemoc Cardenas campaigned on changing the nation's economic policy, rejecting neoliberalism, suspending and then renegotiating the nation's debt, and smashing the corrupt political system of the PRI. His position on the goals of the revolution contrasted sharply with those of Salinas. "The PRD," the Democratic Revolutionary Party that he founded, he explained, "is the heir to those who engaged in the struggle of 1910, seeking to end inequality and poverty and, above all, seeking democracy."[18]

Despite widespread denunciations for fraud, the PRI used its firm control of the government and television to continue implementing its neoliberal agenda. The most dramatic expression of this policy was its promotion and signing of NAFTA. NAFTA established neoliberal principles—ending tariff protection of Mexican industries, allowing foreign ownership of Mexican land, and eliminating obstacles to the operation of foreign-owned businesses within Mexico—at the level of international treaty, making them harder to change by the legislature that might some day be controlled by a non-PRI majority. In 1992 Salinas changed Article 27 of the Mexican Constitution, dividing the land held by communities—the ejidos—into individual pieces of salable private property.

The eventual successor to Salinas, President Ernesto Zedillo (1994-2000), crossed other politically symbolic territory. In order to secure a US bailout in the wake of the December 1994 peso collapse, he channeled the revenue of Mexican oil sales through US banks as a form of collateral. His efforts to privatize parts of PEMEX, the government-owned oil company, were slowed by sentiment so strong that, in the fall of 1996, the national PRI convention passed a resolution against sale of this "national patrimony."[19] Similar efforts to privatize the electric company in the spring of 1999 set off massive protests.

In the summer of 1996 Zedillo surprised the nation when he said, "What we have needed in Mexico, for various years, is to politically debate the economic path by which our country will develop."[20] Shocked, a delegation of top business leaders called on the president the next day. They asserted that Mexico had already experimented with interventionist, protectionist, and statist models of development, all of which had failed. Thus no further debate was necessary. "Only the market economy functions," insisted Claudio X. Gonzales, president of the Mexican

Council of Businessmen. He did concede that Mexico was living through a "surely painful and difficult transition" to the market model. A reporter then had the audacity to ask how it was that during this "painful and difficult transition" Mexico had managed to increase, from 10 to 15, its number of businessmen on the *Forbes* list of the world's wealthiest people.[23]

There was no shortage of critics willing to take Zedillo up on his offer to debate—in fact, they had never waited for an invitation. The Zapatistas convoked an international gathering "For Humanity and against Neoliberalism." The pro-democracy coalition Civic Alliance set up nearly 4,000 polling stations in town squares to gather input from citizens in their "First National Workday of National Condemnation of the Economic Policy of the Government."[24]

Catholic leaders frequently spoke out against government policy. For example, at a national conference to encourage evangelical work, the bishop of Cuernavaca called out for a new economic policy that would privilege "the dignity of the person, ethical values, the universal destiny of what is produced, and, in general, the social reality of the country, principally addressing the needs of the poorest and most marginalized, which includes the indigenous."[25] A gathering of Jesuit leaders from throughout Latin America lamented the "perverse effects" of neoliberalism. Pointing out how economic policies become ideologies, they described how a concept such as the market "passes from being an instrument which is useful, and even necessary to increase and to improve production and to reduce prices, into being the means, method, and final goal that governs human relations."[26]

Perhaps more surprising was that US Ambassador James R. Jones joined the critics list. "I would say maybe 40% to 50% of the population is benefiting from the new freedoms. The other half—or more—are not. I don't believe in artificially redistributing wealth, but this is a little bit like the Depression era in the United States. Opportunities have got to become real for these people."[27]

In January 1997 President Zedillo insisted that, although the country had problems, the economy was clearly in recovery, that more jobs would be created, and that the crisis would be left behind. Yet, when he spoke of new jobs, he did not speak of recovering the value of wages that had been lost to inflation in recent years. Many observers predicted that his policy on wages for the year would result in further losses and it did. He would continue to have trouble satisfying workers. Middle-class debtors, swamped by the peso crisis of 1994 continued nearly daily protests. Nor did there seem to be any end to the internal political problems resulting from the neoliberal model. As the government privatized businesses and cut back on spending, it had fewer resources to dole out to party loyalists. As it continued to favor international investors, it undercut the rhetorical basis of the legitimacy it had maintained for decades, that of revolutionary nationalism. Neoliberalism was clearly ensconced as official policy, but it was not without serious problems.

For Workers and Democracy: The Frente Auténtico del Trabajo

Sometimes it is easier to see something as dangerous, corrupt, materialistic, ruthless, even evil when we are looking at another country. Most readers will see plenty in Mexico that matches those descriptions, but that is not the point. The point is, eventually, to realize that the forces transforming Mexico are also transforming the United States and Canada. The elites that may look ruthless or evil in Mexico are now allies of similar elites, the owners of capital born in the United States or Canada or anywhere, who are transforming the whole world for their own benefit. The point is also to see that people who are intended to be powerless within this political economy are striving to gain the power they deserve. They are able to work most effectively when they work in concert with allies from other parts of the global economy.

The Authentic Labor Front, the FAT, has been the main Mexican labor organization to work with US and Canadian unions fighting the initiatives of neoliberal corporate elites. The FAT stands in dramatic contrast to most traditional Mexican labor organizations. From its origins in 1960, the FAT has been independent from the PRI and from the official charro labor unions. It has survived efforts to co-opt, to corrupt, and to repress it. Many say that one of its great accomplishments has been simply to survive.

Within Mexico, it has won the respect of broad sectors of the population for its consistent integrity and political clarity. In addition to advocating for improvement in the wages and conditions for Mexican workers, the FAT has consistently worked for real democracy, first within labor unions and the labor movement, and then at the level of the community and the nation.

By coming to understand the FAT, we can come to understand that the system transforming the lives of Mexican workers is intimately involved with the changes in the lives of their working-class neighbors to the north. Corporations are organized to transform the world. Now workers are organizing so that they, too, have a voice in the process.

Notes

1   World Bank. 1999. *World Development Indicators.* Table 2.8 "Distribution of Income or Consumption," p. 70-71.

2   "The World's Working Rich." *Forbes* (July 5, 1999): 204.

3   World Bank. The U.S. has the highest inequality of any industrialized democracy.

4   Cumberland, Charles C. 1968. *Mexico: the Struggle for Modernity.* London: Oxford University Press.

5   Zapata, Emiliano. March 12, 1919. "Open Letter to Citizen Carranza." In Hellman, Judith. 1983. *Mexico in Crisis.* 24. New York: Holmes & Meier.

6   President Lázaro Cárdenas went so far as arming workers' militias to prevent a military challenge to his policy of supporting many of the rights guaranteed to workers under Article 123 of the Constitution. General Avila Camacho (1940–46) was the last President with a military background.

7   Russell, Philip L. 1994. *Mexico Under Salinas.* 281-290. Austin: Mexico Resource Center.

8   "Problems for Free-Trade Accord." *U.S. News and World Report* (October 28, 1991): 18.

9   El Fisgón. 1996. "Preparativos." Political cartoon. *La Jornada* (November 23): 5.

10   Ross, John. 1997. "Mexico's Deadly News." *The Nation* (December 22): 4–5.

11   Gutiérrez, Maribel. 1996. "Marcha en Atoyac por los asesinados del PRD" *La Jornada* (November 25): 13.

12   Handelman, Howard. 1997. *Mexican Politics: The Dynamics of Change,* 37–38. New York: St. Martin's Press.

13   Cumberland, 321–322.

14   "Will Mexico Show the Way to Latin Debtor Nations?" *US News and World Report.* (October 9, 1984): 41–42.

15   Gutiérez Garza, Esthela (ed.). 1985. *Reestructuracíon Productiva y Clase Obrera.* Testimonios De La Crisis, vol. 1, 25. México: Siglo veintiuno.

16   Bowden, Charles. 1996. "While You Were Sleeping: In Juarez, Mexico, Photographers Expose the Violent Realities of Free Trade." *Harper's*, 293, no. 1759, December: 50, 44–52.

17   Hellman, 37.

18   Sanner Ruhnke, Jill. 1995. "The Impact of NAFTA on Labor Arbitration in Mexico." *Law and Policy in International Business*, 26, no. 3: 930, Middlebrook 1995: 224, 917–44.

19   Russell, 3, 183.

20   Russell.

21   Dillon, Sam. 1996. "Mexico Drops Its Efforts to Sell Some Oil Plants." *New York Times* (October 14): C2.

22   Márquez Ayala, David. 1996. "El Debate Economico del Presidente Zedillo." *La Jornada* (July 1): 56–57.

23   Vargas, Rosa Elvira. 1996. "Los Empresarios No Dudan: El Camino, la Economía de Mercado." *La Jornada* (July 2): 45.

24   Alianza Civica. 1996. "Con Valor Cívico Realizó la Primera Jornada Nacional de Condena a la Politica Económinca del Gobierno."

25   Pérez Silva, Ciro. 1996. "Programas Económico Alternativos, Exige la Iglesia." *La Jornada* (November 24): 13.

26   Garduño, Roberto. 1996. "Rechazan jesuitas las politicas neoliberales en America Latina." *La Jornada.* (Novemeber 25): 3.

27   Dillon, Sam. 1996. "Have-Nots Need Stake in Mexico, Envoy Says." *New York Times* (December 4): A5.

3.

The Early Years

Corruption, co-optation, repression: the forces that have hobbled democracy in Mexico have also been used to disempower workers in the United States and Canada. The worldwide Depression of the 1930s led to a social pact between governments, labor, and business that increased social supports for average people in exchange for labor leaders' promise that they would restrain their disgruntled followers from tearing down the house of capital. US workers familiar with this history will see that Mexico's charro unions are remarkably similar to the business unions that have shaped their working lives.

World War II stimulated industrial production in much of the world. In the United States, the economy entered its boom years. The "Treaty of Detroit," the five-year contract the United Automobile Workers signed with General Motors in 1950, set the pattern for growing workers' prosperity. In exchange for a cease-fire on labor's complaints, the contract provided corporate employees with pensions, healthcare, and regular annual wage hikes on top of a cost-of-living adjustment. Cold War demands for conformity led the CIO in 1949 to expel 11 national unions with a total of nearly a million members. Among them was the federation's third-largest affiliate, the United Electrical, Radio and Machine Workers of America (UE) which had already withdrawn from the CIO in protest of its conservative policies.

When the AFL and CIO merged in 1955, the conservative George Meany took charge. He presided over two decades of prosperity and workers' incomes rose. But his failure to question the corporate or political leadership of the country in a time of major transformation depoliticized the labor movement and allowed the share of unionized workers to fall, from more than one in three to less than one in five.

While nearly 25% of union members were black, Meany failed to confront the racism that pervaded many unions. His anti-communism would lead him to support the war in Vietnam and, through the American Institute of Free Labor Development (AIFLD), to oppose most authentic workers' movements around the world.[1] AIFLD got along splendidly with the official unions in Mexico.

In Western Europe, as workers slowly climbed out of poverty, they organized politically through Labor, Socialist, Communist, or Social Democratic parties as well as unions. They worked not only to raise their wages but to build governments committed to providing adequate food, housing, education, and healthcare for all citizens.[2]

While World War II did not end poverty in Mexico, it did spark industrialization. In 1940, a mere 10% of its economically active population worked in industry. By 1960, the figure was 20%.[3] The post-war "Mexican miracle" had begun to make a positive difference in the lifestyles of urban, working Mexicans. The area of Mexico City that is now home to the huge international airport was still open land. Most of the workforce in the city had grown up in the countryside. The rural-urban migration was well under way, but the city's development was not smooth, pleasant, or peaceful.

Mexican elites had been struggling to maintain control of the labor movement since the late 1940s. By the late 1950s that control had frayed. While the economy grew steadily throughout the 1950s, growth was accompanied by inflation. Wages often failed to keep pace. Union struggles that began as a result of discontent over falling real wages turned into challenges to the structure of government-dominated unions. Rank-and-file movements emerged to challenge charro leaders in education, telegraph, telephone, electrical power, mining, and petroleum unions, but the most dramatic challenge to the power of government control of the unions erupted in the railworkers' union.

In 1948, when the ruling party imposed its first charro leader on the railworkers' union, it needed military force to do it. Ten years later railworkers rebelled. Workers' demands led to the creation of a Grand Commission for a General Salary Increase. When delegates to this commission began to champion the cause of the workers despite the best efforts of their union leaders, the union's secretary-general called in police to dissolve the commission.

A rank-and-file leader from Oaxaca in southern Mexico, Demitrio Vallejo, developed a plan. He called for a wage hike of 350 pesos per month and a series of escalating strikes until the raise was granted. Trains throughout the country were stopped for two hours on June 26 and for four hours on the 27th. On the 28th the railworkers stopped for six hours and were joined in their work stoppages by petroleum workers, teachers, and students. President Ruiz Cortines intervened at this point and proposed a settlement of 215 pesos a month. Railworkers accepted and celebrated their victory by electing Vallejo and his supporters to head the union.

However, the government-owned railroad and the secretary of labor refused to recognize Vallejo's leadership. Vallejo called for a two-hour walkout on July 31. This time railworkers were joined by striking electrical workers and supported by some sectors of the national teachers union. By August 3 the government intervened again, this time with a different sort of solution. Police and soldiers were sent to raid union halls. Vallejo managed to escape to a railyard in Mexico City, where he called a work stoppage that became nationwide within hours. The government agreed to hold new union elections on August 6. Despite the best efforts of deposed charros to buy votes, Demitrio Vallejo and his supporters won control of the union by a vote of 59,759 to 9. Claiming that no party owned the union, Vallejo promised to restore workers' rights.[4]

Contract negotiations in early 1959 did not go well, and Vallejo called for new strikes in March. When the army again raided union halls, several workers were killed and more than 10,000 railworkers were taken prisoner, as were many supporting petroleum workers, teachers, and students. Vallejo was locked away as a threat to the nation. He would not be released until 1974.[5]

Because of its nationwide scope, its militancy and its frank challenge to the authoritarian PRI-charro system, and because of the overt repression used against it, the railworkers movement of 1958 and 1959 was the central focus of Mexicans concerned about labor rights, better wages, and more democracy. Major strike movements also occurred in unions supposedly representing petroleum, telephone, telegraph, electricity, aviation, and education workers. In each case, movements within the union demanded more democratic representation within the unions and better wages and conditions on the job. These movements drew support from idealistic university students and frequently from teachers. In each case they met repression. For much of 1958 and 1959, the nation was in turmoil over workers' rights.

Repression of unions within Mexico was justified, in part, by Cold War anti-communism that was given added urgency by the victory of the Cuban revolution in 1959. While Mexico's tradition of supporting at least the rhetoric of revolution and anti-imperialism meant that the Mexican government supported Cuba against initial US attacks, its attempts to purge the labor movement of communists and its commitment to capitalist development demonstrated that it would not tolerate left-wing, working-class challenges to the status quo. While rhetorically continuing to champion revolution and the advancement of workers and peasants, the Mexican government did whatever it thought necessary to prevent workers or peasants from gaining any real power.

Though the system of government control of workers through their unions was not quietly accepted, it was firmly in place when the FAT was called into existence in 1960.

Understanding "Christian Unionism"

> Conscious of our rights as workers and of our social responsibility, we signers declare a firm decision to undertake the organization of Christian unionism in Mexico.
>
> The principles that will guide our course at all times will be *(a)* union liberty, *(b)* union democracy, *(c)* independence from all political parties, *(d)* autonomy from government and employers, and *(e)* the constant struggle for the material and spiritual elevation of the working-class.
>
> Based on these principles we found the Frente Auténtico del Trabajo (FAT), that will unite and train unions and workers in a new federation....[6]
>
>   —Declaration of the Constitution of the Frente Auténtico
>   del Trabajo, October 18, 1960

The founding of the FAT in October 1960 was a grand event, with the support of numerous organizations. But grand events and ceremonial support do not in themselves lead to working-class organization. Held at the Mexican Institute for Social Studies, just blocks from Mexico City's central plaza, the event was attended by over 70 people representing a variety of international social and labor organizations affiliated with the Catholic Church.[7] The FAT's founders considered these international organizations representative of "the new union force that will make a contribution to the construction of better perspectives to achieve high standards for the working-class and the forces of the people."[8]

The FAT's relationship to the Catholic Church needs to be understood within the context of both Mexican Catholicism and the changing times. While Mexico is known as a strongly Catholic nation, it has always had a love-hate relationship with Catholicism. It was in the name of the Catholic Church as well as Spain that Cortez had conquered the Aztecs, tearing down their temples and building both a new cathedral and the seat of Spanish government on top of their ruins. Most Mexicans adore their Virgin of Guadalupe, the dark-skinned Madonna who appeared in 1531 to Juan Diego, an Indian, not to his European superiors. Others swear the whole affair was a simple fraud to aid in mass conversions of the indigenous population.

Without a doubt the Church leaders served as a major prop to three centuries of oppressive colonial rulers. In the 1850s liberals gained control of the government and ordained a new constitution, including provisions to break up the extensive land holdings of the Church. Condemning liberal principles of "freedom of speech, freedom of the press, freedom of assembly, the right to vote, and popular sovereignty ... as being contrary to the laws of God and Church,"[9] Church leaders joined wealthy conservatives in going so far as to invite a French occupation of the country under the rule of Emperor Maximillian. It is the defeat of the French by Juarez that is celebrated on May 5th, the Cinco de Mayo. With the liberal triumph, Church lands were confiscated and Church control over education was eliminated. Weddings and birth registries, as well as access to burial grounds, costly burdens previously imposed by the Church on poor peasants, were made civil procedures.

The process of restricting the power of the Church was repeated in the post-revolutionary Constitution of 1917. Articles 3 and 30 made all schools secular. Article 5 forbade monastic orders. Article 27 took all Church properties, including church buildings. Article 130 prohibited any form of political involvement by any formally religious institution, minister, or publication. These articles were promoted not by atheistic modernizers but in the name of "the greatest democrat known in ancient times, who was called Jesus Christ," and against the clergy as "perverters of Christianity and destroyers of human values."[9] As with other provisions concerning the redistribution of private property and the establishment of labor rights, these provisions were ignored or enforced at the convenience of those who controlled the government.[10] The 1917 triumph of the Bolshevik Revolution in Russia, with its subsequent attacks on the Russian Church, gave Mexican bishops the excuse they needed to become firmly anti-communist. They were already anti-revolutionary.

In 1926 the uneasy coexistence of the Church and the now constitutionally anti-clerical government broke into open warfare again. Thousands died in the year-long Cristero Revolt, and it was almost three years before Masses resumed. Reconciliation did not really take place until the late 1930s.[11] Yet, in the context of this politically circumscribed, often vigorously conservative and elitist church, there remained liberationist and democratic tendencies.

The Mexican Social Secretariat (SSM) was created in 1920 as a way for the Church to be active in society despite the restrictions imposed on it by the constitution. The idea for a social secretariat came from Western Europe where it had been inspired by the 1893 pro-worker encyclical, *Rerum Novarum*, of Pope Leo XIII. The Secretariat's first director, Alfredo Mendez Medina S.J., had been trained in Europe, where Catholic unions were common and where unions saw themselves in a revolutionary tradition. Within four years Mendez Medina had developed 350 affiliated organizations with approximately 80,000 members. Mexican Church leaders rewarded this success by replacing him with a more conservative leader who went on to form groups active in the Cristero Revolt and later, the National Association of Guadalupan Workers.

The Guadalupano movement still resonates in Mexico. The Virgin of Guadalupe is a hallmark symbol for Mexican Catholicism. Pilgrims literally crawl on their knees to her, begging for her miraculous intervention in their humble lives. The initial miraculous appearance of this brown-skinned Madonna to an Indian greatly helped the white Spanish convert their native labor force into religious brothers. The Guadalupano movement had a similar goal. This alliance of conservative church leaders and employers sought to eliminate the class-struggle orientation that leftists were imparting to workers in the labor movement. Founded in 1938, the movement encouraged employers to aid workers in establishing shrines in the workplace where they could all pray together at noon. Bosses also organized annual pilgrimages to the Shrine of the Virgin, where tens of thousands of workers were instructed that a good Christian is a good, productive worker who seeks to advance the fortunes of his company. This, along with the Cold War purges of communist union workers, went a long way toward transforming the ideological orientation of many Mexican workers.[13]

In the late 1930s the SSM also started the Casa de Estudiantes Proletarianos (House of Proletarian Students) in Mexico City. Its goal was to train working Catholics to become union leaders with Catholic—i.e., conservative—values and to push out left-leaning leaders. Workers were given six weeks of training in labor law, organizing, speaking, and leadership that apparently proved effective. Within a year they had gained leadership positions in 12 unions in Mexico City and were spreading to other regions. The SSM pulled the plug on the group when they realized that by giving workers the skills they needed to become independent of established labor leaders, they were also giving them the skills to become independent of further guidance from the Church.[14]

In 1948 the Social Secretariat swung back to its progressive orientation with the arrival of Pedro Velazquez, who had been trained in Europe in the tradition of the worker-priest. In the Cold War '50s and within the conservative Mexican church context, Velazquez declared that the goal was to build a more just society that was neither capitalist nor communist, but Christian. From 1956 on, he had to contend with conservative Miguel Dario Miranda as archbishop of Mexico. Miranda had headed the SSM in its turn to the right from 1924 to 1932. He did what he could to limit Velazquez.

In 1955, Velazquez established the short-lived Federation of Free Labor Unions with the goal of starting independent unions. When his inexperience at forming unions in the Mexican context led only to frustration, he decided, "We should not promote Christian unions, rather we should transform the existing ones, principally by training true union bosses."[15] In 1958, in the midst of the national labor upheaval, he promoted the spread of Catholic Working-Class Youth (JOC) and Workers'

Promotion (Promoción Obrera), two groups devoted to social justice agitation and the development of leadership skills among its members. To address the always precarious economic situation of working-class families, Velazquez also urged the creation of Cajas Populares, parish-based credit unions. He established ties with the Latin American Confederation of Christian Unionists (CLASC) and with the International Federation of Christian Unions. All of these would prove important in the development of the FAT.

The Christian workers youth movement, JOC, was started by a pro-union priest, Rodolfo Escamila, in 1947, in the mining community of Tlalpujahua, Michoacan. When Velazquez worked with Escamila to spread JOC nationally in the late '50s, they met with great success. The movement strengthened throughout the '60s as liberation theology gained force. The JOC became a key source for the dedicated young workers who built the FAT from the grassroots in its first decade.

Promoción Obrera found its greatest success with the working-class community of Tepito in Mexico City, where it began in 1958. The members of Promoción's "Grupo Tepito" were employed in shoe-making or construction and most were originally from the state of Guanajuato. Promoción organized group study and reflection toward a goal of social action to resolve the problems of workers. Some of the literature they studied was generated by CLASC.[15] In 1959 Promoción established a formal affiliation with CLASC. From this point Promoción got technical, ideological, and economic support from CLASC. Taking advantage of a 1960 visit of CLASC representative Emilio Maspero, Promoción's Grupo Tepito decided with the support of Pedro Velazquez and Rodolfo Escamila to create the FAT. CLASC, with its experience in union organizing, agreed to provide the FAT with the expertise that the SSM had always lacked.[16]

The Mexican Social Secretariat that gave birth to the FAT embodied a complex history with both progressive and reactionary tendencies. It was originally inspired by pro-working class ideas and forces within Catholic Europe, but it came to exist in Mexico because a frequently reactionary Church had been politically limited by the revolutionary Constitution of 1917. To be able to have a counter-revolutionary influence within an officially anti-clerical Mexico, the Mexican church hierarchy imported a progressive European, who found Mexican workers very receptive to his work. The Church soon corrected course and used the SSM to contribute to the bloody Cristero Revolt and to fight communism through the intercession of the Virgin of Guadalupe. Again turning to Europe for new inspiration, it swung somewhat to the left, creating various working-class organizations, including the FAT. The SSM, which had developed problems with previous workers' movements as it continued to vacillate between its progressive and conservative tendencies, would eventually develop problems with the FAT. It could never be truly revolutionary.

The SSM and the CLASC did commit real resources to attempt to spread the ideas of the new FAT to Mexican workers. Much of the work was that of education, broadly defined. The actual work of organizing independent unions would fall to the workers themselves.

Guanajuato: The FAT's First Contract

Given the tight control of labor relations exercised by the PRI and charro unions, it has been extremely difficult to organize new, independent unions. The goal of the FAT has always been to do precisely that. The barriers to organizing new unions have required that initial efforts take place covertly, *bajo el agua,* below the surface of the water. Early efforts in Mexico City were unsuccessful, due largely to the nature of its initial membership. Most of the original working-class members of the FAT had recently arrived in the capital from the state of the Guanajuato, an agricultural and industrial region northwest of the capital. In 1962 the central focus of the FAT's organizing moved to Guanajuato's largest cities, Leon and Irapuato, where contacts were much better. The strategy soon bore fruit.

Nicolas Medina was crucial to the success of the FAT in Leon. Born and raised as a member of the working-class community of Leon, Medina was unusually well educated. He completed primary school and then continued his studies in seminary. He had also labored in the shoe-making industry. Medina then moved to Mexico City, where he became a member of the Grupo Tepito. He attended the FAT's founding and signed its charter document. Nicolas Medina understood both the Christian and the working-class aspects of the early FAT's goals, and he committed himself heart and soul to them as though he were a priest and this was his mission. He was able to express the vision and the ideology that inspired workers at the international level of the CLASC and at the national level of the SSM in a way that also rang true to his fellow workers.

In April 1962, Medina began the process of *formación* in Leon. Formación, literally formation, could also be called worker education, but beyond merely conveying information and ideas, its goal is to transform the worker in his or her abilities, outlook, and action. It seeks to convert workers who have been shaped in an abusive world of limited expectations into workers who fully realize that it is their right as human beings to be able to live a life of dignity in a fully democratic environment. Its goal is to develop committed people willing to devote themselves to achieving those rights for themselves and their fellow workers, despite the situations that may confront them. It also seeks to give those workers the tools to effectively engage in that world of struggle.

Medina's seminary contacts in Leon served him well. He was able to make connections easily with progressive church leaders. Along with Pedro Lara of Mexico City, Medina began by offering a weekend seminar in the Church of a supportive priest. He drew his first group largely from the JOC group in a shoe-making district. The course addressed such fundamental questions as: What is a union? How does one form a union? What is a collective contract? The seminar was most workers' first exposure to labor law and labor history. It also helped them see themselves in the context of an international effort of unions seeking to respond to injustice.

One of the 15 in attendance at this first training session was a nineteen-year-old, Antonio Velazquez, whose formal education consisted of five years of primary school—quite a lot for a worker of those days. He recalls vividly how new the world looked to him as a result of those two and a half days. And he recalls with joy that the seminar weekend ended with a party at the Rincon Gaucho, roughly translated as the Cowboy Bar and Grill. Seminar participants left the party with the determination to create not only a union, but a federation of new unions in their state of Guanajuato. The next weekend Medina repeated the process in the nearby industrial city of Irapuato.

By late April, that first group of 15 workers in Leon called a meeting of trusted fellow workers. The 60 in attendance decided they would create a union for people in the shoe industry. They pursued the process of formación, spreading ideas and information to the new workers and deepening their own understanding of labor law and the FAT's ideas of what would make a good union. The group chose Jose Torres as their president and Antonio Velazquez as their secretary of labor and conflicts. By the time they were ready to begin the process of registration, Nicolas Medina had left for several months of training with the CLASC in Brazil. They had to invent their process, "with pure Mexican valor," Velazquez recalled.

The young FAT workers knew the formal process called for in the law, and they followed it precisely. They knew that the labor board would not look kindly on a union that was not under the ruling party's control. It could arbitrarily delay or deny their request. However, when they filed their documents with the local Labor Arbitration and Conciliation Board, the board was taken by surprise. On August 16, 1962, the board granted them a registration for their union, the Liberational Union of Shoe Workers and Related Trades.

The FAT workers continued to attract eager new workers, many of them through the JOC, others by recommendations of sympathetic priests. An early problem facing these workers was that while the FAT clearly said that unions must be fully autonomous, with no dependence on or control from any political party, any branch of government, or any employer, they were relying on the Church for their meeting place, for supplies, and for various sorts of support. They determined that they needed to find an office of their own. To afford it they each pledged small weekly dues. When they found a place they could afford, Father Salvador Garcia—who had encouraged them from the beginning—gave them their first chairs, a desk, and a typewriter. Now, like young people finally moving out of their parents' house, they felt more clearly on their own.

This early break was important, and bigger ones would come later. While grateful for the help, they could not allow themselves to be subject to manipulation by an organization with interests other than their own. Nicolas Medina made clear in 1964 the delicate balance between a union having roots in the Church and one tied to it:

> The only doctrine that sustains a true conception of humanity and the world is Christianity.... Nonetheless, we should avoid any discussion of theology within the union context. Practices of any religious sect

have no place within unions ... also, any person without any religious distinction, has the right to organize ... and to live with dignity.[18]

In the early years, the barriers between the FAT and JOC and the SSM were very permeable, as all worked toward a shared vision of greater justice for working people. This vision was strengthened by the ideas of Pope John XXIII and through the Vatican II conference.[19] Vatican II marked a sea change in the Catholic Church, creating a new focus on peace and justice in the present, not merely on salvation in the next life. The Pope's call for the Church to make a "preferential option for the poor" strengthened the resolve of those already engaged in this work and targeted more resources to support their efforts. The priests Medina had known in seminary shared this commitment to social justice work and encouraged their parishioners to become involved. For many of them, this turned out to be working for labor justice through the FAT.

The FAT's first organizing drive in Leon was begun in December 1962 at Calzado America, a small shoe factory employing a dozen workers. The response of the business owner was simply to fire all the workers—regardless of the law. Workers responded to their firing by picketing the owner's house, which was immediately adjacent to the factory. The enraged owner drove through the workers' picket line with his pickup truck in an attempt to do them bodily harm and scare them away.

Previously, most workers in Leon had been so convinced of their own powerlessness that they would never have organized a union on their own, let alone picket a boss's house. The owner was outraged by the workers' lack of submissiveness and shocked at what happened next. Instead of being frightened away, the workers calmly summoned the police and charged the owner with assault. Since this occurred on a Friday evening, the owner had to sit in jail over the weekend until a judge could free him.

The story in the papers the next day was that professional Christian agitators had used violence to get a respected local employer thrown in jail. The FAT workers were overjoyed, not at what the press said, but that the press was talking about them and their new union. Other workers would read and understand.

The FAT's Sindicato Libertario moved into larger quarters in early 1963. They needed a place that could accommodate a hundred workers at a time. They met every Sunday morning for formación. Workers would attend a five-week series of classes. At the end of five weeks, each worker who had stayed with the project was given an assignment to set up a meeting in their neighborhood with new workers. Many of these workers would join the Sunday classes and the process would continue. The FAT was gradually transforming the historically subservient mentality of Leon's workers.

In 1962 the Mexican Congress had passed a law requiring that employers share their annual profits with their workers. Although they had been required to do this by the 1917 constitution, employers were upset that it was finally being enforced. The law was to take effect in 1964. When the FAT agitated for better pay in 1963, employers used the new law as an excuse, saying that all would be better for workers in 1964, if only they would wait patiently. When it became clear to Leon's employers that the FAT would not wait patiently, they called for a "chat" with their local leadership. Seven young FAT workers, including Nicolas Medina and Antonio Velazquez, along with Father Salvador Garcia, attended the meeting.

At this informal meeting, the bosses said they felt that the workers had been using the word "Christian" badly. They should be seeking greater harmony, not greater conflict. The workers remained skeptical of the bosses' vision of harmony. The bosses decided to make things more concrete. They said that since they all wanted a prosperous Leon with no conflict, they could all share from the same pie. They offered each of the workers 50,000 pesos, and they offered Medina a one-way ticket to another country of his choice.

This sum was far more than any of the workers could ever hope to gain legitimately in their lifetime. Because of the vast disparity in incomes between bosses and workers, the tactic of buying off opponents often works quite well in Mexican labor relations. Before anyone could dream too long about how to enjoy such a fortune, Medina stood up and said, "*Que poca madre tienen. Ustedes son como león que cree que todos son de misma condición.*" (Didn't your mother raise you better than that? You are all like a lion that believes everyone is as violently voracious as he.) And they walked out.

Encouraged by developments in Leon and in other locations, the FAT called its first National Council, held November 24 and 25, 1963. In attendance were five regional coordinating committees, four unions limited to specific plants,[20] and four industrial unions,[21] of which three were from Leon and Irapuato.

One of the most interesting documents to come out of this meeting contained a list of the motives for the FAT's continued work. The most enduring of these are:

> Mexican Unionism is badly represented, badly led, and even more badly oriented.
>
> Current unions, tied to a political party and controlled from above, lose their effectiveness in most cases, because the leaders only seek their own comfort and personal advancement, forgetting their pretended roles as union leaders.
>
> The sectarian monopoly that hand-picked union leaders have in labor boards is the reason that there is hardly any legal recognition of independent unions. For all of that, the FAT was born into the union life in Mexico, with a new style and new methods that enlist its action in the service of workers, affirming that its only commitment is to the poor, the workers, the employees and the peasants of the country that want to be protagonists of their own liberation, with the risks that this carries with it.[22]

This national gathering chose Nicolas Medina to be secretary-general, Juan Bruno Cervantes as secretary of labor, and Celerino Velazquez as secretary of organizing. In a nine-page paper, "The Organization of the Workers," which he wrote for distribution through the Mexican Institute of Social Studies, Medina expressed his "revolutionary" analysis of the contemporary situation of Mexican workers and the labor movement.

> The worker is the only one that can resolve his problems, by himself, and no other force has the right to intervene decisively in the solution of such problems.
>
> True unionism should not just be a modification of existing union organizations, but a radical transformation of social and economic structures.... To achieve this in Mexico we first need a Union Movement that materially, intellectually, and spiritually elevates and perfects the worker, making him capable of fully achieving the communitarian enterprise that Real Unionism demands as a solution to the social question.[23]

With Medina taking on national responsibilities, the other young workers in Leon had to do more too. Medina had become a "lawyer" of sorts. Now, Antonio Velazquez and others had to make themselves into lawyers as well. These worker-lawyers knew the letter of the law concerning labor, which in Mexico is quite favorable to workers. They felt able to litigate, to file for injunctions, and to file documents with the local labor board. They often found that the professional lawyers retained by employers were able to slow them down by finding typos or other minor errors in their paperwork. But the biggest legal surprise the FAT "lawyers" got in Leon was when they went to file their first contract.

In 1964, Sindicato Libertario successfully completed negotiations with a small shoe firm, Calzado Gecesa, and was ready to file the FAT's first contract. Their papers all seemed in order, but the labor board claimed that there was no record of the union's ever having received its registry in August 1962. Apparently the union's registry had been "lost." It took weeks of effort, with marches in Leon and in the capital, Guanajuato, before a court would issue an injunction—based on the legal copy of registry the union had retained—to restore the union's registry. Although Mexican law appears generous to labor when one reads it, in practice it is rarely so.

After this first contract, the Sindicato Libertario was able to win contracts at a series of shoe factories in Leon. However, because of the problems they had had with the "lost" registry, the FAT decided to form other unions too. They formed three new unions for shoemakers bearing the historically revolutionary names of 20th of November, Martyrs of Rio Blanco, and Insurgente Ignacio Allende. The four unions quickly organized over a dozen shoe factories. Both within these factories and beyond them—in order to deter further organizing—employers began to improve wages and conditions significantly. The initial contract at Botas Jaca in 1965 brought terms up to the legal minimums. It included wages at least equal to minimum wage, a 48-hour workweek, standards for intensity and quality of work, some limits on discipline, Sundays off, 8 paid holidays, and up to 12 days of paid vacation per year.

In 1964, the FAT organized the May First union for workers in the construction industry. Since there had been little previous union activity in this industry, workers were often paid less than the minimum wage, work hours were long, and paydays were at the convenience of the employer. The May First union always managed to get at least minimum wage and an eight-hour day, plus some basic benefits like registry with the Social Security agency for medical coverage and retirement. The union worked by getting a member hired on a job, then quietly organizing the other workers until they were ready to call a work stoppage. They would then negotiate on the site to get work started again.

In 1967, the FAT won a contract at the German pump-making factory KSB. The factory had opened in 1959 with no union in the plant. In 1966, KSB let the workers know that they would not be paying out the legally required Christmas bonus. Workers began to look around for a union, "and eventually we found the Christians," recalls Pedro Alcaraz. The manager was from Germany with experience in Argentina: both countries with strong union movements. He was used to working with unions and had no problem with them. The 41 unionized workers signed their first contract in November 1967. Since productivity and profits were good, the workers were able to steadily improve both their wages and their benefits. Within a short time, KSB workers had one of the best contracts in town. Over time the workforce grew to over 130 workers.

By 1967 the FAT had more union contracts in Leon than the CTM or any other union federation. Their workers were among the best paid and the most militant. The FAT had become a force to be reckoned with.

Irapuato: Winning Fairness in a Bigger Factory

A similar process had been going on in nearby Irapuato. Initial months of worker education attracted a sufficient core of workers to begin the process of registering unions and organizing plants. A small shoemakers union was formed in Irapuato, but the larger industry developing in Irapuato was clothing.

The FAT began its organizing in Irapuato the same as it had in Leon, by recruiting promising workers through the JOC and on the recommendation of sympathetic churchpeople. Nicolas Medina and others trained them in workers' rights and basic union issues and gave them a vision of a world in which workers were treated with dignity and received a good wage.

One of the first businesses unionized in Irapuato was Ropa Irapuato. This new clothing business opened in 1959 as the first modern, large-scale factory in town. While there had previously been plenty of businesses making clothing in Irapuato, the scale was artisanal. Women sewed in their homes or in workshops with as many as 30 workers. This was the same as the shoe industry in Leon. Ropa Irapuato's young entrepreneur, Francisco Barra, decided he would make clothes in a new way. He modeled his factory after factories in the United States. His goal was to sell to a national, rather than regional, market. When the plant opened, it employed 300 workers, all of whom earned at least the minimum wage and all of whom were enrolled in the Social Security system. This voluntary compliance with legal labor standards was unusual. Barra felt that if he could make his workers happy, they would produce more for him.

While workers organized in Leon had been mostly men, in Irapuato they were mostly women. When Barra found out about the organizing effort he warned many of his workers' parents that their daughters were getting mixed up with communists. Though they worked through the Church, he told them, they weren't really Catholics. They would take them away to work in Cuba or, at the very least, get them pregnant.

The boss's fear tactics proved unsuccessful. In August 1962, the workers formed the Union de Obreros y Obreras de Ropa de Irapuato (Irapuato Clothing Workers Union). Francisco Barra eventually decided that he could negotiate with the union. He recognized them in November.

In December 1964, it came time to negotiate for the first new contract with Ropa Irapuato.[24] Negotiations broke down and the workers declared a strike. The owner, vacillating between pleasing the workers and listening to the more conventional advice of his lawyers and other businesspeople, decided he would pull the machines out of the plant and set up elsewhere with a new workforce. The workers advised him this was not legal, and they set up around-the-clock guards to see that nothing was taken out. When workers caught Barra's relatives bundling sewing machine heads in fabric in the middle of the night, they embarrassed him enough to sign a new contract.

Over time the relationship between the union and the employer improved. By 1969 Francisco Barra had kicked his lawyers out of contract negotiations, and negotiated directly with workers from that time on. As trust improved between the two sides, Barra was able to increase efficiency by reducing his managerial staff to five. The plant ran well until, like a great many other domestic manufacturers in Mexico, facing intense foreign competition and the collapse of the domestic market, it closed in the crisis of 1995. At that time it was employing 200 workers.

It is useful to compare the experience of the FAT with small businesses like the shoe workshops of Leon to that of larger companies like Ropa Irapuato or KSB. The FAT has been able to organize small firms where workers have desperately needed help in improving wages and working conditions, but they have generally faced fierce resistance in those cases. However, when the FAT has been able to organize workers at a larger company with better technology and somewhat more enlightened management, both the company and the workers have done well. Opponents of the FAT have seized on the fact that many of the small firms organized by the FAT have gone out of business, labeling the FAT *el cierre-empresas*, the business-closer. In cases such as Ropa Irapuato we see that bigger businesses were able to succeed for decades with FAT contracts. Most large firms prefer to deal with unions that they can control, but those that have been forced to live with the FAT have found that treating workers more fairly need not cause them problems.[25]

Chihuahua: Taking on Pepsi

The next region where the FAT grew rapidly was the northern state of Chihuahua. Crucial to the success of the FAT's efforts there was a young worker, Alfredo Dominguez. A skilled mechanic, Dominguez had worked at Chihuahua Steel, General Motors, and Volkswagen. His initial orientation on labor relations came through his involvement with the conservative Guadalupanos. His viewpoint began to change in 1962 when he had his first contacts with the FAT through a training program in Mexico City.

His orientation had always been religious, but through the FAT and the Vatican II reforms, he began to interpret labor relations through a combination of history and political economy on the one hand, and the book of Exodus on the other. In both cases, he saw an enslaved population of workers trying to discover their path to liberation.

Dominguez returned to his native Chihuahua and helped the FAT establish a labor training center there. Through the networks of the Guadalupanos and the JOC, the center attracted a core of committed working-class activists. Working quietly within their factories, they identified trusted colleagues who could constitute the core of a new union.[26]

The first organizing success would come in 1963 at the Pepsi Cola bottling plant. One of the workers caught up in the effort was 19-year-old Antonio Villalba. Today both Villalba and Dominguez are on the national staff of the FAT, but on the Saturday afternoon in 1963, when he was asked to attend a secret union meeting, Villalba had mixed feelings. He "knew" that unions existed mostly to collect dues and to en- rich their charro leaders, so he was opposed to them.[27]

Still, young Villalba had nothing else to do, so he attended the secret union meeting the next day, began to imagine new possibilities, and was chosen to be the secretary of exterior. The meeting served as the first as- sembly of Pepsi workers. The slate of officers was confirmed, docu- ments were signed, and the next day the union was registered at the local labor board. The board gave them their registry not because they had met all the requirements, but because they had taken them by surprise.

In that first year, Villalba and many other new labor activists de- voted long hours to studying and learning about labor law, about labor history, and about a new vision of a society that would serve the interests of its majority, the workers and peasants. Villalba recalls his first 25-hour bus ride to Mexico City and the important experience of meet- ing workers from other states. He gained a sense that he was part of something important and growing, a national and international move- ment. It was his first time out of the state.

Within two years the FAT went on to organize unions at Ropa el Diamante, Ropa la Paz, Mercado del Real, Transportes Urbanos, Industrializadora de Cerdo, and Triplay de Parral. The process was harder now. The plywood workers from Parral, almost 200 miles away in the mountains, had to march to the capital city, Chihuahua, demand- ing that their right to unionize be respected. The clothing factories, Dia- mante and La Paz, both already had CTM unions, which they renounced in order to affiliate with the FAT.[28]

When workers from Industrializadora de Cerdo, the pork-packing plant, took their paperwork to the labor board, they were refused a regis- try as an independent union. As a fallback strategy, the workers decided to affiliate with the CTM and later to become independent. They were given their registry with the CTM without any further problems. The CTM then invited the new union's secretary-general to attend a training course in Cuernavaca, just south of Mexico City. According to Antonio

Villalba, the CTM course provided thorough training in "wine, women, and song." When he returned to Chihuahua this leader no longer had an interest in leading his workers to independence from the CTM. Instead he followed the ways of official unions, rose steadily, and became a state leader for the CTM.

What the FAT had gained by their surprise action was soon challenged in a counter-attack. At the El Diamante and La Paz clothing factories, all of the workers were fired. New workers were hired and a CTM union was formed. At Transportes Urbanos enough of the workers were fired to allow the formation of a CTM union. At Triplay de Parral all of the workers were fired. At Mercado de Real just the union leaders were fired. And finally, in 1969 Pepsi Cola fired all of its workers. In all cases a new CTM union was established. The process was not a tranquil one, but whenever they needed support from the labor board or from the police, employers were able to get it. From this experience the FAT learned all too well the workings of what they call the infernal trilogy: "*Charro, gobierno, y patrón, son el mismo cabrón.*" (The charro, the government and the boss are all the same bastard.)[29]

The organizational base that the FAT had established in Chihuahua lived on after these initial defeats. It would soon serve as the basis of a much larger social struggle that spread throughout the state in the wake of the upheavals of 1968.

Notes

1   Freeman, Joshua, et al. 1992. *Who Built America? Working People and the Nation's Economy, Politics, Culture, and Society. Volume II: From the Guilded Age to the Present.* 500, 508–512, 600–604. New York: Pantheon.

2   Esping-Anderson, Gosta. 1985. *Politics Against Markets.* Princeton, NJ: Princeton University Press. Walter Korpi. 1983. *The Democratic Class Struggle.* New York: Routledge and Keagan Paul.

3   Cumberland, Charles C. 1968. *Mexico: The Struggle for Modernity*, 320. London: Oxford University Press.

4   Ortega, Max. 1995. "Vallejo Gana las Elecciones." *Trabajo y Democracia Hoy* (May–June): 50.

5   La Botz, Dan. 1992. *Mask of Democracy: Labor Suppression in Mexico Today*, 54, 69–71. Boston: South End Press. Luna Arias, Jesus. 1995. "Las Huelgas Rieleras y la Represion de 1959." *Trabajo y Democraci Hoy* (May–June): 54.

6   "25 Años de Lucha por la Democracia." 1985. *Resistencia Obrera* 73 (February): 8.

7   Among those in attendence were representatives of the Guadalupanos; the Workers Movement of Mexican Catholic Action, which had no working-class membership; the Federation of Catholic Organizations, known for its work in encouraging churches to keep candles burning eternally; Cajas Populares, which encouraged working-class members to start savings accounts within their parishes; leaders of the JOC; the Promocion Obrera group of nearby neighborhood of Tepito, the only real workers present; and soe people claiming to represent the National Catholic Confederation of Labor, an organization dissolved in 192

8   The FAT initially affiliated itself with the Latin American Confederation of Christian Unionists (CLASC) and with the International Federation of Christian Unions. "25 Años de Lucha por la Democracia:" 8.

9   Cumberland, 185.

10   Cumberland, 264, 265.

11   Cumberland, 264–72.

12   Cumberland, 276–85.

13   "VIVA CRISTO REY! Y LA REINA DEL TRABAJO! Los Trabajadores Guadalupanos." 1979. Anonymous manuscript in the FAT's files, Leon, 6–19.

14   "VIVA CRISTO REY!, 4.

15   Robles, Jorge, and Luis Angel Gómez. 1996. "Las Cooperativas del
           FAT." *Parte del Proyectcto Historia del FAT, Mexico*, Mexico, 1–2.

16   "25 Años de Lucha por la Democracia:" 12.

17   Robles and Gómez: 2.

18   Medina, Nicolas. 1964. "La Organizacion de los Trabajadores." Instituto
           Mexicano de Estudios Sociales, A.C., manuscript in the FAT's files,
           Leon, 7.

19   Encyclicals *Mater et Magistra* (1961) and *Pacem in Terris* (1963).

20   Sindicato de la Fabrica de Textiles y Acabados (textiles), Sindicato de
           Maderas Industrializadoras de Morelia (wood products), Sindicato de
           Trabajadores Mineros y Similares de la Empresa San Carlos los Picos de
           Querétaro (mining), and Sindicato de Trabajadores de la Empresa
           Embotelladora Pepsi Cola de Chihuahua (Pepsi).

21   Sindicato Libertario de Obreros Zapateros, Similares y Conexos de Leon
           (shoes); Sindicato de Trabajadores de Artes Gráficas, Similares y
           Conexos (graphic arts); Sindicato Germinal de la Industria del Calzado de
           Irapuato (shoes); and Sindicato del la Manufactura de Ropa Irapuato
           (clothing).

22   "25 Años de Lucha por la Democracia:" 11.

23   Medina, 5.

24   By June 1964 the FAT had formed 13 unions within the state of
           Guanajuato. It formed the State Federation of Autonomous Unions of
           Guanajuato (FESAG), and managed to get the federation officially
           registered with the state labor board. The FAT itself has never been able to
           gain official national registration. While workers may form a union or a
           federation of unions, unless the government decides to officially
           recognize it, it has no standing within legal labor proceedings. Therefore,
           FESAG can deal with its state labor boards, and its local unions can deal
           with businesses and local labor boards. The nationally chartered industrial
           unions of the FAT can sign contracts in any state, but the FAT itself
           legally has no standing.

25   Velazquez, Antonio. 1996. Oral interview, Leon, July 7.

26   Dominguez, Alfredo. 1996. Oral interview. July 22.

27   This understanding is still common today, as documented in a 1996 study
           done by employers in Ciudad Juarez, on Chihuahua's border with Texas.
           The majority of those surveyed were between 18 and 25, and, as young
           Villalba had been three decades earlier, most of them were opposed to
           unions because they saw them as corrupt and as taking dues away from
           them. They had all been vaccinated against wanting a union. Few workers

then or now can even imagine an alternative—an authentic union of, by, and for the workers.

28   Villalba, Antonio, 1996. Oral interview, the FAT headquarters, Mexico DF, November 22; Méndez, Luis and José Othón Quiroz. 1991. "El FAT: AutogestiónObrera y Modernidad." *El Cotidiano*, 40 (March–April): 37–51.

29   Villalba interview.

4.

Transitions
From Student Uprising to Insurgencia Obrera, From Harmonization to Class Struggle

In the highly politicized late 1960s, forces at work both internationally and in Mexico made it natural for the FAT to link some of its local struggles to national poltical movements. Sectors of the Catholic Church were leaning to the left, students and others worldwide were creating an anti-imperialist New Left and protesting the US war in Vietnam, and labor organizations worldwide were feeling the stirrings of democratic tendencies. In the early 1970s the FAT became an actor with national recognition, known for some of its own struggles and for its part within major labor alliances in what came to be called the *Insurgencia Obrera*, or workers' insurgency. In the process, the FAT forged ties in other countries that became tremendously important in the 1990s.

Liberation Theology
In 1968, the year of the Tet Offensive and student and workers' movements around the world, the Catholic bishops of Latin America met in Medellin, Colombia, and denounced social inequality and class exploitation. This gathering grew out of the Vatican Council II, held in Rome from 1962 through 1965, which declared a "preferential option for the poor." It emphasized that the Church would be found in communities working for social justice, not in buildings or ecclesiastic hierarchies. By 1980 there were over 100,000 Christian communities in Latin America, empowered by the writings of liberation theologists who declared

that "to know God is to do justice."[1] Growing out of the social justice side of the Catholic Church, the FAT was greatly encouraged by these developments.

The Mexican theologian Porfirio Miranda influenced the thinking of many FAT leaders. Miranda denounced conditions in Mexico, where "25 percent of the population monopolized two thirds of the national income, leaving only one third for the remaining 75 percent." No Mexican worker would willingly accept this distribution of income, he reasoned; thus it must be unjust according to the Papal Encyclical *Rerum Novarum,* which declared, "If through necessity or fear of a worse evil, the workman accepts harder conditions because an employer will give him no better, he is the victim of force and injustice." Mexican workers, Miranda asserted, "are being permanently robbed, with the support, approval, and sanction of the prevailing judicial system."[2]

Miranda accepted that the analysis he offered was radical, and that it was grounded in Marx as much as it was in the Bible, but he urged readers of his book, *Marx and the Bible*, to let go of past prejudice and to accept that the two were not in conflict. The true conflict, he asserted, was between biblically rooted Christianity and the injustices of contemporary capitalism.

Activists within the FAT not only read Miranda, they formed close ties with him. The influence of Miranda and of liberation theology in general on the FAT was significant. The FAT's Catholic background put it in the middle of the conflict between the conservative, hierarchical messages of the traditional church and the more radical devotion to social justice. Liberation theology helped to overcome that conflict.

As the '60s moved into the '70s, many FAT activists began to study Marxism and anarchism as a way of understanding the capitalist system that resisted their existence. This caused growing tension between the FAT and CLASC, the Latin American Christian Union Confederation that had supported its creation and development. Following the ecumenical spirit of the times, CLASC had changed its name to the Latin American Labor Congress (CLAT) but remained Christian Democratic in orientation and staunchly anti-communist. In 1973 the FAT supported a multi-union event expressing solidarity with Chilean workers and denouncing the military overthrow of the democratic socialist government of Salvador Allende. CLAT delegates attending the event with the FAT were disturbed by the abundance of anarchist and communist flags and literature. In contrast, the FAT was troubled that Chile's Christian Democratic Party had collaborated with the brutal military coup. The FAT was eager to end any confusion that it still had Christian Democratic ties. The FAT's clear opposition to corrupt, corporatist unions led it to find natural allies, other unions also committed to autonomy, democracy, and social justice, all of which had embraced leftist ideas.

The FAT's fourth National Congress, held in Leon in 1974, marked a turning point. In the strongly politicized language of the day, an official chronicle put it this way:

> The phase of ideological decolonization and separation from the influence of the CLAT advanced.... The insurgent line of the FAT was defined with the following characteristics: a dynamic of class struggle, politicized unionism, ... a disposition towards openness and dialogue with people and groups of the Mexican left, assimilation of middle class supporters transformed by the student movement of 1968 and the process of politicization which it generated.[3]

The Student Uprising of 1968

The massacre of hundreds of demonstrators at Tlatelolco Square—the bloody climax of Mexico's student uprising of 1968—was the result of the collision of two very different forces. One force, the student movement, was part of a worldwide student uprising that was united somewhat vaguely by its opposition to the US war in Vietnam. As such it was both anti-imperialist and anti-capitalist. Perhaps its most vivid expression came in France in May, when ties between the student movement and industrial workers brought the country to a standstill, forcing President de Gaulle to shore up his support from the military, make concessions to both workers and students, and call for new elections.[4]

The second force consisted of Mexico's business-oriented elites, who hoped that by hosting the Olympics in October 1968 they could show the world that Mexico was ready to enter the First World. Mexico's next bid would be in 1994, when it entered into NAFTA. In both cases the glorious plans made by Mexican presidents were spoiled by rebellions from those claiming to represent the excluded majority of Mexicans. In both cases, the Mexican government turned to its military for an effective response.

Beginning in 1968 students protested the distorted priorities of a government that spent millions building stadiums and housing for Olympic athletes while peasants daily flocked into shantytowns surrounding the capital. They demanded an end to repression and freedom for all political prisoners. Included in their list of prisoners were Demitrio Vallejo and Valentin Campa, who had been sitting in jail since the suppression of the railworkers' strikes ten years earlier. The critique of the police extended to criticism of the whole system of authoritarian control. The movement took on a new determination to tear off the mask of democracy and modernity that President Diaz Ordaz hoped to show the world.[5]

When Mexican police brutally suppressed early demonstrations, students throughout the country became involved and a national movement evolved, coordinated by delegates from 128 high schools and universities. When the police invaded the National Autonomous University of Mexico (UNAM) they had the effect of involving faculty and administrators directly in the student struggle as well. By August students called for a national student strike and efforts were made to reach out beyond the academic community.

By mid-August, marches became enormous. The first march following the invasion of the UNAM drew 80,000. School teachers joined the movement with a rally of their own, estimated at 200,000. A combination of beatings, jailings, killings, torture, and bribes served only to inflame the movement.

While the government claimed the movement was the result of foreign agitators who had failed to destroy France in May, demonstrators carried pictures of Mexican heroes: Zapata, Villa, and Juarez. While the CTM and other official worker and peasant organizations supported the PRI by denouncing the protests, the FAT joined democratic elements in the teachers', electrical workers', and railworkers' unions in open support of the student movement. UNAM's radio station spread the movement's views broadly. Marches came to be joined by workers, by parents of the students, by clerks and professionals who left their offices in response to the students' cries of "People, unite!"

The government acted decisively to end the movement on October 2, ten days before the scheduled opening of the Olympics. Ten thousand heavily armed soldiers surrounded Tlatelolco, the Plaza of the Three

Cultures, where an open rally of about 6,000 was taking place. When the order was given, they opened fire on the crowd. Agents within the crowd fired point-blank at students who had spoken from the platform. When the plaza was virtually cleared, troops turned their weapons on the surrounding apartment buildings of the working-class neighborhood that had a history of sympathy toward the students.[6]

No one knows how many people died. The government denied the massacre ever took place. No media coverage of the event was allowed within Mexico. When *LIFE en Español* covered the story, the issue was confiscated and destroyed.[7] Estimates of those killed vary widely, but most agree at least 250 died that night, with a thousand or more injured. Killings in the plaza were followed up with raids in hospital emergency wards. Hundreds were arrested that night and in the weeks that followed. Through this broad-based campaign of terror, the Mexican government put an end to the student movement.

In doing so, however, the government only strengthened the convictions of all of those opposed to its policies. Workers were radicalized. Many former members of the student movement joined in supporting dissident labor movements in the years to come. Still others joined urban or rural guerrilla bands.

While the massacre allowed Mexico to hold the Olympics with few obvious interruptions, it cost the PRI heavily in terms of legitimacy. It revived political outrage in those workers brushed aside in the late '50s. It alienated a generation of students, an important resource in any developing economy. This "generation of '68" now makes up a majority of those demanding the democratization of Mexico. The killings also damaged whatever credibility the government may have had with Mexico's intellectuals, a class with an important role in shaping any regime's legitimacy. When the PRI chose Luis Echeverria—interior minister in 1968 and apparently responsible for authorizing the Tlatelolco massacre—as its next president, it only increased these tensions.

Echeverria worked hard to reverse the damage he had done to the PRI's image. This is not to say he worked to seriously alter policy. He did, nonetheless, call for a time of political opening, and he spoke out against those who had used the political process for the benefit of the few. He spoke out against corrupt politicians and greedy industrialists. Echeverria greatly increased spending on education, but his increases were largely invested in technical institutes, not in the universities that had rallied large number of protesters in 1968. He created the National Workers Housing Fund, INFONAVIT, and provided an initial 100,000 units of subsidized housing to workers' families. But this "pro-worker" reform also had its reactionary side. It served as a reward to the CTM for having supported the government against the students, and it allowed charro unions to channel these major new resources, preventing the sort of democratic opening for which the president seemed to be calling.

Echeverria also created new rural development programs. He often sought out formerly persecuted leftists to manage branch offices. He also encouraged the formation of new left-wing political parties. He managed to co-opt many recent enemies into working within the PRI's system. He was clearly confident that nothing they were able to do, either through small new government programs or through political parties, would pose any significant challenge to the established power structure.

Echeverria's new rhetoric did alienate many private employers, and it did encourage some testing of the waters to see how much democracy would be tolerated. As such it opened the door for what would soon be called the Insurgencia Obrera. We shall see that despite the new president's progressive sounding words, not much had really changed in Mexico's power structure.

Insurgencia Obrera

In the post-war decades, as both incomes and education rose, workers worldwide sought to move beyond the struggle for mere physical survival and achieve a greater measure of dignity in the workplace and respect in the political realm. In May 1968, French workers took over factories, often in defiance of their official leadership. Similar events took place in Italy's "Hot Autumn" of the same year. In the United States, union leadership was content with economic prosperity and limited by its Cold War anti-communism, but years of prosperity left young workers seeking something more: control over the work process. The wildcat strike at the Lordstown, Ohio, plant stands out. Workers shut down the lines, not for higher pay, but for less alienating lives. Throughout Latin America, a gradual increase in industrial employment and worker well-being led to increasing political power for the working class. Reaction to this shift led to a series of military coups—welcomed by the US government—in Brazil (1964), Argentina (1966 and '76), and Chile (1973).[8] While coups did make these countries safer for capitalism, they also fostered years of poverty (enforced with vicious human rights abuses) and put an end to democractic openings. In this context, Mexican workers clearly understood both what they hoped to gain and what they risked.

The Mexican workers' insurgency began in the early '70s with union reform movements, especially among electrical workers and railworkers, competing for power with charros. When railworkers' union leaders Vallejo and Campa were released in 1971 after more than 10 years in prison, they quickly gained control of 29 of the 36 railworkers union locals. When the government refused to recognize their authority, Vallejo formed the oppositional Railworkers Union Movement (MSF).

The democratic tendency among electrical workers was led by Rafael Galvan of the Union of Electrical Workers of the Mexican Republic (STERM), one of three national electrical workers' unions. Expelled in 1971 from the Congress of Labor, the national PRI-dominated union federation, STERM broadened its organizing beyond its original base among electrical workers.

The FAT joined the MSF and the STERM in calling the First National Day for Union Democracy in 1972. Demonstrations were held in more than 40 cities. In 1973 the FAT, the MSF, and the STERM formed the short-lived National Union of Workers (UNT) and held the second and third National Days for Union Democracy.

Never before had the Mexican people experienced a national workers' movement aimed at democratizing unions and challenging the controlling power of the state. People who for years had hoped for something better while passively doing nothing suddenly felt change was possible. In this atmosphere the Revolutionary Teachers Movement (MMR) called for a national strike. Both bank workers and university employees (staff and faculty) began struggles to unionize. Every workers' struggle became part of a larger effort to change Mexican society, to put the country's revolutionary ideals into practice. Since an ordinary strike was now seen as a challenge to government control, the stakes were raised on both sides of the battle.

Under pressure from the government, STERM was forced to merge with one of the charro electicians' unions, with the new amalgam being called the Union of Electrical Workers of the Mexican Republic (SUTERM). Clashes between the two wings of the union resulted in many radicals being expelled from SUTERM and losing their jobs. Frustrated workers broadened their organizing to create the "Democratic Tendency" (TD), incorporating nuclear workers, urban and rural poor, and the various workers' groups already organizing for union democracy. By 1975, a TD-called demonstration in Mexico City drew over 150,000, with participation by independent unions, teachers, students, and neighborhood organizations. Railworkers began to physically occupy union locals, and armed battles were fought in at least three states. Workers fighting to the death against the supposedly revolutionary government was too much for the PRI to allow. By 1975 Vallejo was placed under house arrest. When further purges of TD members resulted in strikes at power-generating stations, the government responded with military intervention. Although TD supporters within the FAT, the MSF, and the teachers' MMR mobilized demonstrations in 19 cities, by 1977 TD supporters in both Puebla and Guadalajara had signed agreements with the charros and the TD movement was formally ended. This wave of Insurgencia Obrera drew to a close.

Although charro unions, backed by government repression, proved more powerful in the '70s, democratic forces were strengthened in numerous ways. The FAT had several of its most widely known strikes during this time. The university unions formed during this time of student upheaval and workers insurgency have remained largely independent of government control. The teachers' movement, MMR, faded, but in 1979 it was succeeded by the CNTE, a vitally important democratic current within the national teachers' union and within the democratizing mobilizations of the 1990s. Subcomandante Marcos, the picturesque spokesperson for the Zapatista guerrillas, also got his political orientation during this period. Although the leader of the charro electricians' union, Leonardo Rodriguez Alcaine, went on to head both the CTM and the CT, he represents the anti-democratic past. Rodriguez Alcaine faces widespread ridicule and opposition that even includes TD survivors in his own union. The movement was repressed, but it did not die.

Key Struggles of the 1970s

The 1970s were a period of intense activity for the FAT. Continuing battles in Guanajuato and Chihuahua, as well as other struggles that gained national prominence, shed light on the problems of organizing independent labor unions in a context of hostility from employers, the government, and the official unions.

Guanajuato

By the late 1960s employers in the state of Guanajuato had become alarmed by the FAT's growth. The conservative nature of Guanajuato is indicated by the fact that during the student uprising of 1968, the only demonstrations held in Leon were massive rallies *against* the students, who were portrayed as part of a communist attack on the Mexican nation. The FAT's endorsement of the students did not go over well here. When a car accident in 1968 caused the sudden death of Nicolas Medina, employers felt emboldened to launch a coordinated counter-attack.

The campaign began in the Pepsi bottling plant and the Fanacal shoe factory just before Christmas 1968. Earlier that year the FAT had organized the workers at the Pepsi plant. On December 23 they were all fired. That same day police were called to the Fanacal shoe factory and all but the most passive workers were told to leave. Simultaneously, 30 new workers, all very muscular and affiliated with the CTM, were hired to replace them. Later that day the CTM filed for the right to represent the workers at the plant. In January, Pepsi hired new CTM workers too. In 1969 the large shoe factory GECESA began a steady process of firing FAT workers until it could break the union. Complaints filed with the labor board did no good.

The supposedly neutral labor board had a clearly negative view of the FAT. In 1970 the president of Leon's local labor board, responding to a request for information on the FAT, characterized the goal of the FAT as socialistic social transformation. While he acknowledged that the FAT had negotiated fairly ordinary contracts, he asserted that the majority of firms that had signed with the FAT had failed. He warned that when the FAT was prevented from setting up its own unions, it would seek to penetrate others, and that its training in both moral and technical matters lead to fanaticism.[9]

Many businesses chose to close as a way of getting rid of their contracts with the FAT. Mexican law requires that a fired worker be paid severance benefits based on the length of their employment with a firm. The FAT was fairly successful in forcing the labor board to enforce that legal requirement. In response to the FAT's successful demands for severence payments to its fired workers, the employers' federation, COPRAMEX, established an anti-FAT solidarity fund. The fund was evidently well enough endowed that some employers with no FAT union began filing claims on the fund. By the end of 1970 most shoe companies organized by the FAT had closed their doors. Most owners then opened other businesses. The FAT's battle for survival was on.

The May First construction union was active into the mid-1970s, but the temporary nature of much construction work, plus a hostile labor board, made it easy to break FAT contracts. Those actively organizing often found themselves blacklisted.

Sacramento Alvarez, a key organizer of the period, insists that because the FAT fought to improve conditions, all construction workers benefited. Employers knew they had to pay at least minimum wage, pay for regular hours, and provide insurance or they might get unionized. Interviewed in 1997, Alvarez insisted: "We fought to improve the situation and so it would be known that there was a union that would fight for the workers. I still haven't lost faith or hope."[10]

Despite the employers' offensive, the FAT still had some contracts in the shoe industry. It both won and lost contracts at small shoe firms during the '70s. When it tried to organize workers at the 500-employee Raudi factory, the company fired nearly all the workers. Public protests won them full severance benefits, but one worker reported getting fired from a job six years later when his employer found out that he had been with the FAT.[11] The era's major organizing feat occurred in 1973, when the FAT won the contract at HILSA, one of the largest and newest factories in Leon. It was the only local manufacturer of shoe soles and heels in this shoe-making city, and it was owned by a former senator, the municipal president of the PRI, and one of the largest real estate developers of the city.

The contracts at HILSA and the German pump-maker KSB demonstrated that the FAT could manage contracts at some of the most modern factories in the area. These also became some of the best-paid industrial jobs in the region. The FAT remained politically combative in many ways, but employer solidarity, amplified by a close working relationship with the local labor board and the CTM unions, took a heavy toll.

Chihuahua

Chihuahua followed close behind Guanajuato in the history of the FAT's early successes. Here some of the most rapid organizing took place and some of the broadest and most militant popular support for the FAT emerged. Here the "infernal trilogy" of charro, gobierno, y patrón responded in force and with devastating effect. Of all the unions established in the early years, not a single one was left by 1980. Even so, three of the four current top national leaders of the FAT emerged from this state. A corps of dedicated supporters remains in the capital city, as well as a new taxi drivers' union. Organizers went on to work with real success in the southern part of the state. And it is in the maquiladora plants of Chihuahua that the FAT went on to fight important battles of the '90s.

The FAT took the state of Chihuahua by surprise when it organized a union at the Pepsi plant in 1963. Each new contract it signed improved the wages and conditions of its members, putting them well in front of any CTM union in the region. In 1969 Pepsi of Chihuahua modernized its plant and secretly signed a contract with the CTM. On June 16 it fired all its FAT workers. The workers struck, but the local labor board declared the strike non-existent since none of the workers belonged to the union with which Pepsi had signed its contract. This blatantly abusive ruling may have been inspired by the fact that the current governor, Oscar Flores, had previously worked for the Banco Comercial Mexicano, which owned the Pepsi bottling plant.[12]

The firings and blatant power ties of Pepsi, the labor board, the local business federation COPRAMEX, and the governor provoked a massive response throughout the mobilized sectors of the region. Railworkers of the MSF, radicalized students, and members of Christian based communities joined the FAT in holding sit-ins and organizing a boycott of Pepsi products throughout the state. Organizing was so effective that it become the base of a political coalition called the Popular Front. An indicator of the coalition's importance as a force for challenging the established power structure is that the local sections of the Mexican Communist Party (PCM) and the conservative National Action Party

(PAN) both became members. The Popular Front was so effective in destroying Pepsi's local market share that the plant had to sell out to Coca-Cola. The organizing effort had other lasting effects as well.

Bertha Lujan was a young student whose family's strong church ties had led to her involvement with groups doing service and promoting links between the university and the working-class community. When the Pepsi firings took place she got involved with the political movement that became the Popular Front. During this struggle she met fellow Chihuahuans Antonio Villalba, who'd been an original member of the Pepsi union and was then the FAT's national secretary of organization, and Alfredo Dominguez, then secretary-general of the FAT. After the Pepsi struggle, Lujan went on to try to organize a union where she was employed at the Chihuahua branch of the University of Chapingo. That experience—eventually successful at branches nationwide—convinced her to stay with labor organizing.[13]

Many of those who had been a part of the Popular Front in 1969 remobilized in 1972, becoming the Popular Defense Committee (CDP). This group came into existence in response to police treatment of a group of radical leftists who had been accused of robbing banks in Chihuahua. The police had avoided a political trial by simply releasing the prisoners in the countryside, telling them to run, and then shooting them in the back. The naked brutality of the area's power structure inspired a massive protest. As the journal *Punto Critico* put it, "The society did not feel attacked as much by the bank robberies as by the actions of the police."[14] This local event united those previously mobilized with the forces of the then nationwide Insurgencia Obrera movement. In addition to the unions, student organizations and militant neighborhood organizations rallied together. When the CDP achieved the firing of the police chief and prosecutor, the group savored the first concrete victory of their broad social movement.[15]

The mass mobilization by the CDP, along with worker mobilization in other states, established a climate in which the FAT was able to organize more local unions. In 1972 they organized workers at the Chihuahua City Water Department, the Pearl tungsten mine, the sawmill of Las Palomas, and a broom factory. The social mobilization led to strong support for the organization and made it difficult for the local labor board to do as it wished—to simply refuse to cooperate with the FAT. The story of Las Palomas shows that the obstructions raised by the labor board can sometimes be too much, even for its own staff.

The sawmill of Las Palomas was located in a remote mountain village. It employed nearly all of the town's men, 140 workers, paid only in script redeemable at the company store. Company stores had been outlawed in the constitution, but the niceties of that document had still not been applied in Las Palomas. The workers were eager to achieve the rights that had been promised them fifty years earlier. Though the FAT had filed all the legal forms required to obtain the registry of the union, the labor board in the capital of Chihuahua was reluctant to cooperate.

The head of Chihuahua's Board of Conciliation and Arbitration declared that the FAT could not get its union registry without an on-site inspection, the costs of which would be borne by the union. Antonio Villalba, organizing for the FAT, agreed to the inspection, and the president of the labor board appointed a law student to do it.

Since the young inspector was afraid of flying, they made the trip by train and truck. In the train the inspector had an allergic reaction to the heat that continued for most of the trip.

At the closest train station Villalba hired a truck and driver. The driver brought along two relatives to help fend off assailants and/or to repair or otherwise rescue the truck as it traveled the mountain roads. Crossing a rain-swollen river, the entire crew had to push the truck through water well above their waists. Villalba remembers the aspiring lawyer at this point screaming heavenward, "*Ay Mama!* Look where your lawyer has gotten himself. What will my kids do if I die here? *Ay Mama!* You wanted me to study the law. Who ever imagined I'd end up like this?"

When they did arrive at the village of Las Palomas, the men affirmed that they wanted the union. The inspector found the employer asleep and hungover. When he was able to wake him, he asked if all 140 men who signed the petition for a union worked for him. "Who else would they work for?" replied the owner. This was evidence enough, given the situation. The lawyer left as soon as he could get the driver to cooperate, eager to return to the relative comforts of the capital city.

When Villalba returned to the capital the next week, he went to the labor board to see if he could finally get the union's registry. The board president began to suggest that the inspection had not been complete, that some detail was lacking, and that the union would have to bring the inspector out another time—at its own expense. Villalba called the inspector in from the next room to see if he was ready for another ride. The inspector, still haggard from the previous journey, immediately insisted, "No! Everything is in order. I'm not going again. Give the man his paper!"[16]

That is how, in spite of the desires of the labor board president, the workers at Las Palomas won their union's official registration in 1972. They soon won the conversion of the company store to a worker-owned cooperative store and wages went up significantly. But those were years when lumber prices were high and there were profits to be made. When profits slowed in 1978, the mill's owners claimed they had lost permission to cut trees. Production stopped. On May 12 several workers were tied up and beaten brutally by the state police until they would sign a paper saying they would give up their union and sell the cooperative store back to the sawmill. Other union members considered it useless to strike, since they were already without work. When the end of the union and the reassignment of the store were made official, the mill owners suddenly regained permission to cut trees. Production resumed in a non-union environment.[17]

In 1973 the government figured that it could best deal with the insurgent CDP by dealing with its separate constituencies. It proceeded to co-opt and to repress selectively. It granted the firing of the police chief and prosecutor responsible for the shooting outrage as a tactical concession (they were later rehired). It promised to grant most of the students' wishes, and actually delivered on some. It granted land and services to some urban squatters. But in 1973 several professors at the university lost their jobs, and the state police briefly occupied the university, arresting key student leaders.[18] With the CDP weakened, the government moved to attack most of the FAT unions through a combination of semilegal tricks.

Within a year the broom factory fired all of its workers and brought in a CTM union. In 1973 the Water Department, which had previously had no union, organized an election for workers to choose between affiliation with the FAT or the CTM. The CTM won the fraudulent election by allowing only office workers to vote, avoiding the FAT's strongest supporters, those who worked in the field away from the steady influence of political bosses. The CTM then followed up its victory by arranging for all known FAT supporters to be fired. In 1975 the tungsten began to run out at the La Perla mine. After striking for six months in 1979 the remaining workers won their full severance payments, but the mine stayed closed. The infernal trilogy had reasserted its dominance.[19]

Cuernavaca and the FAT School

In the early 1970s Cuernavaca, Morelos (about one hour south of Mexico City), saw a broad uprising of workers associated with the FAT. The workers of all the leading unionized factories in the state united to support each other and to defy the leadership of the state federation of the CTM that attempted to control them. The unity of the working class was aided by the support of the bishop, Sergio Mendez Arceo. It was opposed by a unified employers' group, by the CTM, by the state and national governments, and eventually by the arrival of a new "independent" labor federation, the Union of Independent Workers (UOI).

The groundswell began when a disgruntled textile worker, Gabriel Muñoz, was referred to the FAT by a priest, Salvador Garcia, who had been recently expelled from Leon for supporting the FAT. Muñoz and a few friends soon convinced the FAT to open CEFOCEM, a school dedicated to providing education in labor rights and organizing techniques for the workers of the state of Morelos. The school included many FAT militants who had helped build the movement in Leon: Victor Quirroga, Jose Merced, Antonio Velazquez, and Patrocinio Caudillo. Workers from throughout the region attended regularly. Even the bishop attended as a student. The effects were sudden and dramatic. Within six months workers from the school were pressuring for change within every CTM union in the state.

The bishop had already become renowned for his innovative marimba Masses. Now, as a friend of the workers, many called him the "red bishop." The workers came to refer to him affectionately as Don Sergio. He frequently provided support for the workers in his Sunday homilies. His support encouraged many otherwise hesitant workers to join the movement, and, from time to time, he provided a measure of political cover for them. On the downside, because he was such a visible figure his support was over exaggerated. Since Don Sergio had friendly relations with Fidel Castro at the time, the workers movement in Cuernavaca was more easily branded as inspired from Cuba. His role in the Cuernavaca movement is remembered more than that of the FAT, especially since the FAT did not establish any unions outside of the CTM.

Politicians and the media did not take long to condemn the sudden upsurge in independent activities within most unions in Cuernavaca. Stories about CEFOCEM branded it as Cuban subversion and purported to link the school to guerrilla movements. Police were stationed outside to observe who went in and out. Those attending the school now faced reprisals. If they were working, they were fired. If they were not working, they were put on a blacklist, and finding work became next to impossible. Within a year the school was closed, and the local movement lost a valuable resource and focal point. The FAT, always short of resources, unfortunately chose to withdraw some of its staff to pursue work in Leon, Chihuahua, and the valley of Mexico.

In 1972 Cuernavaca's independent union movement gained national prominence at a clothing factory known as Rivetex.[20] The strike was as much against the labor board and national CTM leadership as it was against the company. This strike of some 400 workers was supported by as many as 1,400 workers from other plants who stood with them at the plant gates and in their occupation of the city hall and the town square. As the strike entered its final days the union local's treasurer declared independence: "The CTM and Fidel Velazquez have no business here. Instead of defending us they have attacked us. Here they control no one. The 14 principal unions of this state have separated from that organization, even if the CTM denies it. We will continue in the struggle until the end."[21] Except for back pay, the union won on all its issues, including independence from the CTM.

Echeverria's UOI: Independent from What?

The workers won this important round in the struggle for the right to control their own unions, but they were soon faced with a more subtle challenge. Since the CTM had proven itself incapable of controlling workers in the state of Morelos, the government decided to try a new tactic. It created the Union of Independent Workers, the UOI.[22]

The UOI was part of President Echeverria's effort to maintain control through reform. He hauled an old schoolmate, Juan Ortega Arenas, out of jail to create a new organization of "independent" unions. Ortega had been a member of the Mexican Communist Party until he was expelled in the mid-1950s. He became a labor lawyer but was jailed under President Diaz Ordaz. He could speak a good radical line, and he proved to be a skilled negotiator of labor contracts. His major advantage, though, was the green light he had from the president.

We have seen the myriad difficulties the state has always given the FAT in its efforts to form independent unions. The UOI came into being in 1972 with unions in three strong industrial firms in the critical automotive sector.[23] Their immediate registry by Secretary of Labor Muñoz Ledo was but one example of the state's blessing of this enterprise. Later that year, the UOI made its first overtures to Cuernavaca's Nissan union, which was firmly in the hands of FAT activist Raimundo Jaimes and his supporters.

Jaimes had been through the CEFOCEM school and had spent a month in Venezuela at a CLAT labor seminar. When he took over as secretary-general of the Nissan union in 1971 he retained contact with FAT advisers and made two bottom-line pledges: he would make Nissan live up to the terms of the contract, and he would refuse to be corrupted. The second pledge was immediately tested. During his first meeting with the company, the plant manager told him he was the most capable worker in the plant and that it would be most efficient to settle issues between the two of them. After all, he continued, when the other workers attended meetings they just ate cookies. In fact, Jaimes was such a valuable man that he deserved a real house and a new car each year. He was worth it. It was part of being such a successful leader.

It was very hard to do, but Jaimes said no to these tempting offers. At that point the company changed its tone and began treating him as an enemy. His job as secretary-general meant he no longer had to work on the line. But now the company said he was no longer allowed to enter the plant. Their goal was to get rid of him. Examining union records one day, Jaimes realized two members of his executive committee had already sold out. He asked the general assembly to replace them.

Jaimes's chief goal in renegotiating the contract in 1972 was to reverse the ratio of full-time to part-time employees. It was 70% temporary workers and only 30% permanent workers. This was good for the company allowing it to easily respond to changing demand for its product, but it was terrible for the workers and for the union. The union voted to strike if Nissan did not give in. Since the plant opened they had never had a strike. When Jaimes insisted on this change, the company began to fire workers. Jaimes urged them not to accept a severance settlement. They would get their jobs back, he pledged.

In this tense, pre-strike period, Ortega Arenas, lawyer and director of the UOI, showed up and, as Jaimes later put it, "began to do his work." He offered the support of the UOI unions as well as his legal advice as a negotiator. The union eagerly accepted his offer to help, and the company soon gave in. Ortega Arenas and the FAT advisers, along with the committee of workers from the plant, negotiated a fine contract.

Since the workers at Nissan had clearly shown they no longer wanted a relationship with the CTM, Ortega Arenas suggested their union join with the UOI. The FAT had not pushed the Nissan union to declare itself part of the FAT, as it was unlikely that the labor board would cooperate with them if they did. "The FAT had come to respect the decisions of the workers," Jaimes explained, "not to push ideas. That was not how Ortega Arenas worked."

In an assembly to decide if they should join the UOI or stay with the FAT, Ortega Arenas argued that the FAT was just a bunch of communists more interested in making trouble than in improving their lives. He pointed to the success of his unions and promised their contract would improve still further under his guidance. He had prepared his partisans well, and they actually laughed the FAT advisers out of the room. The majority voted to join the UOI. The labor board quickly cooperated.

Jaimes was disappointed to lose the relation with the FAT, but he was glad to get out of the CTM. He soon found out that Ortega liked to manage "his" unions, not just advise them. At one point, Ortega became angry that the union's executive committee had held a meeting without notifying him first. Jaimes told him that he was just an adviser and they would invite him when they wanted his advice. Jaimes and other workers who remembered what it had been like to be dominated by the CTM began to resist the impositions of Ortega. In November 1973, when Jaimes's term expired, he proposed a new executive committee composed of people who had been educated by the FAT. The FAT slate won, with Jaimes now as secretary of education.

Shortly after the election a worker put out a brochure critical of a Japanese manager named Yoshingo. The brochure called him "Yo chingo," slang for "I screw you." Since this was from Jaimes's department, the company threatened to fire him. They were unable to do it, but, working with Ortega, they continued to seek to rid themselves of FAT partisans.

In the summer of 1975 Jaimes decided he would like to run for another term as secretary-general in the November election. Ortega did an audit of the books and found a large amount of money missing. He blamed it partly on Jaimes and called an assembly to decide whether to expel him or to pardon him; either way he was to be considered guilty. The assembly was held at the end of August, in the largest theater in town, and most of the 1,200 workers attended. After the treasurer stood up and took the blame due to his own bad bookkeeping skills, a worker proposed a motion to leave Jaimes alone. The motion carried.

However, a week later, 45 union members, with the encouragement of the management, filed criminal charges against him for embezzlement. He was arrested on his way to work, then, rather than being taken to a judge for arraignment, he was taken in an unmarked car to a remote rural jail. He feared for his life, but fortunately a fellow worker being released from that jail recognized him and brought the news to other workers and the archbishop who began to apply pressure. He was released on the third day based on the fact that the assembly had already cleared him of improperly using their funds. Jaimes still remembers the shocked look on the chief of personnel's face when he walked back in to work.

Jaimes did win reelection that fall, but things did not go well. He no longer had advisers from the FAT, and he found that many of his friends, who had long worked Monday through Friday on the day shift, were being shifted to weekends and nights. Since the FAT had been thoroughly demonized by the business, the UOI, and the newspapers, Jaimes's association with the FAT often caused him trouble.

He did rely on Ortega and the UOI for advice and recalls that on one visit to the UOI office in Mexico City he was so impressed by this lawyer's skill and knowledge that he told him: "You know so much. You ought to teach the workers what you know because one day you may not be around." Ortega refused, saying if he did, the workers would some day betray him. "That too, was just the opposite of how the FAT worked," Jaimes reflected.

In April 1976 the Mexican economy showed its weakness. The peso was suddenly devalued from 12.5 pesos to the dollar to 26. Inflation was instantaneous. The workers demanded a 100% emergency pay increase. Nissan offered 21% and refused to budge, so Jaimes led his workers out on strike. After 45 days the company refused to make any new offer. Cars weren't selling anyhow. The strikers voted to settle. They got 21%, and no back pay for their 45 days out.

Jaimes was blamed for the long strike and the lost wages. He was removed from the executive committee, but he remained as a worker in the plant. However, he was soon accused of promoting a slowdown, a charge he still denies, and was fired.

The Nissan union had made real strides since the workers began their struggle for control. A careful, comparative study rated union influence on automotive contracts in promotion, employment security, production processes, and conflict resolution.[24] The Nissan plant's first contract in 1966 rated a total score of only 3 points out of a possible 36. Its 1976 contract rated 32 points. The more traditional CTM contract at Chrysler in 1977 rated only 3 points.

The Mexican government considered the automotive sector of its economy one of its most strategic sectors for development. It also placed a high importance on maintaining control of labor relations. In the early 1970s, when President Echeverria chose reform as a means of maintaining control, the UOI played a very important role. With the Insurgencia Obrera challenging government control in many sectors, and the independent workers' uprising in Cuernavaca shattering CTM control of nearly all major unions in the state, the arrival of Ortega in 1972 was no mistake.

Ortega could talk the talk of class conflict, but he always claimed that the forces of the working class were not sufficiently advanced to challenge the state or the capitalist organization of the economy. His anti-political discourse discouraged any alliances with other independent unions. He won real wage increases, improved working conditions, and increased worker input in his factories, but he refused to allow his unions to take part in the street demonstrations of the broader workers' insurgency. The state used the UOI to limit the independence of workers determined to break from CTM control.

The UOI played an important counter-insurgency role in defusing the threat of a movement away from CTM unions. It extracted affordable concessions from within a profitable factory, but it worked with employers to destroy politicized labor leaders like Raimundo Jaimes and to keep the workers off the street. It redirected worker attention to bread-and-butter issues and away from the issues of structural control that were at the heart of the Insurgencia Obrera in Cuernavaca and throughout the country.

The UOI went where it was allowed and encouraged to go. By the end of Echeverria's term it counted at least 85 unions and claimed a membership of 100,000 workers. When government policy changed under Lopez Portillo and Miguel de la Madrid, the UOI stopped growing. It took to the streets in 1980 and 1981, holding massive demonstrations to protest changes in the federal labor law that made it more difficult to register independent labor unions. The UOI even resorted to factory takeovers and rallies at plant gates in efforts to win new unions.[25] However, without his friend the president, Ortega Arenas was confronted with the same frustrations the FAT had always faced. Throughout the 1980s the UOI faded, and in 1997 it maintained unions only in Hidalgo state, where Ortega had another important friend from his school days, the governor.[26]

Employers did not forget the importance of the rebellion that occurred in Cuernavaca. No new industrial plants opened in the area after the FAT opened their labor school, CEFOCEM. Nissan opened two new plants elsewhere, one in Lerma and one in Aguascalientes. While the study of Nissan contracts mentioned above showed the important gains made by the Nissan union in Cuernavaca, it also compared the three Nissan contracts in 1988. The Cuernavaca contract still rated an impressive 33 out of a possible 36 positive points. The contracts at Lerma and Aguascalientes rated a mere two and three points, respectively.[27] When the FAT established its first union in Aguascalientes in the early 1990s, Nissan management protested to the state's governor. Fortunately, the governor felt it was too late to deny the legal recognition. However, when the FAT organized a Japanese-owned auto parts factory there in 1998, the government did begin the process of seemingly endless delays.[28] Nissan had not forgotten what it had learned about the FAT in Cuernavaca.

Internationalism at Spicer

Just as the general climate of the Insurgencia Obrera encouraged more mobilization, each prominent struggle of the FAT led to broader awareness of the possibility of joining a combative independent union. The FAT's strike in the northern industrial city of Saltillo involved most of the city's population and attracted presidential involvement before its resolution.[29] As with many of the struggles unable to be addressed here, it contributed to the awareness of the workers who waged the Spicer strike in Mexico City.

The strike at the Spicer auto parts plant in 1975 helped the FAT refine its ideological and strategic approach to labor issues. Central to their approach was what they came to call *autogestión*, or workers' democracy through self-management; US labor activists refer to it as rank-and-file unionism. After Spicer, the FAT's struggle became even more clearly one dedicated to the empowerment of ordinary workers.

Spicer was a Mexican-owned auto parts company with a license to produce axles patented by a US corporation owned by Manufactures Hanover Trust Company of New York. It also had three US nationals on its board of directors. In short, it was a transnational in a time when foreign corporations faced significant restrictions on what they could own in Mexico. Spicer was ranked 150th on the list of Mexico's 500 largest firms. It supplied axles to most auto plants in Mexico.

Workers at Spicer were represented by a government-dominated union, the Federation of Workers' Groups (FAO). They felt badly served by it. In 1968 in a general assembly, workers refused to approve the slate of officers imposed on them by the union's national leadership. Facing jeers that threatened to escalate to violence if he did not concede to workers' demands, the secretary-general of the union walked out, officially ending the assembly. The business cooperated with the union leaders in firing 23 workers. (Under Mexican labor law a business with a union contract must employ only union workers. When a union declares workers no longer to be members, the business must then apply its "exclusion clause" and fire the workers. Unions often use this process to eliminate dissidents.) Over the next weeks workers conducted slowdowns until the bosses sent in police to drag out another two dozen workers. Then the union was able to regain some sense of control. However, it refused to hold open meetings. In the following year several more workers were fired for promoting the idea of making changes in the union. In 1972, another 10 were fired for suggesting resistance to the charros.

In June 1974 Spicer announced its intention to add a "fourth shift" to increase production by running the plant seven days a week without paying overtime. Workers opposed the idea, as it would have meant drastic changes in their work schedules, days off, and holidays, and required working some weeks in the day and some at night. They knew their union would be no help to them, so they began, with more urgency, to consider forming a new union.

Spicer workers were well aware of the FAT due to the strike in Saltillo, and some of the factory workers had already become FAT activists. The FAT had developed a reputation for being a militant advocate of workers' interests. When the workers showed interest, the FAT supplied advisers. Many of the workers decided they should join the FAT's metalworkers' union, SNTIHA. In August 1974 workers circulated a flier calling for "an Independent Union ... to have a real weapon to use in our struggle against the despotism of the boss and the charros."

After months of meeting and quiet organizing, the workers were ready to act. They submitted the names of 760 of the plant's 800 workers on a petition demanding that SNTIHA, not the FAO, be recognized as their legitimate union. The labor board refused to act in response to their petition. The company responded by firing a hundred workers and by signing an agreement to negotiate with a new charro union, the Miners and Metallurgical Union.

Shifting to the miners meant the petition the workers had given to the labor board was now inaccurate, and they would have to file all over. It also meant that Spicer could hire pistol-toting muscular scabs to fill the positions of former workers. These new employees kept tabs on conversations within the plant and made threats to any workers they thought might continue organizing. Workers called meetings outside the plant, but firings continued. In February 1975 they held their first official assembly as a local section of SNTIHA. In March, they filed a new demand for recognition of their union, but still the labor board refused to acknowledge them or to order an election.

One of the problems in the plant rapidly became a tactical problem for the union. The company had for years been hiring a growing number of "temporary" workers with individual contracts signed for limited periods of time. Some of these "temporaries" had worked in the plant for as long as six years. As the summer of 1975 began the firing of workers continued, with their replacements being drawn from the Miners union. Of course, the first fired were those most active in the FAT union. In July and August 350 temporary contracts would expire. Those workers were expecting to be let go with no right to severance pay. If the FAT waited much longer the labor board could call an election after those workers had been replaced, and the whole effort would be lost.

Finally, on June 30, Spicer workers hung out their banners of red and black and posted round-the-clock guards at the plant's three gates. The strike was on. The strike demands included recognition of their independent union, a legal count to verify which union had majority support, the reinstatement of fired workers and the exclusion of the scabs hired through the Miners union, an end to the use of temporary workers, back pay for strike time, and no reprisals. The demands—with the partial exception of the demand to end temporary contracts and back pay for strike time—were all focused on control, not economic gains. From the beginning, it was a political fight.

Workers had reasons to expect that the company would meet their demands within a week. They had suffered slow production for months, so profits were probably hurting. Also, since they supplied axles for most cars built in Mexico, Spicer would face pressure from customers to settle quickly.

The workers were wrong. Both the Mexican and US owners had deep pockets and many other businesses that they were able to rely on for profits. In the owners' eyes, they were not confronting a simple strike, "but the incarnation of all independent unionism in the country. There was more at stake than one industry; all of private industry was at stake."[30] As the workers eventually realized, "It was not economic logic but a logic of class conflict—workers versus owners—that drove the whole strike. The business was prepared to lose millions and they did."[31]

Suddenly, with very little preparation and no strike fund to draw on, the workers faced the fight of their lives. They had had no union experience prior to their clandestine meetings. They set about organizing themselves to confront their tasks. Since their goal was democratic control of their union, they insisted on organizing themselves democratically. They elected committees to run the strike, gather resources, distribute food, keep workers informed, inform others about their strike, negotiate with the business and the federal labor board, and to guard plant gates. They also established a union school to educate workers.

Delegations of workers from other insurgent union movements and from working-class neighborhood organizations arrived with banners of solidarity. The still vital Democratic Tendency, affiliated with the electricians' union, SUTERM, helped organize the first march in the heart of Mexico City, and the workers chanted, *"Pueblo, escucha, Spicer en la lucha!"* (People, listen, Spicer's in the struggle!)

Support from other unions allowed Spicer workers to provide each family with a weekly allotment of food. Each Sunday the workers held a street party at the plant gates to hold the community together and to boost morale. Various musical groups arrived to offer their talents, and from the workers themselves there emerged some outstanding singers and dancers and even one magician. Several songs were composed as the struggle progressed. The strike gradually became a cultural focus for the Insurgencia and for a number of working-class neighborhoods near the plant. Marches in the area of the plant grew to as many as 5,000 people because of the popular support that had been established.

After more than a month an accord was worked out to end the strike. Since the strike had not been declared legal (though the labor board had not dared to declare it illegal), the agreement was somewhat unusual. In it, the company agreed to recognize the strikers' negotiating committee, to rehire the workers it had previously fired, to extend the contracts of temporary workers by at least four months, to not punish workers for their union activities, and to pay 25% of the salaries workers had lost while on strike. The federal labor board finally agreed to hold an election—when work began again—that would determine which union should represent the Spicer workers. This agreement did not settle the conflict, but with resources running low and repression a real possibility, the exhausted workers decided to take what they could and to regroup while back at work.

With the agreement signed and work scheduled to resume, 300 workers showed up to take down the red and black strike banners and to work their first shift with an expectation of resuming some degree of normality in their lives. The labor board sent observers, but the Miners union also showed up with hundreds of workers it wanted to put into the plant. A tense standoff occurred as SNTIHA workers were determined not to allow the Miners to enter. The police soon showed up in riot gear. This standoff was settled within a few hours as 2,000 supporters from surrounding neighborhoods and supportive unions arrived, marching with their banners of solidarity and wearing looks of grim determination on their faces. The Miners union withdrew its would-be scabs, and the workers entered the factory now clear that the struggle had not ended with the company's signature on an agreement.

Acting as One

Workers refer to the week of August 11 to 15 as the week of *Poder Obrero*, Workers' Power. It was a week of continuous conflict and testing of wills on both sides. The labor board demonstrated that it could be very slow about holding the promised vote to establish which union controlled the plant. It sent an inspector to establish the validity of the signatures on the petition calling for the vote. Each day he would manage to question six or seven workers about their loyalties—all under the menacing gaze of supervisors.

The first serious conflict came the morning of the first day. Within the plant were several workers hired through the Miners union prior to the strike. Viewed as scabs, these workers were subject to verbal abuse and clear hostility by the returning workers. One of them responded by picking up an iron rod and breaking the jaw of one of the FAT supporters. Workers stopped the line and chased the miner out of the plant. They refused to resume work until Spicer agreed to fire the offending miner. The company responded by firing the injured worker. On the second shift, when supervisors tried to discipline a worker for working too slowly, other workers stopped production again. Through shutdowns and clear defiance, the workers insisted that they would be in charge of the pace of production. They held other work stoppages to demand an end to stalling about the election. Occasionally workers in various parts of the factory would break into one of their favorite songs, "We Shall Not Be Moved."

Criticizing the bosses during the strike had been one thing, but maintaining sufficient strength through organization to defy them within the plant had a powerful effect. As one worker explained:

> The first thing to go was fear. We acted as one person, in unison, feeling behind us the strength of the whole factory, all the power. Next we lost respect for the structures of the bosses' power. One supervisor tried to intervene in one of our shutdowns, and we ran him off with yells and a few punches. He had to watch his back as he retreated up the stairs.[32]

The company tried once more, with heavy police support, to inject an extra 150 miners into the factory. Worker solidarity again turned them back. But Sunday night, August 17, the miners took control of the factory. When the first shift showed up on Monday they saw a large police force at the ready, miners inside, and company guards with a list of 164 workers that they would not allow to enter. Workers called an assembly and decided that they would stand together. No one would enter without those the company wished to fire. The company acknowledged their solidarity by firing the remaining 505 workers.

With the support of the Democratic Tendency of SUTERM, the electricians' union, the workers were able to print six million fliers, which they distributed throughout the remainder of the struggle. They conducted nearly daily protests at the Ministry of Labor. On September 10, when the secretary of labor came out, supposedly to have a dialogue with them, they were set upon by 300 riot police, who charged into their gathering with motorcycles. That same day police broke up a march they tried to hold in another part of the city. Two days later police broke up a meeting of the strikers' wives.

The government, throughout the conflict, had shown its tactical support for the owners of Spicer. By simply refusing to allow an election that would give a victory to the FAT's SNTIHA union they made conflict unavoidable. During the strike, when no axles were available for the domestic auto industry, they waived protective tariffs and arranged the importation of similar axles. They provided consistent police support for the owners and the charro unions, and they now intervened to prevent marches from rebuilding the support Spicer workers had enjoyed during the month of July. So, when Secretary of Labor Porfirio Muñoz Ledo—then hopeful of being named to succeed Echeverria as president—urged them to "cooperate with the authorities so that through dialogue and conciliation we can resolve the situation," they did not give him the quiet solution he had hoped for. When Muñoz explained to FAT leader Alfredo Dominguez that the FAT would never be allowed to organize in the automotive sector—that it was reserved for the UOI, but he could offer them more contracts in the shoe industry—they still did not give in.

Nonetheless, time, repression, and intransigence were demoralizing the workers. In a desperate effort to rekindle support for the movement, on September 30, thirty leading strikers and their main legal adviser sat down at the Labor Ministry and declared themselves on a hunger strike.

This tactic did renew interest in the Spicer struggle. Newly unionized workers and professors at the massive UNAM held a two-hour sympathy strike, conducting 142 different meetings to discuss the struggle in their various work units and to reaffirm the message that the Spicer struggle was part of the struggle of all Mexican workers for basic labor rights.

Spicer workers gathered material and political support from 120 union organizations throughout the country, from students, and from people in the streets. They also drew material and political support from the CLAT in Venezuela and Costa Rica, from the Catholic-associated World Federation of Labor (CMT), including a CMT affiliate in Quebec, Canada, and CMT affiliates and a metalworkers' union related to Spicer in Belgium and Holland. After 21 days of hunger strike, the wives of the 30 famished men occupied the fifth floor of the labor ministry. Three thousand workers showed up to support them; supporting demonstrations were held in Europe and Canada. This was the first time that a Mexican labor dispute had achieved international support.

International support had a particular effect on President Echeverria, then nearing the end of his term. Due to his seemingly progressive policies of "democratic opening," along with leadership in the North-South dialogue and occasional defense of the Cuban Revolution, many Third World governments were discussing the possibility of his leading the United Nations. He needed to solve this conflict before it went on much longer. Many of the workers expected that when they finally got the attention of the president, justice would be done. After all, they were primarily asking for the right to form their own union according to Mexican law. But on October 23 he declared,

> The problem of Spicer will never be solved by the Christian Democrats controlled from Venezuela, nor if its workers are manipulated to create union problems in other factories throughout the country.[33]

This rhetoric was carefully crafted to align the FAT with the Christian Democratic party that had been discredited in the eyes of most workers by its support of the military coup that had toppled Chile's Allende. It also attacked the FAT as non-Mexican and as a manipulative force responsible for labor unrest throughout the country.

When Echeverria imposed a settlement that took no account of the law, these workers confronted the shock of further disillusionment. As one man explained in the final general assembly of Spicer workers, "We learned the meaning of worker solidarity and of class struggle. We became conscious of ourselves as workers and that our interests are different from those of the bosses and the government."[34]

The settlement imposed on the workers partially responded to some of the economic issues, but it gave no ground on the fundamental political issue of the workers' right to form their own union. The settlement named the Miners union as the recognized union at the plant. It offered 485 of the 612 strikers the chance to return to work either as members of the Miners union or of no union. These workers were also offered a lump sum equal to nearly half their lost wages. Those not allowed to return were granted 100% of lost wages and 100% severance pay. One hundred of the temporary contracts would be converted to permanent positions.

In the final assembly, workers decided to leave each worker free to choose, but the majority chose not to return to Spicer under those conditions. With their dignity intact, the 612 workers attending the final assembly sang "We Shall Not Be Moved" and "We Shall Overcome" before marching out with fists in the air, vowing to "create one, two, three, hundreds of Spicers" wherever they worked in the future.

Those workers who did choose to return were harassed into changing their minds. Once again, the words in the agreement meant little. The company did not want workers who would keep alive the memory of their defiant struggle. Then, to further obliterate the memory, the company changed its name to Ejes Tractores, S.A.

Self-Management

Two aspects of this struggle are of special importance for understanding the struggle of the FAT in the 1990s. They are international solidarity and autogestión. That workers saw themselves in an international context is obvious in the Spicer workers' choice of songs from the black civil rights movement and a slogan based on the Vietnam War. The international links that the FAT established during this struggle, particularly those with the CSN of Quebec, were maintained from that time forward despite the eventual break of the FAT from the CLAT. The support of the CSN was important in building the current FAT headquarters building in the 1980s. This link also laid the groundwork for outreach to Canadian unions in the 1990s, when the FAT spearheaded Mexican opposition to NAFTA.

During the strike, workers had to organize themselves. They chose forms of organization that reflected both their distrust of leaders who might turn into future charros and their desire for real democracy. They developed a form of direct democracy known as autogestión, or self-management. As much as possible, decisions were made by those responsible for living with the decisions' consequences. During the strike they were often made by the groups responsible for different plant gates. They were made in committees carrying out tasks like fundraising and publicity. Inside the factory they were made in departments and by different shifts. Decisions affecting everyone were made by the general assembly—all workers meeting, discussing, and voting as equals.

The following is taken from a recent FAT brochure titled *Autogestión*. It was drawn up by Jorge Robles, a worker whose first involvement with the FAT came through the Spicer struggle.

> We understand *autogestión* as a series of principles that together create the basis of a self-managing society.
>
> **Direct Democracy:** Interested parties are the ones that make their decisions, without delegating to intermediaries the responsibility to decide on their affairs. Consensus is the predominant form of decision making, resorting to votes only in extreme cases, thus avoiding the tyranny of the majority and permitting, when possible, minority positions.
>
> **Direct Action:** If participants make their own decisions without intermediaries, in direct action they also carry out their own agreements without intermediaries.

Mutual Support: We work to develop the concept of solidarity as an ethical principle at work wherever we participate, and wherever we advise, beginning with ourselves.

Outgrowth: We seek to apply these principles of *autogestión* in the community, extending our influence in all sectors and all regions, as well as in our personal life. We cannot promote *autogestión* in our union or our cooperative and be intolerant tyrants in our personal relations, in our family, with our friends, or with co-workers in our organization.

Education: Study and practice will permit us to consider a broader range of alternatives and to make better decisions.

These basic principles of applied self-management, which we adapt to the circumstances of each case, are applicable in any organizational setting, from the small union or cooperative, to the neighborhood, the community, society itself. None of the principles takes priority over any other; none can be sacrificed for the sake of another. All five must be taken together.

Autogestión—self-management—is not just a long term goal; it is the practical method for getting there. Means must be consistent with their ends.

These principles were applied in the Spicer strike and gave real strength to that struggle as workers were able to achieve directly—at least within their own organizations—the goal they were struggling for in their strike: meaningful control over their own affairs. It is something that sets FAT unions apart from those dominated by the charros and the PRI.

During this period of transition the FAT became a presence known nationwide for its ability to inspire workers to confront previously hopeless situations and to win wide-spread support from their communities. New communities of FAT activists were established in many states. Breaking all church ties while building alliances both nationally and internationally, the FAT clarified its vision. Abandoning its original notion that Christian capitalists could be called to a more just relationship with their workers or that the government was concerned with the welfare of workers, they now saw that workers would gain only when they were organized to confront the infernal trilogy. To do this they would have to begin by democratizing any ground on which they stood.

Notes

1   Gutierez, Gustavo. 1971. *A Theology of Liberation*, 175. Maryknoll, NY: Orbis.

2   Miranda, Porfirio. 1974. *Marx and the Bible, English Version of 1971 Marx y la Biblia*, 5, 6. Maryknoll, NY: Orbis Books.

3   "La Historia del FAT en Sintesis." 1995. *Resistencia Obrera*, 141 (October): 4.

4   "France, history of, The Fifth Republic." *Encyclopeadia Britannica on-line*. http://www.eb.com:180/bol/topic?eu=119352&sctn=1#s_top.

5   Katsiaficas, George. 1987. *The Imagination of the New Left*, 47–48. Boston: South End Press.

6   This account of the student movement draws most heavily on Hellman, Judith. 1983. *Mexico in Crisis*, 173–86. New York: Holmes & Meier Publishers.

7   News of the events did get out internationally, even if coverage was quite limited. The *New York Times* (Oct. 4–7, 1968) at first reported the official death toll of 20, but within days reported student claims of up to 300 missing. The only magazine listed in *Readers Guide to Periodical Literature* to offer coverage was *Sports Illustrated*, "Tragic Battle between Students and Troops." 29:36–38, October 14. Despite this limited coverage, students staged support demonstrations in Paris, Managua, Santiago de Chile, and New York.

8   Weis, W. Michael. 1997. "Government News Management, Bias and Distortion in American Press Coverage of the Brazilian Coup." *Social Science Journal*, 34:1, 35–58. Houtzager, Peter P. 1998. "State and Unions in the Transformation of the Brazilian Countryside, 1964–1979." *Latin American Research Review*, 33:2, 103–143. "Former Dictator Arrested for Stealing Children during Dirty War." *NACLA Report on the Americas*, 32:1, 1. 1991. "Memories of the `Dirty War.'" *U.S. News & World Report*, 1, 9. Ford, Anibal, and Jorge Elbaum. 1998. "Reflections on Contemporary Argentine Culture." *NACLA Report on the Americas*, 31:6, 35–39. Kornbluh, Peter. 1999. "Declassifying U.S. Intervention in Chile." *NACLA Report on the Americas*, 32:6, 36–43.

9   Ramírez Martínez, Ramón. 1970. Letter from JLCA of Leon to José González Alvarado of Monterrey. 2 pages.

10   Alvarez, Sacramento. 1997. Oral interview at his home in Leon, April 22.

11   Vilchez, Jose Cruz. 1997. Oral interview at FAT in Leon, April 22.

12 "Pepsi Cola: Primer Sindicato del FAT in Chihuahua." 1978. *Resistencia Obrera*, 7 (July): 8.

13 Lujan, Bertha. 1996. Oral interview at FAT in Mexico, DF, November 26.

14 "Chihuahua: La Verdad Sobre los Asaltos." 1972. *Punto Critico*, 4: 19–21.

15 Villalba, Antonio. 1996. Oral interview. November 22.

16 Villalba interview; Góngora, Janette. 1990. "Cómo Se Obtiene un Registro Sindical en el Culo del Diablo." *Trabajo*, 3–4 (Summer–Fall): 99–103.

17 "Las Palomas de la Paz." 1978. *Resistencia Obrera*, 7 (July): 3.

18 Huacuja, Mario, and Jose Woldenberg. 1976. *Estado y Lucha Politica en el Mexico Actual*, 87–89. Mexico, D.F.: Ediciones "El Caballito."

19 Robles, Jorge, and Luis Angel Gómez. 1995. *De la Autonomia al Corporativismo: Memoria Cronológica del Movimiento Obrero Mexicano (1900–1980)*, 89, 99. Mexico, DF: El Atajo Ediciones; Lujan interview; Villalba interview; "En Chihuahua: Ha Terminado una Batalla. La Lucha Continua." 1979. *Resistencia Obrera*, 23–24 (November–December): 10.

20 The following account of the conflict at the Rivetex plant is based largely on an unpublished, incomplete manuscript, "La Huelga de los Trabajadores de la Confeccion," with no author's name or date. It was provided to this author by Gabriel Muñoz, a witness to many of the events in Cuernavaca.

21 Anonymous. "La Huelga de los Trabajadores de la Confeccion." 45–46.

22 This account owes much to an extended interview with Raimundo Jaimes in Cuernavaca on July, 17, 1997. But it also draws on numerous published works. De la Garza, Enrique. 1991. "Independent Trade Unionism in Mexico: Past Developments and Future Perspectives." In *Unions, Workers and the State in Mexico*, edited by Kevin J. Middlebrook, 153–84. San Diego: Center For U.S.-Mexican Studies; Robles and Gómez, 111; Montiel, Yolanda. 1991. *Proceso de Trabajo, Acción Sindical y Nuevas Tecnologías en Volkswagen de México*. Mexico, DF: Ediciones de la Casa Chata; Othón Quiroz Trejo, José. 1997. Oral interview, Mexico, DF. July 14; Sánchez Diaz, Sergio Guadalupe. 1978. "Sobre la Unidad Obrera." Paper presented at the Encuentro Sobre la Historia del Movimiento Obrero. Puebla, Mexico: Universidad Autonoma de Puebla.

23 Initial UOI contracts were with Euzkadi Tires, Acros, and DINA, the nationally owned car and truck manufacturer.

24 Middlebrook, Kevin J. 1995. *The Paradox of Revolution: Labor, the State, and Authoritarianism in Mexico*, 242–44. Baltimore: Johns Hopkins.

25 1981. "Unidad Obrera Independiente." *Organizacion*, 4 (August): 22–29.

26 Quiroz Trejo interview.

27 Middlebrook (1995), 280-81.

28 Martinez, Benedicto. 1997. Conversation in Mexico, DF. July 14; Martinez, Benedicto. 1999. Oral interview, Ciudad Juarez. June 19.

29 This strike was at CINSA-CIFUNSA. Camacho, Manuel. 1975. "La Huelga de Saltillo, Un Intento de Regeneracion Obrera." *FI XV-3* (Jan-Mar): 1-38; Robles and Gómez. 1995, 110.

30 Trejo Delarbre, Raul. 1976. "Lucha Sindical y Politica:

31 Anonymous. *Poder Obrero: Testimonios de los 121 de Lucha de los Trabajadores de Spicer,* 10. Mexico, DF.

32 *Poder Obrero,* 24

33 Trejo Delarbre, 88.

34 Trejo Delarbre, 90.

5.

In the Era of Crisis

The economy of Mexico grew steadily from the 1940s through the early 1970s, decades referred to as "the Mexican miracle." Granted, it was not growth with equity. Productivity increased much faster than wages, so the rich got richer while the poor got richer at a slower rate. Although inequality increased, many people were becoming somewhat better off and the official phrase "stabilizing development," which the PRI used to describe its economic policy, was somewhat accurate.

If the years of the '50s and '60s were relatively good years for workers, the '70s and '80s were decades of tumult and uncertainty. Workers' demands for democracy grew along with growing wages and led to the years of the Insurgencia Obrera. To counter this and other threats to PRI power, President Echeverria declared a shift from "stabilizing development" to "shared development."

Echeverria increased spending on social services, promoted new programs for peasants and workers, and drastically increased state investment not only in infrastructure but in direct industrial production as well. The government invested heavily in the steel, energy, and transportation sectors necessary for a modern economy. The number of state-owned enterprises increased from 84 to 845.[1] Echeverria also asked industrialists, who were used to years of protective tariffs, to begin making better products at lower prices.

Mexican business was not at all pleased with the new economic policy of shared development. The poor and middle classes got a larger share of the nation's income, while the share going to the richest 20% dropped from 64% to a mere 55%.[2] The wealthy responded by shipping much of their savings out of the country. Inflation escalated and government indebtedness increased by over 700%. In 1976, the last year of his presidency, Echeverria was forced to devalue what had long been a stable peso and to ask the International Monetary Fund (IMF) for assistance. To get help, he was obliged to impose an austerity package, slashing the government's social and industrial programs he had so recently increased.[3]

Within the government, economic planners agreed that they needed to reorient the economy. They disagreed on whether to improve the country by focusing directly on Mexican workers and consumers or by making Mexico more attractive to foreign investors. One group favored focusing on creating jobs in an economy geared to production of consumer goods and making real improvements in basic nutrition, health, education, and housing. Others, the tecnicos, pushed to focus on reducing inflation and increasing the country's integration with the global economy. The tecnicos took power with the election of Echeverria's successor, Jose Lopez Portillo. One of his colleagues, Ricardo Garcia Sainz, explained frankly that their plan for progress was based on "support for and incentives to capital, with sacrifice and effort from the working class."[4] The discovery of new oil fields and drastically increasing prices for oil allowed the government to obtain huge foreign loans and spend lavishly. Unfortunately, while Mexico was on its way toward "progress," public-sector debt rose from $19.6 billion in 1976 to $92.4 billion in 1982.[5]

In the early 1980s interest rates rose sharply around the world, largely to stem the inflation that had been spurred by the rise in oil prices. Oil prices had also stimulated an expansion of oil production in areas like the North Sea, as well as in Mexico. Combined with a nearly global decline in economic activity, this led to steadily falling oil prices. With oil revenues down and the interest on its enormous loans soaring, Mexico declared in August 1982 that it could no longer pay its foreign debts.

Making matters worse was the behavior of Mexico's own business sector. The reforms of the mid-1970s had reduced the amount of protection offered to Mexican industrialists. By the end of the decade, they found it more profitable to invest in real estate and banks in the United States. Morgan Guarantee Trust estimated that if the $55 billion that had left the country from 1975 to 1985 had been invested domestically, Mexico's foreign debt would have been a very manageable $12 billion instead of the $97 billion it reached.[6] In 1982 an outraged President

Lopez Portillo declared that the Mexican bourgeoisie had "stolen more money from our country than the empires which have exploited us since the beginning of our history."[7] In a desperate effort to stanch the country's financial hemorrhaging before he left office, Lopez Portillo nationalized the nation's banks and imposed foreign exchange controls.

Lopez Portillo had hoped that the bank nationalization and debt moratoriums would raise his standing as an economic nationalist and give his government the popular support needed to stop the economic collapse. However, his moves were adamantly rejected by both domestic and international business elites, who cared little about popular support. Since the cooperation of these elites was necessary for the success of any financial plan under consideration, before he left office Lopez Portillo was forced to approve an agreement with the International Monetary Fund committing the Mexican government to a neoliberal economic future. In order to be able to pay its debts—the key concern of the IMF—Mexico agreed to lower its budget deficits, diminish public-sector spending, and lower real wages.[8]

The "miracle" had been revived, briefly, on borrowed money. When the bubble finally burst, the crisis was on in earnest. The solution to the crisis was modernization, or the neoliberal model. Using this solution, Lopez Portillo's successor, Miguel de la Madrid, and other US-educated economists managed to coax a recovery out of the economy in the early '90s, and began to sell dreams of a new miracle.

De la Madrid: Administering the Crisis

Miguel de la Madrid had been an economic planner in the Mexican government since the time of Echeverria. His presidency (1982–88) announced the triumph of the economic technocrats over the more traditional elements of the PRI. He whole-heartedly committed the Mexican government to the principles of the global economy.

As one treasury official explained the new economic regime, "In order to pay the external debt, the government had to ... gather resources from the society and transfer them abroad."[9] By 1988 debt payments reached 60% of the public-sector budget. Excluding those debt payments, public spending declined by a shocking 60%.[10] From 1983 to

1988 spending on education declined by 29.6%; spending on health dropped by 23.3%.[11]

While Mexico became a model debtor, the effects of the new economic policies on ordinary Mexicans were devastating. Infant mortality climbed for the first time in decades. By the end of the decade average caloric consumption had fallen to half the level recommended by the World Health Organization. Consumption of milk and meat became luxuries and declined by nearly 50%.[12] Put another way, in 1981, the cost of a family's daily basket of foodstuffs (tortillas, bread, pasta, flour, cookies, crackers, rice, beef, pork, fish, milk, eggs, vegetable oil, beans, and sugar) was less than 60% of the minimum daily wage. By 1984 the same basket of goods would cost them 120% of the day's income.[13] While the workforce grew by eight million people during de la Madrid's term, the total number of jobs declined by 400,000. Employment in the industrial sector fell by nearly 12%.[14]

While previous presidents had harmed workers, or at least limited the gains of labor unions, they had always managed to portray themselves as defenders of the working class. De la Madrid committed Mexico to a policy clearly opposed to workers' interests. In order to pay off debts, the country was compelled to increase its export earnings. Since oil no longer offered a magic solution, workers and peasants would be made to pay. Domestic consumption would be cut. The lure of cheap, controlled labor would attract foreign investment in export-related industries.

Official unions proved no brake on this policy. While Fidel Velazquez of the CTM threatened a general strike if wages were not immediately adjusted to make up for losses to inflation, other government-affiliated labor federations like the CROC and the CROM—eager to gain at the CTM's expense—offered no resistance at all. De la Madrid responded with a flat "no" to Velazquez's calls for justice for the working class and for loyalty to the goals of the revolution.[15] When Velazquez failed to take action, he exposed his earlier "militant" calls for what they were—empty posturing.

For de la Madrid, the holders of foreign debt were now more influential than those who had traditionally made up the rank-and-file of the ruling party's corporatist alliance. The tecnicos who shared his vision of Mexico as an efficient, world-class competitor also shared a disdain for the old-style patronage politics of their predecessors that guaranteed a steady flow of resources to people who had traditionally supported the party, regardless of their inefficiency or corruption. The tecnicos called the old-style politicians and labor leaders "dinosaurs."

The tecnicos knew that rebuilding the economy required pleasing both international investors and major Mexican capitalists, all of whom had the option of investing in other countries. They knew that workers and peasants had nowhere else to go, and that they were experienced in suffering. The tecnicos would do what they thought best and let the others adapt.

In 1986, over the objections of the official unions and many Mexican business organizations, de la Madrid committed Mexico to the General Agreement on Tariffs and Trade (GATT). This removed many of the remaining protections for domestic industries, and it offered improved access to many export markets. Some of Mexico's largest manufacturers did well under this regime. However, a great many less efficient businesses closed, destroying jobs by the tens of thousands and earning the increased hostility of domestic businessmen who could not keep up with the new global order.

Struggling to hold wages down, rein in inflation, and keep the badly abused labor movement in line before entering an election year, de la Madrid called upon the corporatist traditions of Mexico and convoked the leaders of labor as well as those of business. Together, in December 1987, they agreed on the Pact of Economic Solidarity, or simply, *el Pacto*. The Pact put caps on both wage and price increases. Labor gave up any hope of regaining what it had lost in wages, but it gained access to a greater amount of subsidized food to be distributed through official union networks. This was the old-style politics the dinosaurs knew and loved. They would soon find out if it was enough to maintain the loyalty of their memberships.

Another factor troubling the stability of the PRI's machine-like control of Mexican society was the aftermath of the 1985 earthquake. The September quake leveled buildings throughout Mexico City, leaving approximately 7,000 dead and 30,000 homeless. The government's response was limited and channeled through corrupt PRI networks of favors for clients. The result of the government's deplorable response was a flowering of civil society and the emergence of many non-governmental organizations, such as the Asamblea de Barrios (Neighborhood Assembly), with its masked hero, Super Barrio. The new networks of self-help facilitated activities outside of the PRI-controlled infrastructure. Independent politics began to be possible in the capital city. The PRI's neglect of the people was no longer without cost.

The ruling party's commitment to neoliberal economic policies that sacrificed the vital interests of the majority of its traditional voters was bound to have political consequences. Members of the PRI who challenged those policies and sought to influence the selection of the next president became known as the Democratic Current. Led by Cuauhtemoc Cardenas, son of former president Lazaro Cardenas, eternal symbol of policies in favor of the now neglected workers and peasants, they were expelled from the party in late 1986. Cardenas won the backing of a number of small center and left-wing parties and ran for president in 1988 as the head of the National Democratic Front (FDN).

Cardenas rallied the support of most of those who had been hurt by the policies of de la Madrid. Workers and peasants abandoned the PRI in record numbers. The most significant deserter from the official labor movement was Hernandez Galicia, better known as La Quina, the head of the powerful petroleum workers' union. La Quina not only failed to direct his workers to vote for the PRI, he urged them to vote for Cardenas, a man who would never privatize Mexico's oil holdings, an action under consideration by tecnicos in the PRI, including their presidential candidate, the economist Carlos Salinas de Gotari.

On the night of the election, July 6, 1988, Cardenas seemed to be taking a significant lead when all of a sudden the electoral computer system "failed." By the time it was repaired and the tally was completed—a week later—the PRI had "cooked the data" to show that Salinas had won. Salinas was given 50.4% of the vote—by far the lowest vote count ever for a PRI candidate. Cardenas was officially awarded 32% of the vote—the highest ever for an opposition candidate. We will never know the true outcome. The FDN claims that Cardenas won 42% to Salinas's 37%. Other election surveys show Salinas with a slight victory, but well below half the vote. Perhaps the most significant poll was one taken nearly a year later by the *Los Angeles Times* that reported that 74% of the population did not believe Salinas had actually won.[16]

The years of crisis had led to a democratic mobilization unprecedented in post-revolutionary Mexico. For all but a privileged few, the

'80s were justly known as the lost decade. The arrogance of the tecnicos and the grave damage done to the material fortunes of average citizens had apparently led to an abandonment of the PRI. Last-minute goodies were no longer sufficient to buy the votes of a majority. The PRI's tecnicos had had to resort to the anti-democratic skills of its dinosaurs in order to maintain control.

Labor During the Lost Decade

Wages, however they are measured, fell catastrophically during the '80s. One study notes that the average factory worker's weekly wage dropped by 66% between 1982 and 1985.[17] Another author notes that by 1987 the real urban minimum wage was only slightly more than half of its 1980 level, and the share of the GDP accounted for by wages had fallen from 42% to 30%.[18] Yet another reports that total real wage income fell by 40% under de la Madrid. While workers in the manufacturing sector lost less than other working and poor categories in the period, manufacturing still lost nearly 12% of its jobs.[19]

Workers did not accept this radical attack on their livelihoods with tranquillity. Yet their resistance was well controlled by the state. One simple means of control is the ability of labor boards to deny the legality of strikes. In 1987, for instance, with inflation at its highest levels, unions filed over 16,000 strike petitions with Federal Conciliation and Arbitration Boards. Only 174 of these, about 1.1%, were legally recognized.[20] Official unions also helped manage the process by accepting most of these rulings and quieting their workers.

Yet there were numerous instances of local unions defying government policy, often confronting their national leadership in the process. Cutbacks in government spending in the social sector led to rebellions in the unions of Mexico City's subway system, the Metro, and in the public health system. Workers of the Metro managed to reform the leadership of their union in May 1981. They democratized internal governance, emphasized solidarity with other unions, and won real pay increases. The de la Madrid administration decided it would not tolerate so much deviance in such a strategic location. Workers loyal to the previous leadership held a rump assembly, elected new leaders, and immediately had their illegitimate election approved by the federal labor board. When workers objected, police forcibly ejected them from their union head-quarters in October 1983. Thirty-five of the top democratic leaders were then fired.[21] Healthcare workers in the Mexican Institute for Social Security confronted both falling wages and falling budgets with which to deliver health services to the citizenry. Since leaders of the official union, the SNTSS, refused to oppose government policies openly, workers formed a Democratic Current within the union. They held unauthorized work stoppages in 1984, '87, and '88 and had some success at limiting the cuts, but they had to contend not only with their union leaders, but with other factions of co-opted workers.

The government also prevented union democracy in the government-owned Telefonos de Mexico. Francisco Hernandez Juarez, leader of the telephone workers' union STRM since 1976, had been perceived as a militant defender of the rank-and-file, but when he negotiated new rules in response to technological modernization, the rank-and-file turned on him. They called a general assembly of the workers and occupied union headquarters. Hernandez Juarez responded by occupying the main switchboard of Mexico City as a way of striking back at militant operators. He then called on the secretary of labor and Fidel Velazquez to intervene in his favor. They did, and dissident leaders were removed. As one worker put it, the days of union democracy had "passed into history in order to enter the era of 'modernization.' "[22]

A variety of other repressive measures were used against union dissidents. Democratic forces within the national teachers' union (SNTE) were punished with the 1983 closing of the Normal Superior teachers college, which had served as a source of democratically minded new teachers. In 1984, the government developed a new tactic to deal with unions: bankruptcy. To punish SUTIN, the independent union of nuclear workers at the state-owned URAMEX, Mexico's congress voted to close the company. It then reorganized the operations, opening the way for foreign investment and getting rid of the troublesome union.[23] Facing hard times in the steel industry and a resistant union movement, the government closed its Fundidora de Monterrey steel mill in 1986, thus terminating jobs for all the workers. In 1988 it closed Aeromexico in the midst of a strike, suddenly declaring bankruptcy. After a brief period of down time, the airline was reorganized and workers were selectively re-hired with a new union and a new contract, all in apparent violation of labor law.[24] In one of the most creative responses of workers to the onslaught of the 1980s, 3,500 miners held a work stoppage dressed in only their boots and their hard hats.[25]

Though there were occasional small victories for workers, the period is summed up in the title of a book by two sociologists who followed events of the period closely: *State Modernization and Worker Response: History of a Defeat.*[26]

The FAT Confronts the Crisis

It should be clear to the reader by now that it has never been easy for a worker in Mexico to earn a living, nor to try to improve his or her lot through a labor union. The new economic model adopted in the mid-1970s and implemented with ever more vigor since the early '80s has only made it harder. When the key goal of the economy became generating foreign exchange to pay back international debts, anything that interfered with that goal became an obstacle. The situation was similar to the early years of Mexico's Spanish colonization, when the goal was to extract as much gold and silver as possible, regardless of the fact that native Mexicans were dying off by the millions. Thus spending on social needs became a problem, and labor unions that challenged government policies or that tried to raise wages were a problem. The FAT and its allies were clearly a problem.

One of the first serious catastrophes facing the FAT as a result of the new economic policy was that many of the companies they had unionized simply went out of business. We have seen that government policy often denied the FAT the right to organize large businesses, and that employer federations and large corporations resisted the FAT tenaciously; thus most of the FAT's unions were in small to medium-sized businesses. Many of these had benefited from tariff protections and were inefficient compared to companies that sold similar products on the global market. When tariffs were reduced or eliminated in the 1970s and '80s, firms were forced to modernize or close.

The FAT in Guanajuato

While the FAT had its first successes in the state of Guanajuato, establishing a strong presence in the shoe industry of Leon and in the clothing factories of Irapuato, by the early '90s it had lost nearly all of its contracts in these two sectors. The stories of this period tell us much about life during the crisis and much about the importance of the FAT.

HILSA and CIZSA

The strike at HILSA and CIZSA in 1979 reflected both the coming crisis and the ability of the Lopez Portillo regime to compromise with workers. The FAT had organized the CIZSA shoe factory and the HILSA rubber sole factories in the early '70s. The factories each saw relatively good times for the next several years, but an account by a CIZSA worker suggests that the firm was making plans to rid itself of the unions. It was opening additional shoe factories with non-union workers and supplying them with materials charged to CIZSA's account.[27] Both factories were owned in part by the president of the local PRI, a state senator, Alfonso Sanchez Lopez, locally known as Don Alfonso. The senator's family also owned five additional shoe factories, one shoe machine supply and repair business, two additional businesses in shoe soles, and various banking interests. As a union member described it, "The Sanchez Lopez family had made a great accumulation of capital through exploitation of wage labor and usurious banking."[28]

In December 1978, Don Alfonso simply announced that he could no longer pay his workers their wages or their Christmas holiday pay. Nor did he reopen either factory in January. When workers finally declared a strike on March 2, 1979, the local labor board did the senator the favor of declaring the strike legally non-existent. With the support of other FAT locals, the workers put on a de facto strike that lasted through late June.

The strikers held marches and public convocations. At the first march from the factory to the central plaza, Alfredo Dominguez, from the national leadership of the FAT, spoke of Don Alfonso as the embodiment of the PRI, insisting that the PRI didn't want to pay workers. The senator resigned his party post the next day. The FAT broadened its attack with events such as a local symposium featuring national journalists denouncing the unfair press coverage of the strike, and another event with an anthropologist, a sociologist, an economist, and a political scientist analyzing "The Labor Conflict of the Workers of HILSA and CIZSA in Light of the Social Sciences." They intruded on the CTM's May First Labor Day parade. They marched on Mother's Day, and their children marched in honor of the International Year of the Child. They even composed *corridos*, songs telling the history of the conflict. They succeeded in winning so much popular support that the wives of the employers provided workers with weekly baskets of food. The involvement of the senator and the major debt owed by HILSA to the government-owned supplier of raw materials eventually led to federal intervention and the strike was settled.

Workers at HILSA won 90% of their back pay and vacation money, as well as half-pay for their strike time. Workers at CIZSA did not do as well, many losing their jobs but receiving severance pay, others getting half their back pay and losing their jobs a few years later. On new footing, HILSA managed to do well through the 1980s, being the main supplier of shoe soles and heels to the region's shoe industry, but in the early 1990s Don Alfonso sold it to a businessman who saw it as a cash cow, extracting as much capital from it as he could in a short time. He then sold it to a larger firm that produces Neolite shoes in Mexico.

The new firm has several other factories where workers earn half as much pay as the HILSA workers. It has refused to invest new capital into the HILSA plant and it often refuses to pay the benefits called for in the contract. Dirty, noisy, hot, and lacking in safety equipment, the once state-of-the-art factory has decayed. A whole section of it, damaged by fire, has never been repaired. The firm is also badly in debt again, but the workers were able to block management's attempt to sell off machinery to pay off debts. By 1997 workers felt the company wanted to provoke another strike so it could go out of business. Nonetheless, HILSA paid one of the best wages in town, so workers sought to maintain their place of employment.

The courts have already awarded the workers ownership of some of the machinery in lieu of overdue benefits. But the workers do not have the leverage they once had over the very personal local owner, Don Alfonso. Confronting a more modern business with plants in many locations producing for transnational corporations, the workers placed their hopes in Mexican labor law and in their own tenacity. In the spring of 1999 HILSA stopped paying workers, and the strike began. The labor board ordered the business either to rehire the workers and pay them back salaries or to pay them the severance benefits they are due. But management—unable to cut HILSA wages as low as they would like—claimed that the rigidities of Mexican labor law lead to economic failure. They chose simply ignored the law and opened a new factory. In August of 2000, workers maintained their vigil at the plant gates. One worker explained, "Yes there is hunger, misfortune, cold, and rain, but none of us is moving from here until they do us justice."[29]

The Shoe Sector

Botas Jacas was a much more typical employer of the FAT's unionized workers in Leon. They had organized the business early, in 1965. The employer was torn between his visceral hatred of unions and his church's instruction that employers should treat workers with justice. The demands of the workers in the first contract negotiations in 1965 had been quite basic. Workers should get at least the legal minimum wage and work a 48-hour week. They should also get the holidays and vacation days required by law. A survey of union records for 83 shoe-makers showed their average age to be 21 and their average education less than three years.

In 1981 the 75 workers of Botas Jacas won a contract that called for a five-day week with benefits that included 13 to 31 days of paid vacation per year on top of holidays, a Christmas bonus equal to 25 days' wages, life insurance, a 10% punctuality bonus, scholarships, honeymoon and funeral benefits, and full pay for the head of their union. They had clearly made progress. But their employer was aging, and his nephews—educated at business school in Monterrey—had increasing influence in managing the enterprise. Although the company was profitable, the nephews knew that their labor contract was far more generous than others in the area. In 1983 they refused to sign a new contract with the union, closed the business, and eventually agreed to severance pay for the remaining 25 workers. Shortly thereafter they reorganized and reopened with a new, cheaper, non-union workforce. They are now one of the most prominent makers of boots in Leon. To this day FAT loyalists in Leon insist that—on his deathbed—the owner of Botas Jacas summoned the FAT's lawyer, Victor Quiroga, to ask his forgiveness for breaking the union.

Throughout the '80s other factories closed, some to reopen with no union contract. Attempts to organize at other shoe factories, such as Din-Din in 1986, resulted in new forms of CTM-labor board collaboration.[30] By the end of the '80s the FAT had been driven out of Leon's shoe industry, with the lingering exception of HILSA.

The legacy of the FAT continues to aid Leon's 150,000 shoemakers, though. In order to avoid a FAT unionization drive, most employers provide a measure of security first won by the FAT. They pay a guaranteed salary, even if work is slow, and although salaries are less than $10 a day, they are twice the salary paid by the new General Motors plant just 10 miles outside of town.

Irapuato: Workers with Open Eyes

In the neighboring town of Irapuato, the FAT had organized a variety of unions, including shoemakers, bus drivers, restaurant workers, and campesinos. But the FAT's major work in Irapuato had always been in the town's large garment manufacturing industry. Through the '80s and '90s this industry went through a transition, first adjusting to the economic downturn and the market opening due to GATT, which led to a round of closings, and then to the arrival of the maquiladoras: businesses set up with Mexican or foreign capital that sold batches of production on contract to international clothing labels.

At the start of 1982, total employment in Irapuato clothing factories was 3,500. By year's end it was barely half that number. One of the union locals that died that year was at Ropa Acero. It had been organized in 1966 and its 150 workers had, through various struggles, improved their pay and working conditions. They were making twice what women in unorganized shops were getting for the same work. In midsummer, the boss closed the factory, insisting that he couldn't compete. The women at first refused to go on strike, preferring to negotiate to try to save their jobs rather than giving the owner an excuse to close. But meanwhile, they kept an eye on the plant, knowing that the owner might try to take out finished garments and machines to reduce his assets before meeting his responsibilities to them. One night they mobilized 30 angry women to stop his attempt to "rob" himself. Eventually they negotiated a severance package that exceeded the legal requirements, and the business officially closed. Women at non-unionized shops or those organized with the CTM often got little or no severance pay, regardless of the law.[31] The business eventually reopened, without a union, as did others. The restructuring of the '80s left little room for just treatment of the workers.

The FAT did manage to hang onto its union at Maquiladora Pantalones de Irapuato until the factory closed in the economic crash of 1995. One of the women who lost her job then, Griselda Angel Gonzales, had worked there for 13 years. She spoke highly of the union that bore the proud name of Libertad when it was first organized in 1963. The workers got advice from organizers like Antonio Velasquez, but they always had to make their own decisions. "It's not like the CTM, where they make people act like robots," she added. When she lost her job, she used her settlement money to open her own small shop and now employs 11 workers. She insists she pays them over twice the minimum wage, plus benefits, while other shops now offer only the minimum wage.

What she appreciates about the FAT is not just the skills and the confidence she gained as a member, but also the political awareness. The FAT was always involved in politics and sponsored talks that usually drew over half the membership. She insists that workers need to be interested in politics. She says when wages go up by 8% in response to price hikes of 20% that's politics. "Some people say 'I may as well lay down and die, because it makes me so angry, but I can't do anything about it,'" she explains. "What they ought to do is shout about it, denounce it!"

Griselda had come to the FAT office to use an expensive sewing machine that she could not afford to buy. She was using it to make up some samples for a potential buyer. She explained that the FAT had gotten some machines donated so it could train women looking for work in the town's factories. The training improved the women's chances of finding work, and it might someday lead to new organizing. But she pointed out that most factories were now hiring women straight out of small villages.

> They tell them, "Watch out. Don't stop by that FAT union or we will
> fire you." Why? Because they know that at the FAT people will work
> to open their eyes. And they don't want people with open eyes.

If the FAT gets inside a factory, the owners close it. That's why the FAT is so small. That, and the fact that workers are conformist and lazy—well, not really. They are afraid of what will happen if they open their mouth. They could get fired, and they need to bring food home to the family.[32]

The very real increase in hunger, unemployment, and desperation brought on by the years of crisis produced fears in workers that facilitated Mexico's adjustment to the global economy—at their expense.

KSB: A Dwindling FAT Workforce

In addition to HILSA, only one other FAT contract remained in force in the state of Guanajuato by the end of 1999. The KSB plant, the German pump-making plant unionized in 1965, continued to employ 40 FAT members; their value to the firm was evidenced by the fact that they were paid over four times more than comparable workers.[33]

Through the 1980s and '90s KSB had to go through a series of adjustments to the changing economy. In the early '80s it attempted to respond to globalization by exporting part of its production. The company expanded production and opened a foundry in nearby Lagos with a FAT contract identical to the one in its original plant. Sales abroad did not go well and the company, in trouble, took on some Mexican partners. The Mexican investors insisted on a Mexican manager who was determined to get rid of the union. He closed the Lagos plant and opened a new, non-union foundry and assembly plant in the neighboring state of Queretaro. Over time, it seemed, he wanted to transfer all production there. At one point the new management attempted to move machinery out of the Leon plant to Queretaro. FAT workers blocked the move and threatened to use their contacts with KSB's German union to bring pressure there. The machines stayed put.

The more experienced workers in Leon have proven indispensable for repairs, and they still produce the largest and most complex of the KSB pumps. But the plant that employed 160 workers in the early '80s now employs a mere 42 workers. Most of them seem happy, and they are proud that their experience makes them better workers than those in the now much larger Queretaro plant. While FAT advisers in Leon feel that the KSB workers are being undermined, the union members seem content with their overtime and their relatively high wages. They do not attend FAT political events or training sessions as did the workers from the HILSA plant. While the FAT advises, the workers themselves make their decisions. FAT advisers fear those workers may be coasting toward oblivion.

CRISA: Frozen Fruit for Global Trading

Many of the FAT's members whose union jobs no longer exist remain active in other aspects of the FAT's work (as discussed in Chapter 6). These dedicated activists have allowed the FAT to keep a high profile and help set a standard for the conditions of all workers. Employers who abuse even these minimal rights sometimes find that their workers turn to the FAT for help, either as individuals or collectively. One struggle that is on-going as this book goes to press is that of the workers who pack frozen strawberries and other fruit for the Congeladora del Rio (CRISA) plant in Irapuato. The plant is owned by Arthur Price, who also owns Global Trading of Greenville, South Carolina.

The workers at CRISA approached the FAT for help in May 1999 when they were denied the profit-sharing they felt they were legally guaranteed. They worked from 8 to 15 hours for between $5 and $10 a day in harsh conditions. Some of the workers were as young as 12 years old. Workers filed a legal petition demanding representation by the FAT. CRISA responded by firing 200 workers and claiming that another union already represented the workers. The State of Guanajuato brokered an agreement calling for the reinstatement of all the workers, but so far only a few of the workers have been rehired.[34]

One aspect that makes this case distinctly interesting is that the FAT has gotten a great deal of support from unionists and grassroots activists in the United States for the strike. Arthur Price has responded personally to e-mails with a variety of interesting lies both defaming FAT members in Mexico and threatening US supporters with arrest if they come to Mexico. While pursuing legal avenues in Mexico—a long and uncertain process—the FAT is also considering calling for a boycott of Global Trading's strawberries in the United States. Initial research has shown their berries to be used in jam, yogurt, and ice cream products that are popular throughout the country. Other research indicates the company may be considering closing the Irapuato plant rather than recognizing a legitimate union. Another interesting wrinkle in this case is that Vicente Fox, president-elect of Mexico and former governor of Guanajuato, has all the influence needed to make CRISA abide by its agreement. To date he has done nothing.

Meanwhile, encouraged by international support, the strikers maintain their vigil outside the plant, demanding "reinstatement of the 200 workers fired at CRISA; freedom to join the union of our choice, chosen through an election; and better working conditions, hygienic conditions and protection for the work we do."[35]

In the Valley of Mexico: Sealed Power

The FAT has a variety of unions, large and small, in Mexico City and the surrounding state of Mexico. Perhaps the best known of these is the union of Otis Elevator Workers, which is a national union that encompasses plants and service operations in the capital and around the country. The FAT has also begun organizing new unions in the huge and diverse service sector. These unions work in close cooperation with the national leadership to meet the needs of local members and to work in coalition with other unions in trying to influence national policy. During the '80s and since, this close cooperation has been crucial to the success of union struggles.

The story of Sealed Power is an important one for at least three reasons.[36] First, the initial organizing effort is a valiant story that deserves to be recorded and that has lasting resonance within the national leadership of the FAT. Second, it allows us to see a successful instance of a union recapturing a plant that had fled to a non-union area in order to escape the FAT. Third, it deals directly with the issue of a union's role in increasing the productivity of its employer's operations.

Sealed Power is a brand of piston rings used in the engines of many Ford, Chrysler, General Motors, and Nissan vehicles. In the early 1960s US investors built its Mexican plant in the industrial town of Naucalpan, in the state of Mexico, just outside the limits of the Federal District of Mexico City. Before it even started production, the plant had a CTM union contract for the purpose of regularizing labor relations, not representing the workers. During the Insurgencia Obrera of the 1970s Naucalpan was a center of militant union organizing. Unions at neighboring plants formed an alliance to support each other. The union at Sealed Power, though, served as an arm to support the arbitrary punishments and general corruption of the plant's management. Workers slowly began to organize for a change.

One of those workers, Benedicto Martinez Orozco, had been born in a Mige Indian village in the southern state of Oaxaca. In the mid-1960s after his father, a village leader, had been shot in a dispute, Martinez joined the army, patriotically inspired to follow the example of a previous Indian from Oaxaca, the former president Benito Juarez. Martinez rose rapidly through the enlisted ranks, attracting the attention of influential officers, who facilitated his education. When he came to understand that the army was being used to kill students and workers in 1968, he resigned and joined the ranks of young industrial workers in the nation's capital. Eventually he landed in the foundry at Sealed Power.

There he met Daniel Lopez, one of eight children born and raised in working-class Mexico City. Daniel had completed secondary school by the time he was 15, while helping his father and his uncle collect and re-sell scrap metal, bottles, and used magazines. After a string of jobs he found himself assigned as a helper to Benedicto at Sealed Power. They played together on the company basketball team. They also shared complaints about abusive treatment by their supervisors and simple dreams about how nice it would be to have a decent place to eat their lunches at work. One day they calculated that the company could pay each of their salaries by selling only two of the thousands of piston rings they made each day.

The leadership of the CTM union was very lax. It did follow the legal requirements of holding occasional general assemblies and electing union delegates, but the delegates were generally expected to do nothing. Both Daniel and Benedicto won positions in union elections. Daniel says he won not because he had ideas or class consciousness, but because he was a good talker. Benedicto was elected after a general assembly at which he asked the CTM leader why workers could never get anything out of their forced savings accounts. Benedicto and a few other workers began attending an independent "union school" held at the nearby Harper Wyman plant, where they learned how to print up their own literature and how to solicit contributions on the street during a strike.

In May 1978 the union's contract expired without an agreement being reached on a salary increase—an obvious necessity given on-going inflation. The union local struck, giving both management and union leaders the first real indication of the level of resentment building within the workers. The strike was settled after 39 days, a period during which many of the workers were exposed to the more militant consciousness of workers in factories around them. Several of the workers determined to do better the next year. When CTM leadership only laughed at them, they began to investigate the possibility of forming an independent union.

With contract negotiations looming in May 1979, a core of workers secretly began to plot. Daniel and Benedicto conspired to make the May first Labor Day march an organizing event. Using their position within the CTM local, they made it mandatory for all workers to march in the parade, or be fined three days' salary. They bought sour oranges to pass out to the hot, thirsty workers and generally planned to make the day miserable. During this march they grumbled their complaints about the CTM and talked about the need for a change. By the time they got to the National Palace, where they were to thank the president for his support of the workers, they thrust their fists in the air and shouted out together, "The workers, united, will never be defeated!" In the next few weeks, they were able to sign up more than half the workers to form a new union.

At this same time workers insisted on a decent salary increase, but they were discouraged in their efforts not only by their employer but by their regional CTM leader. But workers had elected their own negotiating committee, which managed to get a 20% raise, even though the government policy allowed only a 13% increase. At the next general assembly they voted to get rid of their CTM leader and they determined, quietly, to move forward on forming their own union. In mid-June they began circulating word that they would hold a general assembly to declare its formation. When management and the CTM found out that they were planning to hold the assembly at the independent Euzcadi Tire union hall across town, they got suspicious.

Management sensed they were losing control, and on June 24 they fired Benedicto Martinez. He refused to sign a severance agreement, but he agreed to change his clothes and leave. Then, rather than going to his locker to change, he went back to the shop floor to say goodbye to Daniel. Without thinking, Daniel hugged him and they both sat down, determined not to leave voluntarily. They had no idea if the workers would be ready to support them. The supervisor told them not to be ridiculous, to get up.

Daniel got up and began to shut down machines. He called out to other workers to support Benedicto. They too stopped their machines. They demanded the boss explain why he was firing Benedicto. The boss yelled back: "I don't have to explain. Now get back to work if you don't want to lose your jobs!"

Daniel asked the workers if they were afraid, and they yelled back, "*No!*"

Seeing the workers line up behind Daniel and Benedicto, the boss called Daniel a "damned communist" and told workers not to fall into his trap of trying to lead them into a commie union. He was clearly shaken by the workers' solidarity. Encouraged by this show of force, Benedicto agreed to leave when the police arrived. But word spread and workers on the second shift had a similar work stoppage.

The next day the business decided to face the facts. The workers had taken a stand with Daniel. They called him to the office and said: "Look, our mistake was not to fire you first. But what we need is steady production. What do you need? A house? A car? A future for your children? If you can promise us steady production, we can give you what you need."

Daniel thought of his family and of a new house, but at the same time he thought of the other workers standing on their machines with their fists in the air and of the dreams he had shared with Benedicto. He refused to take the bribe and was fired.

That Saturday the workers held their first independent general assembly. There they elected a new executive committee with Daniel as secretary-general and Benedicto as secretary of labor, and they committed themselves to form an independent union. They also made plans for Monday. None of them would enter the plant unless the fired workers were reinstated.

Monday morning management proved pragmatic. They had been shocked at the work stoppage and by the sudden display of militant solidarity. The plant manager had recently arrived from Belgium, where he had closed a plant due to labor difficulties. He may not have wanted a similar loss here. So that morning the bosses opened the gates wide to all the workers and told them to go ahead and form an independent union. They now claimed that the firings had been a mistake; that they had come at the request of the CTM union. The new committee began negotiations immediately. And, in spite of their attorney—who wanted to lead them into another government-affiliated union federation—the workers eventually found the FAT. In November they voted to join the FAT's National Union of Iron and Steel Industry Workers (SNTIHA) by a vote of 270 in favor, one opposed, and two abstentions.

The union was elated at their victory but aware of the limitations of merely continuing to improvise, so it dedicated itself to the process of formación. Workers met every Monday after work for an hour to discuss topics such as how to organize a strike, how to bargain collectively, how to lead a meeting, and how to speak in public. They also had presentations on labor history and on wars in Central America. They analysized Mexican society and watched films on social topics. During the first year, they had general assemblies twice a month.

Relations were not smooth, but the new union developed an ability to negotiate directly with the company. Unknown to the workers, management had decided to build a new plant where it could escape the independent union and train new workers in an environment that had never known what a militant union could be. It followed Nissan's lead and bought land in Aguascalientes, 400 miles to the northwest.

By 1982 negotiations were deteriorating to the point that a strike looked likely. At that point the Mexican auto parts conglomerate the Condumex Group bought out Sealed Power. Condumex was hesitant to take on a FAT union, but Sealed Power fit their business plan, and they knew and approved of the plan to move to Aguascalientes. For a while Sealed Power's head of industrial relations plotted with managers of other companies that had SNTIHA union contracts to destroy the union nationwide. However, upper management decided to change course. They appointed a new manager of industrial relations, who came to terms with and began to develop a more direct, respectful style of negotiations with the union, which by then was headed by Benedicto Martinez, Daniel Lopez having moved to a position in the national leadership of SNTIHA.

The subsequent years exemplify a fascinating dualistic aspect of capitalism. Both sides understood well that they were class enemies.

They sought to get as much out of the other side as possible, and they viewed the other as an antagonist. At the same time, they both saw themselves as partners in the same enterprise and knew that their economic fortunes depended on the productivity of the other. Thus, what may appear below as hypocrisy or cynicism is also the pragmatic implementation of contradictory goals.

An official company history of the relations between the SNTIHA union and the new Condumex management of Sealed Power declares:

> The company was at a fork in the road. We could chose total confrontation, regardless what it cost to get rid of the union, or we could try to win over the workers so they would once again look upon the business with affection and regain respect for their union representatives. We chose the latter course.[37]

Benedicto Martinez also speaks of developing relations of respect and trust with the new director of industrial relations at the plant.

> Thanks to the presence of the new director, a new relationship developed. We developed frank communication and we strengthened the idea of playing fair. For example, we discovered ... [that] some people were due less than what the company was paying them. And we told him, "Manuel, we don't want to take advantage." That's how we established relations on a new level. An environment of mutual respect developed and deepened.[38]

Yet, in spite of this relationship of "mutual trust," Sealed Power went ahead with its plan to rid itself of the old plant and its union. While the factory was closed for the Christmas break of 1983–84, the company secretly moved all of the machines used in finishing the piston rings to its new plant in Aguascalientes. Work began there later that year. Before the new plant was even completed, the company had signed a protection contract with the CTM. New workers were hired from the surrounding countryside, and most had no knowledge of labor rights or unions. Most also had no experience with the expectations of industrial life either. Problems of attendance, turnover, low quality, and uneven work slowed the company's plan to shift all production to the new plant.

Workers at the older plant pledged 10 pesos a week to the organizing drive, and Benedicto Martinez began spending three days a week in Aguascalientes. The organizing process proceeded covertly for months. Martinez did not care to test whether Sealed Power managers would tolerate their organizing plan, and he definitely did not want to alert the CTM or other local businesses. Because many of the Sealed Power managers knew him, Benedicto stayed out of sight in his hotel room except to meet with workers interested in leaving the CTM. They met in small groups in parks or cafes. Eventually they were able to elect one of these workers to the executive committee of the new plant's CTM local. He then served as both a source of information and a helpful influence.

The old plant's union asked to visit the Aguascalientes plant. It took three months of negotiations with both the management and the CTM to approve the trip. This trip allowed Benedicto to appear overtly within the plant to people he had previously met only in secret. Workers began a dialogue and found out that those who worked in the Mexico City factory were getting twice as much pay as those at the new plant. Workers from the new plant made a visit to the old one and dialogue continued. At the prompting of the covert FAT supporter, the CTM's secretary-general suggested that they form one common union. Benedicto replied, "Well, if you insist."

The organizing committee in Aguascalientes managed to get a second member onto the executive committee and was able to lead the local leader, Agapito Jimenez, around by the nose. They supported his calling an assembly in which he proposed changing unions, but they suggested that, since he had the most direct CTM ties, he abstain in the actual voting. They filed papers calling for a vote for a new FAT union, choosing to use the FAT's newer and less well known metalworking union, STIMAHCS. This may have been an important point, because when the management of the nearby Nissan plant eventually figured out that the FAT was moving into town, they complained to the governor. After all, they had moved to Aguascalientes to escape the sort of informed militancy that the FAT had instilled in its workforce in the 1970s. But by then the election had already been held and the governor refused to interfere.

STIMAHCS won unanimously except for the abstention of Agapito Jimenez. At the first general assembly of the new union, workers elected a new secretary-general and demanded that Agapito account for the local union's money. Outraged, he refused, saying the CTM had told him it was his money to use as he wished. They bid him good riddance and vowed to make their finances a matter of open record in the future. Thus, within four years of when the Aguascalientes plant began work in its new location to escape a FAT union, the FAT unionists had secured control of both plants.

Compared to other examples of businesses that have gone to extremes to resist the FAT, this gentle but serious combat is unusual. After going to great lengths to escape the FAT by moving, Sealed Power did not really resist the successful effort of the FAT to organize its new workforce. Neither did it completely acquiesce. In 1996 a researcher discovered that—as part of its productivity efforts—the company was conducting surveys of its Aguascalientes workers that included questions about how the workers viewed their union, their wages, their benefits, and their work efforts.[39] These could clearly be used to subvert the union. In 1997 the CTM won some support within the workforce and challenged the STIMAHCS union for the right to represent the workers.

Days before the October 9 election the state government threatened the workers that if they didn't vote for the CTM they would never find work in the state again because workers there reject "foreign independent unions."[40] Potential officers were offered new cars if they supported the CTM. The independent STIMAHCS, nevertheless, won a resounding victory: 427–1. Given the involvement of a hostile state government and the covert opposition from management, the union is preparing for future problems by continuing the formación that has helped its members resist intimidation and co-optation so far.

Productivity and Quality of Work Life

Another area of cooperation and combat has been the whole notion of productivity. One of the key goals of Mexico's neoliberal economic policy has been to increase its exports by becoming competitive on a world-class scale. Part of this process has been an effort to increase the productivity of its manufacturers and of their workers. Progress here has been terribly uneven. Many medium and small businesses have never had the capital to invest in the latest technology. For them increasing productivity has meant trying to get workers to work longer and harder for less pay. For businesses like Sealed Power, it has meant investing in new technology and training its workers, as well as finding new ways to organize the work more efficiently. The FAT has entered into this area of increasing productivity with its eyes open but with a recognition of the need to engage.

Nowhere has the emphasis on productivity been higher than in Mexico's automotive sector. Throughout the 1980s, Sealed Power was the sole domestic supplier for piston rings in Mexico. In the late 1980s one of its key customers, Ford Motor Company, notified Sealed Power that it would have to achieve its quality standard, "Q-1," if it wished to continue selling to Ford. In February 1989 Ford wrote to Sealed Power:

> Through this communication Ford of Mexico recognizes the outstanding ongoing performance of your company.... Therefore we are very pleased to grant Sealed Power de Mexico the Q-1 Vendor Award.
>
> Ford business culture demands excellence.... The Q-1 Award is the result of our joint efforts for continuous improvements in quality and productivity.[41]

The award was celebrated by the company, and it inspired researcher Joaquin Peon Escalante to focus on Sealed Power and the FAT for his case study on "Total Quality." Reviewed in the FAT's own newspaper, *Resistencia Obrera*, the business-oriented case study discussed the unusual cooperative relationship that had developed between management and union after the years of initial conflict.[42]

When the company first began taking the issue of productivity seriously, it tried to impose a plan. The workers whistled to show their disgust when the notion of productivity was raised within the general assembly, and management's plan went nowhere. But within the union, workers began discussing the issue. Benedicto Martinez, then the union's secretary-general, insisted "If we don't deal with this, we don't have any future. The country itself needs profound changes in the quality of its products and services. We want a better country, and we want the change to benefit the workers."[43]

As a result of these discussions productivity began to improve. Management backed off from its control mentality. If managers saw three or four workers chatting in the aisle they just passed them by. The sense of greater freedom in the workplace benefited both the workers and the company.

What made the process of improving productivity work was that both sides were amenable to open communication and both, thus, had access to accurate information, and that built trust. Sealed Power's management spoke clearly of the advantage of dealing with an independent union like the FAT.

> We saw sincerity, strength, and commitment in this independent union. There is a clear lack of communication or even contact between workers and their leaders in many of the official unions. We decided that instead of a problem the new union presented an opportunity.... The democratically elected leaders truly represent the interests of their workers.[44]

The direct communication allowed the development of new work processes that improved quality and productivity. The FAT newspaper pointed out that this showed that "an independent union is not a business-closer, nor are we the unapproachable, closed-minded radicals that many bosses still call us."[45]

Yet the "good relations" that developed are not without controversy. Martinez says that dealing with management on issues of productivity is "like walking on the razor's edge." In many cases the efforts to increase productivity through quality circles or just-in-time production are simply "modern slavery." "If someone wants to be your friend and he asks you for your watch, giving it to him is not a way to maintain good relations. It's just abuse. And if a company asks you to sacrifice while they are doing well, that's not good relations. That's abuse."[46]

A walk through the Aguascalientes plant in November 1996 revealed machines humming and relaxed workers doing their jobs but comfortable with the idea of stopping to shake hands and talk. The factory was clean and appeared relatively safe. Workers were happy with the pleasant cafeteria that provided good food at subsidized prices, with their on-site union office, and the ready access they had to management. Martinez recalls:

> At one point we noticed an increase in production from 1,000 to 1,500 units per day in part of the plant, so we asked union members what was going on. Some said they used to read two comic books a day, and now they only read one. We reduced the amount of wasted time by making the workplace a more comfortable place to be.[47]

An official statement of the FAT on productivity emphasizes that "Total Quality" has to include improving the quality of workers' lives in ways that include education, housing, nutrition, culture, and time to relax. Only if the workers see real benefits from increasing productivity does it make sense for them to contribute, and if they do not contribute, productivity will rarely increase. While investment in new technology is part of the picture of improving productivity, the other part is investing in the workforce by establishing greater trust between workers, their union, and the employers.

The FAT document recognizes the need to increase productivity in Mexico given the realities of the global market, and it makes a strong argument that those unions that democratically represent the interests of their workers play an essential role in any real progress. Only democratic unions will be able to establish the honest communication and the sense of shared interest that are required to make real gains. It points out that the government dreamed that NAFTA would attract enough investment to make the country competitive on a global scale. In reality, investment has touched only part of Mexican industry, leaving most of the nation's workshops unable to compete. Many of those that do attract modern investment still lack high productivity. The document concludes that if Mexico is serious about increasing its productivity, it must also modernize its system of labor relations by allowing workers to form unions that are capable of representing their interests in the dialogue with their bosses. Thus revisions of NAFTA should include protections for workers, just as much as protections for capital.[48]

The reality of the productivity situation at Sealed Power continues to be mixed. The 1996–98 contract dealt with productivity in at least two ways. Workers received a bonus of between 3% and 7%, depending on the percentage of their department's production that passed quality standards. Individually, their pay was based on how many skills they had mastered within their department. A worker who had progressed through the six stages from the lowest to the highest could have increased his or her pay from 29 pesos per day to 50.74 pesos per day. In 1996 pesos, that meant that the top production worker could have earned nearly $7 a day—not a huge share of the earnings of a large corporation given that the workers were achieving world-class precision at levels of productivity comparable to those of skilled operators in the United States or Canada.

Management was disappointed that few workers chose to pursue the highest skill levels. The union maintained that compensation for training time was insufficient, as was the pay increase for extra learning.

The debate has continued with neither side satisfied, and neither side willing to trust that the relative improvements they have received from the other side is what they deserve to get. Each side has taken pride in the improvements they have achieved thus far. Yet management has continued to be open to replacing the STIMHACS union with one from the CTM that would allow them a more authoritarian approach, such as that used across town at the Nissan plant. The union has continued to walk carefully on the razor's edge, mindful of the need to produce a product that can compete in a global market and mindful of management's continued desire to more fully exploit its members.

PROVISA: Founding an Industrial Cooperative

The history of the plate-glass workers who eventually formed PROVISA reflects well the last four decades of the life of Mexican workers. Their first factory was built during the growth years of the '60s. In the 1970s the workers of two plate-glass factories struggled to form an independent union. In the initial years of crisis in the 1980s, they struggled to keep their plants open, eventually forming their own producers' cooperative. In the 1990s, challenged by international competition, they struggled to modernize.

In the late '60s, entrepreneur Francisco Campos Herrera hired local peasants with little or no formal education to build and operate the Alumex glass factory in an area that was still cornfields on the edge of Mexico City. After seeing the initial success of Alumex, Francisco's brother, Pedro, opened a second plant, Vidriera, near by. Until that point, a company based in the northern city of Monterrey had produced nearly all the plate glass in the country. Within a short time, Vidriera and Alumex came to supply nearly 10% of the national market.

During the early years, as the workers built the Alumex plant and began operating it, they had close, informal relations with the owner. Francisco Campos would eat lunch with them each week. He'd bring out meat, avocados, and tortillas and say, "Eat, it's yours, you've earned it." He would frequently ask them, "Help me, help me, please," and they would work overtime with no pay. But when they began to ask him for the vacation time with pay that was due to all Mexican workers he explained: "The little calf is barely born. We have to wait until it gives milk. For now, there are no vacations."[49]

Working conditions were hot and unsafe. Workers were not issued safety equipment, nor were they enrolled in the government's medical insurance and retirement system. When they were injured, they were referred to a nearby midwife for treatment. Pay was low, and there were no benefits at all. When in 1971 the workers decided to see if they could form a union, they were told they were already represented by the CTM. When the CTM glassmakers' union delegate for their state—their union representative—finally showed up at the factory at a meeting called by the workers, he apologized, saying he had previously been too busy to visit them. The workers were so fed up that they hooted and yelled at him. For this, three of the workers were fired. This settled things down for a bit, but the workers did not forget.

By 1972 workers were aware of the fact that they were paying union dues and still working under the same dismal conditions. They began to organize again, demanding such basics as gloves. Again, a few of the leaders were fired, and the movement died down.

In 1974 production intensified at Alumex with the installation of a new oven. Injuries also increased. Again workers sought to organize. Then, in the midst of this time of Insurgencia Obrera, the idea of an independent union was in the air and in the minds of many workers. The FAT had been advising a group of workers at the Vidrio Plano plant since 1971, and by 1974, workers at Alumex also sought out the FAT's help. Antonio Villalba of the FAT began to advise them, and on August 3 the Alumex workers called an assembly to constitute their new independent union. Informants—"dogs with big ears," to use the workers' expression—named names, and the next day the leaders were all fired. But this time workers were prepared to resist.

The fired workers held demonstrations at the Alumex gates. Workers inside defiantly yelled in support of them. They also wrote "REHIRE!" on each new sheet of glass produced. The 21 fired workers managed to survive through collections on the street, through support from the insurgent Electrical Workers union, and through contributions from their fellow Alumex workers. Yet many of them were beaten at the plant gates by paid thugs, and some were hauled into jail, where they were also beaten and asked who their leaders were.

At this time the Campos brothers were feuding. Pedro, the owner of Vidriera, needing skilled workers for a new oven, hired the workers fired by Francisco. This took the financial pressure off those workers, but workers within Alumex continued to demand their reinstatement. They also began a slowdown and "allowed" numerous defects into the glass they were making. By May 1975, Francisco Campos accepted the FAT-affiliated independent union at Alumex and rehired the workers he had previously fired. By August they achieved recognition from the state for their new union.

Workers at Vidriera were also organizing for a switch from the CTM to an independent union, in part as a result of conversations with fired Alumex workers who had been hired at Vidriera. The CTM leader, apparently in collusion with Alumex's owner, Francisco Campos, threatened a strike at Vidriera just as the new oven there was coming into full production in early 1975. Workers took advantage of this by telling Pedro Campos they would not comply with a CTM strike order if he would recognize their independent union. He agreed, thus easing the way for an election that the FAT won over the CTM by 100 votes to 10.

While workers at both plants had won their new unions, they still had no experience of what a democratic union could be. The first years were difficult years of learning. But many of the workers attended the union school organized by the FAT. General assemblies were held, and when attendance initially proved low, small fines were imposed to encourage fuller participation. In addition to general assemblies, the workers organized assemblies by shifts and by departments to more readily deal with problems they faced. With encouragement from the FAT they also visited workers on strike at other plants. Given the widespread political mobilization of this period in the late 1970s, these visits gave workers a sense that they were a part of a larger workers' movement. Just as the Electrical Workers union had supported them during their organizing drive, they now offered political and economic support to other workers. By meeting with workers from other factories, they developed a sense of class consciousness, which was necessary to overcome the subservient and isolated ways of thinking they had absorbed in the years before they unionized.

The workers' new organization, awareness, and training in how to function as a union led to concrete advances. Workers at both plants were—for the first time—enrolled in the government healthcare system. They got new safety equipment, work shoes, uniforms, vacation bonuses, Christmas bonuses, and wage hikes that were generally 5% above the cap set by the government.[50] But these gains were not won without provoking resistance and a new unity from the owners.

In 1977 the workers at Vidriera elected new leadership, with very effective and militant men as secretary-general and secretary of labor. In 1978 their boss, Pedro Campos, devised an innovative way to get rid of them: the new union leaders were kidnapped in broad daylight. One was even taken off the bus he was riding home—at the point of a machine gun. They were held captive for over a week, fed only tortillas and water, and beaten repeatedly. Upon their release, the workers were fired. The contract said that a worker with more than four absences in a month could be fired with no severance pay. Campos denied any responsibility for the affair, but pointed out that the workers were evidently in danger. He *generously* offered each of them a huge severance package and suggested that perhaps they would be in less danger if they accepted it and quit. Workers called a general assembly to discuss the issue and voted to allow the leaders to take the money and leave, but they were clear that combat had been joined.

In November 1979 Pedro Campos stopped production at Vidriera and told the workers the plant was finished. Meanwhile, Francisco Campos told workers at Alumex that they were superior workers, and warned that they should never be as troublesome as those of Vidriera; their good behavior was why they were still working. This ploy to divide the workers failed. While workers at Vidriera filed a petition to strike for breach of contract, workers at Alumex slowed production by half and seemed to have frequent accidental breakages of what they had produced. Workers at Alumex also filed a petition to revise their contract or strike.

The two union committees worked closely together on legal issues. They held joint demonstrations and joint parties. After 18 days of work stoppage, the labor board ordered Vidriera to resume production. Workers at both plants made only modest improvements in their contracts, but they had saved the unions and grown in solidarity.

One worker, looking back on this period of testing, recalls:

> We discovered that workers have made and continue to make everything that exists in our society, and just as we transform the nature of

raw materials, we can also transform the nature of organizations, including unions, business, and society itself.[51]

In 1980 both Campos brothers granted generous raises but stopped paying into the union dues fund and the union-administered loan fund. They began making loans directly to more compliant workers. When these efforts to divide the unions' base from their leaders also failed, the bosses made their final attack. In August 1981 they stopped paying the workers and they left the plants.

The workers decided to keep showing up and keep making glass, holding up their side of the bargain. They kept producing for nearly three weeks, until supplies ran out. In the process they also learned what they had long suspected: that they did not need bosses to be able to make glass. In the meantime, they also filed a petition to strike for breach of contract. A strike was legally declared on September 1.

Legally, if the owners of a Mexican business want to stop production, they are required to pay severance pay to their workers based on their years of service to the firm. If they truly lack the money to pay the workers, they are required to turn over assets of the business to satisfy the workers' claims. Meeting these obligations was never the Campos' intention. We have seen that other businesses came to use the tactic of bankruptcy as a way to rid themselves of unions. The owners wished to reopen the factories with non-union labor or to move their accumulated profits into other investments, such as real estate or bank stock in the United States.

Closing a factory without a union would be sufficient to get rid of most workers. Closing a factory with a corrupt union could often be managed by making sufficient payments to union leaders so that they would direct workers to accept a smaller settlement than what they were due. Neither of these tactics worked with the unions of Vidriera and Alumex. Here the strategy became one of delay. How long could workers persist in their claims before they would take other jobs and drift away? Workers won every legal issue in front of the labor boards, but each victory took time, and each was followed by a new delaying tactic.

Meanwhile workers had to guard the plants to be sure the owners would not remove glass or equipment. They maintained themselves on a strike fund they had set up and on contributions they could raise in the streets, but as time passed and financial collapse hit much of the economy, contributions evaporated. Most workers eventually took whatever work they could get, but they stayed in contact with their union and made contributions to support a core group that stood guard at the factories and continued to fight the legal battles. They all got together for assemblies and for parties to keep alive their unity and their spirits.

Finally, in 1983, the workers were awarded both plants and the glass inside them. That summer, when the businesses were finally put up for sale, with the proceeds to go to the workers, the CTM made it public that it was going to buy the plants, effectively discouraging other buyers. Some workers were eager to sell the plants at any price to get some money for all their suffering, yet the economic collapse of 1983 meant that all offers were quite low: too low for many of the workers. They proposed working the factories on their own.

The Workers Take Charge

Early in 1984, in closely divided votes, assemblies approved the plan to put the plants to work, yet it took until October to get the plants running. Workers sold the glass they had in inventory in order to raise some initial working capital. They also had to negotiate with suppliers of gas and raw materials for credit when those businesses were still owed money by the prior owners. Other workers relined the furnaces and made repairs to get the business ready to operate again.

It was more than three years from the time of shutdown to reopening. One articulate worker explained: "We defended our right to work and our right to live. Nothing more, nothing less. By this we defended our right to joy, to music, to celebrate, and to our rebellious cry of liberty. What grand acts of militant solidarity we lived in those years."[52]

The legal form of the new business is that of a capitalist corporation, the Union of Producers of Plate Glass of the State of Mexico, Incorporated, or PROVISA for short. Yet the internal organization is one guided by principles of democratic socialism and autogestión. Workers own the means of production, and they ultimately make all the decisions through various committees and the general assembly. The general assembly now is no longer that of a labor union, but one formed by the workers as shareholders.

The new situation facing the workers inspired one to write:

> We compañeros have in front of us the great responsibility: to demon-
> strate that we Mexican workers know how to make things, and to fully
> maintain our ties to the democratic workers movement and not forget
> that, thanks to other workers, we have been able to realize the dream of
> the whole working class.... We now confront the competitors in the
> market, our own internal divisions, the intervention of the authorities,
> and the responsibility to produce not just glass but also new men.[53]

With the exception of producing "new men," workers have faced all
of these challenges and met them with sufficient success to survive. Internal divisions continue to exist. An early problem was that many of the
workers had preferred to sell out, but were required to stay with the business as workers or get nothing. Some of these workers, delivery drivers,
were caught stealing—taking out a load with twice as much glass as
called for on the invoice. Others spent as much of their energy criticizing
as they did working. But these problems began to fade when, after the
first hard years, profits were earned and distributed.

An enduring division derives from the different skilled jobs within
the plant. Those workers who work at the top of the ovens receiving, cutting, and handling the new, hot sheets of glass suffer conditions of tremendous heat and an unrelenting pace. These few workers feel they
should get extra pay for their difficult work, but since they are but a minority of the workforce and since decisions are made by majority vote,
they have not been able to win this concession.

Another enduring division is that between manual and managerial
work. This division has been lessened somewhat by the fact that the majority of those now working in managerial areas like purchasing, sales,
and accounting have moved into their jobs directly from the shop floor.
An administrative council made up of five workers oversees the implementation of policies adopted by the general assembly. The council
must approve all major investments and purchases, but its work is
largely in response to the efforts of the general coordinator. This coordinator is a professional manager who is not a shareholder and whose
background is that of business, not labor. The workers recognize the
need for this sort of expertise, and, despite their democratic structures,
they are, to a large extent, dependent on this one man's ideas and decisions. However, they are also the ones who hire him, and they have the
power to fire him.

In 1984, when the business reopened, Gustavo Velasquez, a very successful businessman who is also devoted to the ideals of the FAT provided this coordinating guidance. After several years of other managers, Velasquez returned in the late '90s to manage the firm, which again teetered on the verge of bankruptcy in the wake of the economic crash of 1994.

The influence of managers is tremendously important, but it is not without limits. Velasquez recalls that one manager wanted to buy a piece of property adjoining the factory in order to make improvements. Workers decided to distribute profits as income rather than investing in the land, a decision that Velasquez feels hurt the company. But workers had followed the suggestions of other managers—to try making new kinds of glass and to start up a third oven—and both had cost them huge losses.

In the summer of 1996 PROVISA decided to stake its survival on modernizing its main ovens to recycle heat and thus cut fuel costs dramatically. These modifications had never been attempted on an oven like theirs. Working alongside engineers from the United States, PROVISA crews made the modifications and—through experimentation—learned how to run the reworked ovens. Fortunately this investment paid off and the plant has again been making a profit.

Having solved this technical problem the workers face a new threat, the arrival of a French transnational, St. Cobain, which has begun to sell imported glass. As a partial response to this challenge of international competition, Velasquez found a buyer in Texas who wants glass cut for picture frames. PROVISA will have to keep innovating to meet the challenges of the global market. What they lack in capital, they will have to make up for with the gains they can produce as a cooperative, non-alienated workforce.

In the beginning of PROVISA, the FAT advised workers to spend a fair amount of time on formación, addressing the information and attitudes they would need to function well. With the plant in their own hands, some workers thought they could take it easy. But clearly, they had to be at least as productive as before. No one wanted to work at a killing pace, but they learned to work more effectively by improving communication and cooperation. If bosses were not going to tell them what to do, they had to understand the process, and to coordinate their efforts, by themselves. They also saved the energy they had previously spent looking over their shoulder to see if the boss was about to crack the whip. Walking through the plant now, workers can take pride in seeing their colleagues working efficiently without supervisors.

Some managers have encouraged a more democratic life than others. The current manager, Valasquez, has urged workers to place a renewed emphasis on formación, saying without it, technical improvements of the ovens will not be enough. As part of this process of on-going education, the factory entrance was changed to include a lending library of books workers may read during lunch or take home with them. Many workers and some family members have learned to read in workshops at the plant. In the fall of 1996 a weekend retreat at the FAT's rural center in Temamatla involved most of the workers. The next PROVISA newsletter carried interviews with one worker who attended and another who used his weekend to earn extra money for his family. The first found the discussions "*bonitas,*" saying he had never been at such an event, which had dealt with technical aspects of making glass, how to work more effectively in teams, and how to improve companionship. The one who did not attend said many of his friends found the events good, but he wondered why, if money is short, they should spend it on such activities. But he then went on to say he would like to see training not just in glass making but in music, drawing, and theater as well. The May 1997 newsletter reported that of the 49 suggestions adopted at the fall conference, 30 had already been implemented. The other 19 would require money for implementation, but the worker-owners anticipated being able to make those investments "in the medium term." Although not perfect, the process appears to be one that seriously engages the attention of the workers and that makes a difference in the life of the factory.

PROVISA workers, most with very limited formal education, have accomplished a great deal. It is common to hear them speak of gaining dignity and of having something to pass on to their children. Many of them feel they are setting an example that can let other workers know what can be done. They have faced the challenges brought by the years of crisis. They carry a sense of on-going, often exhausting struggle that they wear with an air of rugged pride.

Notes

1   Centeno, Miguel Ángel. 1994. *Democracy Within Reason: Technocratic Revolution in Mexico*, 181. University Park: Pennsylvania State Press.
2   Handleman, Howard. 1997. *Mexican Politics: The Dynamics of Change*, 122. New York: St. Martin's Press.
3   Morris, Stephen D. 1995. *Political Reformism in Mexico: An Overview of Contemporary Mexican Politics,* 182. Boulder: Lynne Rienner.
4   Centeno, 188.
5   Handleman, 124.
6   Handleman, 131.
7   Centeno, 190.
8   Handleman, 126.
9   Centeno, 198.
10   Centeno, 192.
11   Middlebrook, Kevin J. 1995. *The Paradox of Revolution: Labor, the State, and Authoritarianism in Mexico*, 258. Baltimore: Johns Hopkins.
12   Centeno, 207.
13   Middlebrook, 258.
14   Centeno, 200; Middlebrook, 258.
15   Middlebrook, 260.
16   Handleman, 80–81; Morris, 70.
17   Measured in constant (1970) pesos, wages fell from 964.87 in 1982 to 327.28 in 1985. De la Garza, Enrique. 1991. "Independent Trade Unionism in Mexico: Past Developments and Future Perspectives." In *Unions, Workers and the State in Mexico*, Kevin J. Middlebrook (ed.), 177. San Diego: Center for U.S.-Mexican Studies.
18   Centeno, 202.
19   Middlebrook (1995), 258, 265.
20   Middlebrook (1995), 165.
21   Laredo, Gustavo Lopez. 1995. "El Movimiento Democratico en el Metro, 1983–84." In *Las 100 Luchas Mas Importantes del Movimiento de los Trabajadores*, A.C. Centro Nacional de Promocion Social (ed.), 87. Mexico, DF: Trabajo y Democracia Hoy.
22   Ortiz, Rosario. 1995. "Los Telefonistas Toman el Local Sindical, 1982." In A.C. Centro Nacional de Promocion Social, 85; Morris, 58.
23   Sanchez, Victor. 1995. "El Poder del Estado Contra el SUTIN, 1984." In A.C. Centro Nacional de Promocion Social, 89.

24   Nequiz Gonzalez, Jesus. 1995. "Huelga y Quiebra de Aeromexico." In A.C. Centro Nacional de Promocion Social, 100.

25   Becerril, Andrea. 1985. "Real del Monte, los Mineros Se Desnudan." *La Jornada* (May 25).

26   Mendez Berrueta, Luis H., and Jose Orthon Quiroz Trjo. 1995. *Modernizacion Estatal y Respuesta Obrera; Historia de una Derrota.* Mexico: Universida Autonoma Metropolitana.

27   "Reseña de la Sección CIZSA." Anonymous four-page typescript addressed to "Compañeros," the FAT, Leon, 1979.

28   Cauldillo, Jose Luis. 1985. "Relato de Dos Huelgas: HILSA Y CIZSA." Unpublished typescript.

29   Fabiola Martinez. 2000. "En Guanajuato, repudio patronal al sindicalismo." *La Jornada*, August 1.

30   "Din-Din Violacion al Convenio 87 (OIT)." 1987. *Resistencia Obrera* (February): 15–16.

31   Taibo, Paco Ignacio II. 1997. *Insurgencia Mi Amor*, 662–66. Mexico, DF: Ediciones El Atajo.

32   Gonzales, Griselda Angel. 1997. Interview at the FAT office in Irapuato.

33   Regular weekly pay was US$75 but large amounts of overtime brought them to about $125.

34   Campaign for Labor Rights. 2000 "Mexico: CRISA Update." February 24.

35   Oral Testimony of Margarita Diaz Lara, February 23, 2000, in Eugene, Oregon. Transcript available from Campaign for Labor Rights: CLR@igc.org.

36   This section on Sealed Power is based on the following sources: Oral interview with Daniel Lopez Garcia, July 15, 1996; oral interviews with Benedicto Martinez Orozco, July 16, 1996; July 23, 1996; November 22–23, 1996; July 1, 1997; Morris, John T. 1997. "The Strategic Terrain for Independent Union Organizing in Mexico's Auto Parts Sector: Opportunities and Constraints." Paper presented at the XX International Congress of the Latin American Studies Association, Guadalajara, Mexico; Peón E., Joaquín. 1990. *Calidad Total: Casos*. Edited by Joaquín Peón Escalante, Vol. 3: *Sealed Power Mexicana (SPM)*. Mexico, DF: Fundación Mexicana Para la Calidad Total, A.C; "La Lucha de los Trabajadores de Sealed Power (II Parte)." 1980. *Resistencia Obrera*, 34 (October): 2–3.

37   Peón, 4.

38   Peón, 5.

39   Morris, John T., 14.

40 "Recuentos por Titularidad del Contrato del STIMAHCS FAT." 1997. *Resistencia Obrera*, 148 (October): 6.

41 Peón, 1.

42 "Reconocen el Profesionalismo de un Sindicato Independiente:" 3.

43 Peón, 5.

44 Peón, 6.

45 "Reconocen el Profesionalismo de un Sindicato Independiente." 1990. *Resistencia Obrera*, 115 (April): 3, 3.

46 Martínez interview.

47 Martínez interview.

48 Alcalde Justiani, Arturo. "Elaboracion de una Propuesta Sobre Productividad." Five-page statement issued by the FAT, Mexico, DF.

49 Gómez, Luis Angel. 1990. *Vidrieros: La Experiencia Sindical del los Obreros de Vidriera y Alumex*, 23. Mexico: Información Obrera/ Equip Pueblo/ Unión de Productores de Vidrio Plano del Estado de México.

50 Gómez, 41, 51.

51 Aruajo, Arturo. 1988. *Unión Provisa: Una Aventura Libertaria para Contarse*, 7. Mexico: FAT/ Información Obrera.

52 Aruajo, 21.

53 Aruajo, 26, 32.

6.

The FAT as a Social Movement

Mexico's economic crisis of the '80s hit the FAT hard, closing many of the factories where it had unions and inspiring other employers to break FAT-affiliated unions. But, as FAT leaders often point out, while the main emphasis of the FAT has been on organizing workers into democratic labor unions, the group has always looked beyond the factory floor to its mission of social transformation. The breadth of the FAT's vision includes:

> a *worker-managed society* with the direct participation of workers and civil society and a *democratic political and economic system* whose decisions begin in grassroots organizations—the factory, the cooperative, the peasant organization, the neighborhood, and social organizations—and remain democratic at the local, regional, and national levels.[1]

Clearly unions should be an important part in achieving this vision, but the other organizations are vital to this work as well.

Just as the Vidriera glass factory was transformed into a worker-run business, so the FAT has supported other workers in transforming businesses into worker-managed cooperatives. In fact, there is a whole sector of the FAT devoted to cooperatives of workers, farmers, savers, and consumers. Other sectors of the FAT include the peasant sector and the new urban settlements sector, and the FAT puts a strong emphasis on addressing women's issues throughout all its sectors.

In addition to these sectors, the FAT has broadened its efforts into what it calls "para-sindical" work, educating and advising workers regardless of their union affiliation. In regions where they have lost several union locals, the FAT is still an active presence in its community's working-class politics.

Para-Sindical Work

A simple illustration of para-sindical work is that the FAT offers training and expert advice to hundreds of union locals that have no formal ties to it. Local union leaders may feel it is not politically expedient to declare themselves openly as a FAT union. They may, however, be committed enough to serving their members that they actually want to do a good job of negotiating an improved contract. Since ordinary unions do little to empower their rank-and-file leaders, they may seek advice from the FAT on a variety of issues. A November 1996 training conference on collective bargaining drew committees of three or four workers from union locals around the country. Approximately 25% came from university unions, and another quarter came from other unions with no formal ties to the FAT. The gathering featured training from FAT members with decades of bargaining experience as well as top lawyers and sympathetic economists.

Workers were taught how to analyze contracts, the meaning of relevant laws, the way to calculate benefit changes separately from wage changes, how to adjust for inflation, and how to make reasonable demands and win them. Participants also heard presentations on national political and economic policy. Most rank-and-file workers entered without a clue and left feeling much more capable. And the simple act of participating in the event gave them all a taste of what life within a democratic union that values the rank-and-file could be. They left feeling part of a broader society of workers dedicated to advancing worker interests, not just the power of union leaders. Those not directly affiliated with the FAT would likely stay in touch for further support.

One interesting group attending the conference was the executive committee of a factory whose efforts to join the FAT in the 1970s had met bitter resistance from both the owners and the government. These workers knew they would face considerable obstacles if they tried to affiliate immediately with the FAT. Their plan was to work within their local to improve wages, benefits, and working conditions, while educating the workers. Eventually they might feel ready to try to break out of their charro-dominated union and join the FAT. In the meantime, they would function as much like a FAT union as they could.

Examples of the FAT's helping non-affiliated unions in Mexico City abound. One of these is the case of the workers of the government's ministry of fisheries who organized themselves into an independent union in 1977. That made them, SUTSP, the largest government union not affiliated with the PRI and the only one to elect its officers through secret ballot. To eliminate this deviant union, the government combined the fisheries ministry with other ministries dealing with the environment and natural resources in December 1994. When the independent union tried to update its papers in January 1995, it was told it no longer existed. At this point it lost access to many of its union resources and came to the FAT to use office space and to hold occasional meetings.

The FAT also helped the fisheries workers to file a complaint with the International Labor Organization in Geneva, Switzerland, whose ruling helped SUTSP regain legal recognition—technically. As a result, the new union that the government had organized had to be temporarily disqualified until a new election could be held to determine who would represent the workers. In the meantime the government union, although technically disqualified, continued collecting members' dues, created 700 paid staff positions to organize for the elections, and had access to government resources such as offices, telephones, and trucks, while the legally recognized union, SUTSP, remained cut off from all resources and direct access to workers. The new election was held, and the government union—not surprisingly—won. At this writing the independent union has again won the right to exist and to represent its members, but the government agencies continue to refuse to deal with it. An interesting test of the new Fox administration will be whether or not such governmental lawlessness continues.

The FAT has also made its Mexico City offices available to leaders from a dissident local of the Social Security workers union, SNTSS, even when one of their officers was jailed, supposedly for corruption in 1996. In 1998 the government fired 270 of its "temporary" workers, employed in the bureau of statistics, INEGI. The workers, some of whom had worked for INEGI for as many as 20 years, had sued for their rights as permanent workers, a status held by only 25% of the ministry's 20,000 workers. The workers, who had also declared themselves members of an independent union, had been told to withdraw their suit or be fired. They refused and were fired. Dozens of the fired workers employed in outlying states slept at the FAT headquarters while protesting their case in the capital. This willingness to provide support for non-affiliated workers engaged in the same struggle for greater working-class rights is one of the ways that the FAT extends its influence well beyond its official membership.

In the city of Leon, where FAT unions had such a strong presence until the '80s, the FAT remains an important presence within the city, largely through para-sindical work and through its other sectors. The FAT enjoys a strong staff of two formally educated lawyers as well as two lawyers that got their education during the struggles of the '60s and '70s. These lawyers spend much of their time representing individual workers who have work-related legal conflicts. Their services are nearly free and the FAT has a reputation for honesty and integrity as well as effectiveness, so their offices are usually full. These contacts have sometimes led to direct intervention within factories to try and win a better contract or form an independent union. Even though many of these struggles have been lost due to massive resistance and governmental policy, they have kept the FAT presence alive in the minds of both workers and employers. In this way FAT organizers feel they have been a check against even worse abuses.

The FAT in Leon advises a number of affiliated unions in the region surrounding it. Its offices also house a food cooperative and a credit union. It serves as the base for CODIM, a very active group working on women's issues. Many of the core participants in each of these activities are drawn from the memberships of unions that no longer hold active contracts. Those members still find the FAT an important center for addressing some of their economic needs, a base for their political activity, and a place to maintain and extend friendships. The same can be said for many FAT centers around the country.

The Women's Movement of the FAT

The FAT officially committed itself to work on women's issues in 1990. The economic realities of the '90s made this ever more important. Participation of women in the official workforce doubled, rising from 17%

in the 1970s to 35% in 1997. In the dynamic maquiladora sector of the north, employers hire more women than men, for they are seen as more docile and adaptable.[2]

Women have been active within the FAT as leaders from fairly early on. One of the most visible of these women has been Bertha Lujan, who supported the FAT first in 1968 as a student in Chihuahua. She continued to work as an activist, forming a union at the University of Chapingo, where she was doing clerical work, and supporting cooperatives of all types before taking a one-year position with the FAT's national office in Mexico City in 1977. She has been an important part of the national staff since then. When the FAT reorganized itself in 1990 to have a less hierarchical national structure, it decided that each of its four regions, each of its four sectors, and each of its six commissions would have representation in a national council. Daily operations would be run by a three-person "National Coordination," at least one of whom, henceforth, would be a woman. Lujan became the first woman in the national coordination, where she was responsible for the FAT's international relations and its work with civil society within Mexico.

In 1990 the FAT began working explicitly on women's issues in Mexico City. They sponsored activities such as cooking workshops that also engaged women in broad discussions of health, self-esteem, gender roles, and the economic environment. If the FAT had organized workshops on any of these themes directly, the only women to attend would have been those who were already quite advanced in these areas. Cooking workshops proved a more effective outreach mechanism. Union women, housewives, and professional women attended and shared their experiences.

Some within the FAT criticized this work, saying that they should be spending all their resources on organizing new unions. But Matilde Arteaga Zaragoza, the first national coordinator of the FAT's programs for women, sees women's activities as necessary long-term work. Women who come to cooking workshops might start out completely unapproachable on the issue of forming a union. Through their contact with the FAT, they advance in their understanding of social and economic issues. Several young women who attended a cooking workshop in the San Jaunico neighborhood of Mexico City went on to form a union where many of them worked. They had become very well organized and quite militant, going out on strike when necessary.

Conchita Lopez, the organizer for women's work in the southern part of the state of Chihuahua, explained how she sees the work. "We begin by simply sharing the experience of being women, and on that foundation we build everything. Because machismo is so ingrained we have to do a lot of work on self-esteem before we can do much more."[3] She explained that they deal with issues the women want to pursue—the family, couples, domestic violence, health, the environment, work—looking at the role of women in each area. Lopez's experience in her small town of Villa Lopez is an indication of the controversial power of feminist organizing. Local leaders had in the past appointed Lopez as supervisor of local elections—a position requiring a strong but neutral person. But officials ended her role as elections supervisor once she began the work she calls "awakening the women."

In Leon, women of the FAT organized the Women's Center for Integral Development and Organization (CODIM). CODIM's outreach brochure proclaims, "This center wants to be a space that is useful to you, woman, if you want to work for a more just society where all—men and women—have absolutely the same rights and obligations, if you want to work against unjust social structures that make possible the special oppression that women suffer." The center offers legal advice on labor, family, criminal, civil, and commercial law. CODIM also provides training on family, work, and child education issues and helps in organizing unions, cooperatives, urban or rural community groups, and groups of people demanding housing or public services.

One group that CODIM has organized is made up of women over the age of 45 who have virtually no possibility of obtaining work in a society where ads frequently state that job applicants must be under 25. None of these women have Social Security or health benefits. They have formed a cooperative kitchen that does catering. In addition to helping the women start their business, CODIM has stimulated their social and political analysis. CODIM invited these and other women of Leon to a series of meet-the-candidate nights so the women would be informed and involved voters and so the candidates would have to address women's issues.

CODIM's work with women has attracted attention at the level of the state government. "We get invitations as CODIM," says Angeles Lopez, "that we would never get as FAT."[4] Based in Leon, Angeles Lopez is a labor lawyer, organizer, and mother of two. In 1997 the FAT's national membership chose her to coordinate its work on women's issues nationwide. Lopez was also chosen to provide leadership for all the NGOs of her state—a significant recognition since most NGOs work with middle-class women.

CODIM works closely with the women of Irapuato who used to be employed making clothes. When their factories were closed and their FAT unions were broken in the 1980s they remained in contact. In the 1990s they have been able to influence state law, creating statutes against sexual abuse and expanding sentencing options for domestic violence. What used to be simply jail or nothing now includes counseling, training in communication and conflict resolution, and sometimes referral to women's organizations like CODIM.

The FAT has also been working on women's issues within its own unions. The work has not been easy. At the Sealed Power plant in Aguascalientes the union offers a monthly workshop for women on gender issues, sexual health, and self-esteem. FAT organizers would like to get women to feel confident enough to speak up more at union meetings. In this rural area, such progress is slow. The FAT also would like to make childcare a union issue. Currently it is seen as a problem only for women. But with women working in all three shifts, some feel the issue must be addressed by all workers.

As part of an outreach effort at the PROVISA glass cooperative, FAT staff women sent information home to the wives of the all-male workforce informing them of a food cooperative. The information discussed prices in relation to the men's wages. Some of the men complained they didn't want their wives to know how much they were earning.

In spite of such opposition, the FAT is thoroughly committed to working on women's issues. Angeles Lopez asserts, "Since the objective of the FAT is the struggle for democracy, if half the population is excluded, we need to deal with it." So the work in the unions and beyond continues. This means working on issues of equal pay, ending sexual harassment, ending discrimination such as the forced pregnancy tests now required by some employers, improving safety, and raising the abilities of women to participate equally in all areas of the nation's economic and political life.

Women's work has also afforded the FAT with more opportunities to connect internationally. Angeles Lopez represented the FAT and CODIM as part of Mexico's delegation to the 1995 UN women's conference held in Beijing, China. As part of its strategic alliance with the United Electrical Workers, the FAT has also hosted tours of US union women and it has, in turn, sent groups of its women to tour and speak in the United States on women's, labor, political, and economic issues. Such exchanges build solidarity, strength, and understanding on both sides of the border. Women representing unions from Italy, France, and North America attended the National Congress of the FAT in 1997 and witnessed the many strong women of the FAT lead the whole federation to a rededication to these efforts. As Annie Labaj of the Canadian Autoworkers Union said, "When we are all working together and you include women's issues, you make the whole movement stronger."[5]

The Sectors of the FAT

Most of this book is dedicated to the life of the union sector of the FAT. Unions have been the first and the primary focus of the FAT, but from early on the FAT has been involved in a variety of other activities, some of which are now the main projects of the FAT in some regions. In addition to unions, the FAT has a sector for *campesinos* (peasants), for *colonos* (residents of new urban settlements), and for cooperatives. After much debate the FAT decided not to create a separate sector for women's issues, but to integrate that work into all of the sectors.

Campesino Sector

With a quarter of Mexico's workforce still engaged directly in agriculture, the FAT sees the campesino sector as a necessary part of its broad effort to democratize the life of Mexico's workers. Nonetheless, the campesino sector is a fairly small part of the FAT. It is strongest in the region of southern Chihuahua near the city of Jimenez, where the national coordinator of the campesino sector, Ramon Ramirez, has dedicated his efforts since the late 1960s.

Until 1991, Article 27 of the Mexican Constitution provided that any group of 20 or more campesinos in need of land could petition the government to give them land that was not in use, whether it belonged to the government or to private owners of huge properties. The law even stated that the best land available was to be given to the peasants. In practice, little land was transferred to peasants, and much that had been was worth very little. These communal lands were called *ejidos* and, like unions and many other social formations, they were usually organized by and their members were loyal to the ruling party.

Ramon Ramirez was part of a union of ejidos linked to the PRI for a couple of years, but in 1968, when election time came around and all the ejido members were expected to vote for the ruling party candidates, many looked for alternatives. It was then that organizers from the FAT won Don Ramon over as a lifelong activist.

As in its para-sindical work, the FAT offered Ramirez's union of ejidos a source of information, advice, and coordination for a broad range of problems the campesinos often confronted, ranging from expanding ejido lands to marketing products to getting members out of jail. The key to all was formación: education and orientation on one's basic rights. As with labor issues, the law on agrarian reform provided many rights, but the practice of the law was often another matter. The union of ejidos helped campesinos to get land, to defend the land they had, and to avoid losing it when they got in credit trouble. Though the group was established to serve ejidos in a relatively small area, news of its expertise and combativeness spread and the FAT soon had to provide help for a much greater area.

In one instance the Agua Fria ejido was awarded land and began to develop a walnut grove in one corner of it even before the many years of paperwork were completed. When the former owners of the land saw the wonderful improvements, they began to plot to be sure that in the final survey the grove and the new irrigation wells were left outside the ejido boundaries. The FAT made sure that when state surveyors came to finish their job, they were accompanied by engineering students from Chihuahua who had been involved in the FAT's early organizing in that city. The grove was saved. At that point the FAT helped the community establish a producers' cooperative for the walnut grove. They farmed the rest of the land in individual plots as they had always done, but over time they came to see that they were making more money in their walnut co-operative. Together they gradually converted their whole ejido to growing nuts.

Zaragoza is an ejido of 40 families that is associated with the Jimenez ejido union. One of its senior members, Agustin Herrera, remembers when the FAT first appeared in his area to help campesinos "learn to defend our rights." When a member had a problem, they would all chip in a peso. When a member was jailed unjustly, the FAT would organize people to get him out. Mostly he recalls what a difference the FAT made in his life. This tall, confident, well-spoken man says that when he first attended FAT meetings he was afraid even to speak. He had had no schooling, and he considered it a sin to talk about problems. He knew only how to work hard and to avoid troubles.

Formación not only taught him his rights, it broke the monopoly on thought the PRI had in his community. He found his voice. The FAT meetings he attended became his school. Meeting peasants and workers from other states and other countries served as his university.

In 1991, President Salinas reformed Article 27 and put an end to the ejido system. Now all communal lands have been divided up into individual plots that each person has the right to keep or sell. Salinas argued that this would lead to greater efficiency in agriculture. Those willing to invest in the land could buy out those who no longer wanted to work it. Restrictions on foreign ownership were eliminated. Community rights were wiped off the books. Those most able to buy have been huge corporations and wealthy individuals.

Ramon Ramirez feels the countryside is reverting to the way it was under Porfirio Diaz. The Mexican Revolution is being reversed. When this tall gringo researcher and two locals showed up in a car at the Zaragoza ejido, Agustin Herrera initially refused to come out and talk to us. He was sure we were land buyers. Don Ramon is discouraged. "It was hard when we began, but our main argument was that the law gave us the rights Zapata and so many others had died for. Now the law says we are obsolete." But Martin Garcia Quintana, current coordinator of the union of ejidos of Jimenez, is unwilling to give up. He organizes regular Sunday meetings for formación, and Agustin encourages his young relatives to attend.

Life in Mexico's often harsh countryside has never been easy. The tecnicos now seem bent on driving peasants off the land and into the factories, much as England did in the days of Charles Dickens. At the FAT's 1997 National Congress, Victor Quiroga from Leon spoke about the ideals of the FAT being tested in the campesino sector.

> We take two steps toward our utopia and see that it is four steps farther off. So we take four steps and see that it is eight steps farther off. If we take eight steps, it's sixteen steps farther away. So what good is our vision of utopia? It keeps us walking.

Cooperative Sector

Cooperative forms of organization fit well with the ideals of the FAT because they are owned and run by the members. Ideally, they are democratically managed in a way that not only represents but empowers the members. Within the broad definition of the cooperative sector, we find production cooperatives, consumer cooperatives, savings and loan cooperatives, agricultural cooperatives, and housing cooperatives. Co-ops are found in urban areas, peasant areas, and in indigenous communities.

In the history of the FAT, consumer cooperatives associated with unions were the first to develop. Through bulk buying and the elimination of markups for profit, these co-ops allowed members to stretch their wages further when buying food and basic household items. At the same time, peasant groups advised by the FAT developed cooperatives dedicated to feeding and marketing animals, or marketing vegetable crops. In the 1970s credit unions that had started as small savings groups associated with church parishes realigned themselves with the FAT. In the '80s, as more and more businesses failed, the FAT developed producer cooperatives.[6] In the '90s the FAT's cooperative sector had almost as many members as its union sector.

Of the FAT's producer cooperatives, PROVISA is the largest. A smaller cooperative is Paraiso, a women's cooperative that produces marmalades from local fruit in the small village of Temamatla outside of Mexico City. Inspired by a women's discussion group held at the FAT's retreat and training center in Temamatla, the Paraiso co-op gives part-time employment to a group of 10 women. To this author, the pineapple-coconut and guava jams both taste as though they had come—as the name implies—from paradise. Another small producer cooperative is El Atajo, a part-time editorial cooperative that produces small runs of books consistent with the goals of the FAT. Recent works include a major source for this book, *De la Autonomia al Corporativismo* by Jorge Robles, a collection of essays on labor struggles titled *Insurgencia mi Amor* by the popular novelist Paco Ignacio Taiblo II, and the novelistic account of the travails of a telephone operator who becomes a union activist, *A Dónde Desea Hablar?* by Carolina Velasquez. Since the 1980s many communities have formed cooperatives that combine both a credit union and a consumer cooperative. The FAT headquarters in Leon has one small office with a two-person staff that serves as the consumer co-op's office and credit union. Another room, approximately 15 by 20 feet, is stocked with basic foods, cleaning supplies, and toiletries. The credit union staff also takes payments for the groceries. Recent years have seen a rapid expansion of such co-ops in the Puebla-Tlaxcala region, which now has two in urban areas, nine in peasant communities, and seven in indigenous communities.

Cuernavaca is home to the largest and most successful of the FAT's cooperatives. The 5,000 members of Cooperativa Bandera have built themselves an impressive facility, which is home to a modern credit union; a well-stocked grocery; a general store stocked with clothing, shoes, and household appliances; a meeting room; and a pleasant courtyard kitchen. Just a few doors away, members have recently completed a building supply store. While its size and general affluence sets it apart from the FAT's other co-ops, it does exemplify the philosophy that guides all of the FAT's co-ops, a philosophy and way of functioning that differ from those of apparently similar US cooperatives. The majority of co-ops within the FAT belong to the Independent Cooperative Unit (UCI), which defines itself as:

> the organization of various cooperatives and cooperativists that strive to bring about an authentic cooperativism that reflects the interest of working people, that practices *autogestión*, that places its members in administrative positions and operates its cooperatives well without following the forms or the injustices of the capitalist system; a cooperativism that promotes the development of new women and men who serve as the seed of a new society that we propose to build.[7]

One of the distinctive features of these credit unions is that initial deposits of members (up to one month's salary) are non-refundable.

This is a major commitment for most Mexicans and can take two to three years to accumulate. These deposits become part of a communal resource upon which all can draw. Additional savings do earn interest and can be withdrawn. Members may take out loans at interest rates well below those charged by commercial banks. They also have access to the services that the cooperative's accumulated resources enable it to provide.

A fundamental difference between the FAT's co-ops and the more capitalistic ones that also exist in Mexico and that are the rule in the United States is that participation in the FAT's co-ops is restricted to the working class and poor by a policy setting a maximum income level for membership. The coordinator of UCI explains, "We don't allow the bourgeoisie to enter because they'd like to take over and use the money of the poor for their own purposes." Since the co-op is run entirely by the members, they have decided to avoid the conflict of interest they see as inherent between those with wealth and those who must constantly work to get by. An orientation brochure explains the folly of letting foxes in the henhouse. A member put it abruptly, "You can't be both with God and with the Devil."

Bandera Co-op traces its roots back 35 years. Years of accumulation and a large membership have led to the impressive array of services available. Members receive benefits in communal services, but they also get a yearly share of the co-op's earnings, based not on their investments, but on how much they use the services and how much they participate in the work of the co-op. After the building supply store gets running, they are considering constructing a large hall with a bar and restaurant. They could rent it out to conventions and use it to make money off the tourists. It would also provide a space where the membership could all meet together. With over 5,000 members, they have to hold the general assembly and annual meetings in several shifts.

Pedro Romero, guiding spirit of Bandera and of UCI, is a former priest who is still willing to preach his ideals:

> [H]uman beings can live in peace and harmony, without exploiting each other. Mutually we can protect ourselves, combining our individual abilities for the common good, sharing with justice the riches that we produce with our work. We have faith in humanity and we have no doubt that together we can build a better world.[8]

Romero found the credit union's current manager, Jose Luis Cuevas, selling encyclopedias. Although this young man had only completed eight years of schooling, he has become an excellent manager without losing touch with his membership.

The Bandera co-op's large meeting room provides a space for the required two-hour membership training and doubles as a simple dormitory when regional meetings are held. The co-op also hosts a film series and a variety of educational activities. Romero explains that the co-op's mission really has three "phases." The first is to help people meet their basic needs. This it has been doing well, distributing goods to its membership without marking up prices for profit. Since it operates as a wholesaler the members also avoid the 15% sales tax charged at other businesses. The second phase is to educate its members to understand and to change society. The third phase will occur once people realize that if they don't like the current society they can build a better one based on "justice, starting today, in the community." He laments that most members are happy with the first phase and don't want to commit themselves to anything more.

Still, Romero sees signs of progress. When the co-op first began, membership meetings rarely lasted more than an hour. Now they can last up to five hours with better participation and far better discussion. "Real democracy takes time," he notes. And he attributes the change to member education. He likes to think that the political awakening of Cuernavaca—it voted less and less for the PRI in the 1990s—may have something to do with the work of the co-op.

Bandera means flag in Spanish, and the flag of the Bandera cooperative carries the traditional green and yellow of credit unions and co-ops throughout the world. It also carries the black of the anarchist movement, the source of early writings on autogestión: both work and rule by the members. Romero insists: "We seek more than democracy. We are trying to build a society built and controlled directly by the workers." A variety of cooperatives of the FAT are working daily throughout the country for this radical goal.

Colonos

The FAT's sector of urban colonos has no parallel in the rest of North America. Like most cities in the underdeveloped world, many Mexican cities are ringed with squatter camps or shantytowns built and occupied mostly by rural people uprooted from their traditional homes by the economic upheaval of recent years. Generally these newly occupied areas have few, if any, basic services. By providing organization for a "colony," the FAT can help its residents (*colonos*) put pressure on local authorities to provide water, improve bus transportation, and see that schools are built. The FAT can also help them to generate employment, organize cooperatives, and develop many of their own resources. Individuals who become engaged with the FAT in these communities often become involved in the FAT's other sectors. The most successful example of such organizing has been going on since 1980 in the city of Gomez Palacios, in the north-central state of Durango.

Domingo Mazcorro was an industrial worker in the city of Chihuahua who became involved with the FAT in the early 1970s. When the steel mill where he worked, Aceros de Chihuahua, went bankrupt in 1979 he moved south to Gomez Palacios, where he began to organize. On March 27, 1980, he led 420 families in an occupation of 35 acres of unused land on the edge of town. They called the community the Popular Workers', Peasants', and Students' Front (FOCEP). The name describes three sectors of the population working together in common cause, and that is what the community had to manifest.

Land occupations are not uncommon in Mexico, where large landholders leave much of their arable land unused and where there are many people who can't support themselves on whatever dry, barren land they have inherited or been able to afford. Organizing people to make a land occupation is only the first part of the task. The next part is defending the land from the government and from the nominal owner of the land, neither of whom want land to be taken without a legal purchase. In this case, FOCEP set up barricades at all entrances and refused to allow police to enter. Only if they were able to defend themselves would these impoverished people be able to negotiate to make the land legally their own.

The community of some 2,000 people divided up the land into family plots of 10 by 20 meters. Streets were laid out in the dirt, and people began to build their houses from whatever scrap material they could collect. Gradually they replaced cardboard or tar-paper walls with adobe bricks, made from their own dirt, or cement blocks, if they could afford them. Since the streets initially were simply dirt, they were badly rutted and nearly impassable in the rain. FOCEP got together a small fleet of old cars that provided a taxi service within the community. Because the community still refused to allow municipal police to enter, the taxi drivers also served as their police force, keeping an eye on outsiders, breaking up fights, and occasionally hauling people into their own jail.

The community rapidly organized a cooperative store to provide food and basic supplies. They established their own medical clinic, and skilled craftspeople formed a cooperative to provide carpentry, plumbing, and electrical services. In December 1983, FOCEP took over an adjacent 50 acres of land to expand the community. By 1999 the combined FOCEP community had more than 17,000 residents. That is just over 5% of the population of Gomez Palacios, but the cohesiveness and militancy of FOCEP, along with broad support from the surrounding community, give it tremendous weight. The main street of the community honors the FAT with a name unused in any other city in the country, "El Frente Auténtico del Trabajo."

Domingo Mazcorro knows that Mexican law says that any group of at least 20 workers can form a union, but he knows well that getting a union registered requires either submitting to the charro hierarchy or building enough force to get what one wants in spite of the charros. With thousands of people organized, FOCEP has that force.

FOCEP formed its first union in 1984, a vendors' union, for people who sold food at small stands throughout Gomez Palacios. Traditionally vendors got permission to have their stands from an operative in the PRI. FOCEP residents demanded that vendors have the right to organize themselves independent of the State. When the government denied their request, thousands of people blockaded City Hall. They got their registry. Later that year, they organized a union of the workers at the annual fair by shutting the fair down until they got their registry. By 2000, they had a union of temporary workers for the fair in nearby Torreon, and for cockfights, horse races, and baseball games throughout the region. This provides regular work for members of their community at better wages than temporary workers had ever earned before.

In 1985 they organized a transportation union, providing bus service in Volkswagen vans between downtown and outlying neighborhoods. Initially the government denied them the right to operate and seized the vans for operating without permits. The community then seized an equal number of city buses and held them until they got both their vans and their permits. The following year they were able to expand from their initial 23 vans to over 50. In 1987 they began organizing taxi unions. By 1999 they had six taxi unions with over a thousand taxis, providing service to Gomez Palacios as well as the two adjoining cities of Torreon and Lerdo. Currently the FAT is seeking to build on these unions to obtain a charter for a nationwide transport union.

In 1987 the community organized a union for the wedding photographers of the region. They also reached out to the surrounding countryside and organized a union of agricultural day laborers. They now work with Ramon Ramirez of Jimenez to provide assistance to ejidos in the area. In 1989, FOCEP elected members to the city council of Gomez Palacios, and they sent Domingo Mazcorro to the state legislature for a three-year term. As in many countries, legislators enjoy immunity from criminal prosecution while in office. Mazcorro used his immunity to facilitate two new land takeovers, one in the adjoining city of Lerdo and the other in the state capital, Durango. In each of these, the process of forming cooperatives and unions began all over again.

The militancy of the colonos is reflected in the name chosen for the new community in Durango: Division del Norte, the name used by the masses of peasants who fought under the region's revolutionary hero, Pancho Villa. One wonders if the PRI did not see Domingo Mazcorro and his supporters the way PRI founders must have seen Villa when they tried to take control of the Revolution for their own elite interests. Mazcorro has been kidnapped once and, in 1994, was forced to flee the state for a year after he and FOCEP blockaded the Pan American Highway at the edge of Gomez Palacios to force then president Salinas to stop and listen to them.

The process of expansion is continuing. Mazcorro is proud of their musicians' union, which represents 25 musical groups. In 1996 women at a sewing factory 25 miles north of Gomez Palacios appealed for help. They were sewing batches of jeans for Levi's, Wrangler, Lee, and other popular name brands, but they were hired for only three weeks at a time. This way the business never had to pay them any benefits and never had to pay severance during a layoff. With support from FOCEP and the cooperative sector of the FAT, the women discovered that the business had been started as a cooperative in a government-supported regional development program. But the workers had no control in this government-organized co-op.

Only two of the women had worked there from the beginning, but they were able to lead an occupation of the plant. Since these women were technically members of the original co-op, they could not be charged with taking it away from anyone. Eventually, the women ended up with the building and the machines. They offered the previous manager a job—cleaning the restrooms and cooking lunch—but she refused it. Now these 40 women have job security, benefits, and some sense of control as they negotiate production with the global garment industry.

Domingo Mazcorro is now the national coordinator of the FAT's sector of new urban settlements. Within this sector one finds all the other sectors: peasants, co-ops, and unions. The FAT has had remarkable success in this remote part of Mexico. It is a poor region, and "with more hunger," Mazcorro says, "comes more exploitation." He has also found that when that hunger is combined with effective organization much can be done. He says:

> [Mexico is only a] simulated democracy. Just speaking up is risky. If we don't have a movement, the government will not listen; they will repress us. But the community is a beach head, and from our first landing, we have been moving forward.[9]

The years of crisis brought a harsher political and economic environment in which to organize authentic unions. Its problems were systemic and could not be addressed within the bounds of any specific workplace. The FAT's response was to diversify its tactics. Where it could not move forward by forming new unions of its own, it would organize women's groups, cooperatives, and urban communties, and it would support peasants. Here the FAT not only addressed immediate needs of specific workers, they also demonstrated an alternative model of social development. Needing to educate its own workers on how to deal with new legal government policies and new corporate strategies, it also helped educate workers trapped in less democratic unions. Through this covert para-sindical work and through overt alliances with other unions, the FAT extended its influence as an agent of change throughout the Mexican labor movement.

Notes

1   Statement of Purpose adopted at the FAT's 11th National Congress, November 1997. Emphasis in original.

2   Frente Autentico del Trabajo. 1997. *Informe Politico*, official document of the 11th National Congress of the FAT. Oaxtepec, Morelos.

3   Lopez, Conchita. 1999. Oral interview, June 16. Villa Lopez, Chihuahua.

4   Lopez, Angeles. 1996. Oral interview, July 14. Leon, Guanajuato.

5   Labaj, Annie. 1997. Oral interview, November 29. National Congress of the FAT, Oaxtepec, Morelos.

6   Luján, Bertha, and Luis Angel Gómez. 1991. "El Cooperativismo en el FAT." *El Cotidiano*, 40 (March–April): 43, 51.

7   Unidad Cooperativista Independiente (UCI). 1996. *Manual para el Buen Socio*, training manual for members of Cooperativa Bandera, 21. Cuernavaca, Morelos.

8   Unidad Cooperativista Independiente (UCI), 1.

9   Mazcorro, Domingo. 1999. Telephone interview, July 17; Martinez, Benedicto. 1999. Oral interview, June 19, Ciudad Juarez; Villalba, Antonio. 1999. Oral interview, July 17, Ciudad Juarez.

7.

Confronting NAFTA
and the Global Economy

The North American Free Trade Agreement, NAFTA, revealed a huge gap between the economic and political elites and the vast majority of workers, not just in Mexico, but in the United States and Canada as well. In each country it was pushed through the legislatures in a clearly anti-democratic manner.

In Canada, the 1989 election was a three-way race. Based on well-grounded fears of losing national sovereignty, having the social safety net dismantled, and losing jobs, candidates for the Liberal and New Democratic Parties made opposition to the US–Canadian Free Trade Agreement a major part of their campaigns. While together these parties attracted the votes of a majority of Canadian voters, the Conservative Party received the biggest individual share of the votes, took office, and passed the deal as promised. The NAFTA vote was just a continuation of Conservative policy.

In the United States, NAFTA was brought into the 1992 presidential campaign when Ross Perot claimed that it would produce a "giant sucking sound" of jobs being lost to Mexico. Incumbent George Bush, who had been promoting the deal since its beginning, continued his support. Bill Clinton spoke out of both sides of his mouth, assuring workers that before he would ever support NAFTA he would have to be sure jobs in the United States would not be lost, and assuring wealthy contributors that the United States would protect the interests of its corporations. If we add the 19% who voted for Perot to the vast majority of Democratic voters who expressed opposition to NAFTA in opinion polls, we have to conclude that the majority of voters in 1992 thought they were voting

against NAFTA. If we add in those Republican voters who had supported the candidacy of Pat Buchanan before he was rushed off the campaign stage by leaders of both his party and the press, shocked at his
making a surprisingly effective reactionary, isolationist pitch against
NAFTA, we would have even larger numbers clearly opposed.

Safely in office, Clinton joined the Republican Congress in pushing
NAFTA through. To do so he had to negotiate side accords on labor and
the environment that have proven as toothless as critics at the time predicted, but gave representatives some cover for their vote. To win passage of this free-trade treaty he finally resorted to protectionist deals on
textiles, citrus, sugar, wheat, and peanuts, essentially buying the votes
he needed from regions that feared competition.[1]

In Mexico the fraudulent election of 1988, coupled with a rub-
ber-stamp Congress, meant that President Carlos Salinas faced little
overt political opposition in getting NAFTA approved. He simply made
sure that it was barely discussed in the legislature and that only
like-minded government officials and heads of major Mexican corporations were invited to negotiating sessions. The only leader of an official
union to oppose his economic policies was the head of the oil workers'
union, La Quina. He failed to instantly embrace the candidacy of Salinas, and his reputed covert support for Cardenas was matched with victories for the challenger in major oil producing areas. On January 10,
1989, the army blew his front door down with a bazooka, and he was
locked in jail for the next eight years (on charges that could have been
justified at any time over the previous three decades).[2]

Salinas was convinced that modernizing Mexico's economy required turning it over to large private interests regardless of nationality.
He had promoted such policies as a government technocrat, and as president he continued the policy of privatizing government enterprises such
as the national telephone company, the huge Cananea copper mine, the
two major airlines, the banks, and some television stations. The
privatizations were often accomplished over the objections of the workers (with the aid of over 300 army troops in the Cananea case) and generally by way of sweetheart deals to close allies of President Salinas or his
brother, Raul. These give-aways were on top of Salinas's alteration of
the Mexican constitution to privatize the ejidos, the communal agricul-

tural lands. But, his crowning act of economic policy was NAFTA, known in Mexico as the Free Trade Treaty, or TLC.

Mexico's key goal in negotiating NAFTA was to gain an advantage in attracting foreign investment. Even before NAFTA went into effect, in anticipation of Mexico's improved access to the US market, investment poured in. Foreign investors dumped piles of money into the Mexican stock exchange beginning in 1991. Direct foreign investment in plants and equipment went mostly to the maquiladora sector. Both investment and exports rose sharply with the advent of NAFTA, while wages fell after the first year.

Maquiladoras are located mainly along the border with the United States. Generally they import sophisticated components from other countries, assemble them into products, and re-export them. The combination of cheap labor and direct access to the huge US market was successful in attracting foreign money to Mexico.

The Salinas plan to accelerate the ownership of Mexico's economy by fewer and wealthier investors, Mexican or foreign, was not well received by all. On January 1, 1994, just after midnight when NAFTA officially took effect, Mayan Indians wearing ski masks or bandannas occupied the city of San Cristobal de las Casas in the southern state of Chiapas. The Zapatistas, as they called themselves, declared war on the Mexican army, "the basic pillar of the dictatorship under which we suffer.... To us, the free-trade treaty is the death certificate for the ethnic peoples of Mexico."[3] Open war raged for several weeks, then settled down to the war of attrition that the government has waged since then.

Open warfare in Chiapas was not the only difficulty facing Salinas and the PRI in the 1994 election. The presidential candidate anointed to succeed Salinas, Luis Donoldo Colosio, was assassinated in March, possibly by elements within the PRI. To assure that this instability would not lead to a financial crisis and the election of a left-leaning government, the US Treasury and the Federal Reserve quietly put up $6 billion to support the Mexican peso.[4] With the economy seemingly on track and wages rising for some, the PRI candidate, Ernesto Zedillo—another US-trained economist—was elected president. The economy did not collapse until December.

At the start of December it took three pesos to buy one US dollar, the same as it had been for years. By the end of the month the rate was

5.7 to the dollar. The peso continued to drop over the next months to over 7 to the dollar. By March 1999, the rate was 10 to 1.

With the collapse of the peso, prices of nearly everything shot up. Wages could not keep up with the rapid inflation. In the manufacturing sector, real wages sank by 25% in the first two years. Many wages in the economy are pegged to the minimum wage; a quarter of the population earns less than the minimum, while another third earns less than twice the minimum.[5] In 1995 and 1996 the real minimum wage sank nearly as rapidly as the industrial wage, but had already been sinking steadily since the early 1980s.

Workers had been distrustful of Salinas, and some had openly opposed his policies. But for a few years official unions had managed to recover some of their workers' wages, and most never dreamed of complaining. With the collapse of real wages under Zedillo, popular support also collapsed. While the Zapatistas raised the cries of the indigenous peoples of the South, workers in many independent and semi-independent unions took to the streets to denounce the policies of the government, and middle-class debtors, suddenly facing bankruptcy, joined the fray. Finally, in the elections of July 1997, the PRI lost control of the Congress, and Cuauhtemoc Cardenas of the left-wing Democratic Revolutionary Party (PRD) won control of the government of Mexico City. The ability to run the economy for the benefit of the few was being challenged more effectively than ever before.

NAFTA had been imposed against the interests of the majority of North Americans, but this violation of democracy stimulated a burst of democratic organizing in all three countries. The PRI's loss of the presidency in July 2000 confirmed that commonsense notion that one cannot abuse the majority of one's people and win elections forever. This loss was preceded by effective citizen organizing throughout the country—much of it in the independent labor movement. Similar organizing began to transform orientations in the United States and Canada, leading to the defeat of Clinton's fast-track authorization, the events of Seattle, and more. The process continues.

The FAT Responds to the Global Economy: RMALC

When it became apparent that NAFTA would be proposed as a follow-up to the US–Canadian Free Trade Agreement, the FAT began to look for allies in the two countries to the north. The FAT's US contacts had been limited to ties it had had with the United Farm Workers union in the era of Cesar Chavez. The AFL-CIO had limited its ties in Mexico to official unions. It had especially close ties with the CTM since they were both members of the International Confederation of Free Trade Unions. Yet the FAT did have good contacts with Quebec's French-speaking National Union Confederation (CSN). The CSN had left the Catholic Church–linked World Federation of Labor during the same period the FAT broke its ties. The two unions had stayed in touch since the 1970s. The CSN had already been working with other Canadian labor federations and organizations opposed to the bilateral treaty between the United States and Canada. This broad coalition had already established ties to concerned US unions. Based on these links, the basis for tri-national cooperation grew. These early tri-national contacts led to a 1991 meeting in Zacatecas, Mexico at which like-minded Canadian and Mexican NGOs and unions were joined by the US-based NGOs and the United Electrical Workers (UE). Because the FAT was the leading Mexican industrial union to openly oppose government policy, many labor activists throughout the United States and Canada became interested in it.

In April 1991 the FAT played a key role in helping to found the Mexican Action Network Confronting Free Trade (RMALC). This network included several FAT unions, unions from various universities, environmentalists, women's groups, academics, the National Association of Democratic Lawyers, and labor representatives from two political parties, the PRD and the PRT, as well as peasant organizations and other NGOs. The group proposed to enter into the NAFTA negotiation process that was being conducted entirely by the elites. From the beginning RMALC members insisted that they were not flatly opposed to the concept of a tri-national treaty on commercial relations, but that the treaty needed to reflect the needs of the majorities of working people, not just the interests of business classes.

By late April RMALC convened a meeting of organizations from the three countries. Participants issued a joint statement declaring their intention to influence NAFTA negotiations. They realized that none of the governments wanted to allow the voice of working people to be heard within the negotiations. They also realized that few citizens in any of the countries were getting any information about the realities of what was being negotiated. They decided that, from that point on, whenever the official delegations met to negotiate, they would also be present to try to at least get the word out to the press. Since the NAFTA negotiators limited their remarks to the press to generalities, such as, "The meeting was quite fruitful, making substantial progress toward significant goals," RMALC and its Canadian and US friends were welcomed by the press as a source of news to fill the vacuum left by official sources. At events held in the United States, official press conferences were held only in English. The union action networks won press attention by providing translation into both Spanish and French of both the official information and their own.

The Canadian Action Network found a contact within the official Canadian delegation who leaked a working copy of the treaty, the Dallas Draft, dated February 1992. RMALC hurried to translate the 600-page top-secret document and released it to the Mexican press in late March. They also marched on Congress, where they presented a copy to the Chamber of Deputies, saying, "If the President won't inform you, the citizens' organizations will so you can fulfill your historic responsibilities to the country."[6]

When the negotiators met in Mexico in July 1992, RMALC made a public march on the negotiators' hotel with a public letter outlining their proposals. The press picked up the bait at the hotel doors and reporters persuaded aides to the secretary of commerce to come out and receive the letter. RMALC used a similar technique later to get their proposals on the side accords put before the negotiators. While they hoped that government negotiators would take at least some of their ideas into account, that was not the only point. With these techniques, RMALC had broken the government's monopoly on the news.

RMALC's efforts got a draft of their ideas into the hands of the official NAFTA negotiators. As far as we know, those ideas were completely ignored, but no labor or environmental groups in the United

States or Canada can claim any more influence. In all three countries, labor succeeded in gaining influence only indirectly, by mobilizing their membership and by educating the public. They then used that awareness to try to have some influence through their nations' legislatures.

As of this writing, RMALC remains active, publishing studies of the Mexican economy and its place in the global economy. Seen by the media and the public as an important and credible source of alternative economic data and policy ideas, RMALC currently has over 100 affiliates in Mexico. The FAT remains fundamental to the network, providing offices in its national headquarters. RMALC's executive committee meets weekly under the coordination of Bertha Lujan, national co-coordinator of the FAT.

In its publications on NAFTA, RMALC has pointed to the obvious imbalance of economic power between its economy and that of the United States and Canada. The cover of one of its books is simply a map of North America showing the yields of corn in tons per hectare. From north to south they are 6.2, 7.0, and 1.7 respectively.[7] Opening the border to free trade has meant that poor Mexican farmers can no longer sell their most traditional crop. Since the advent of NAFTA there has been an acceleration of the flow of peasants into the cities, into the maquiladora factories, and into the United States. Economists would argue that this is a positive movement of labor to more efficient uses. The official trade unions in Mexico predicted that NAFTA would lead to more and better jobs. The results have been an increase in jobs in maquilas along the border, with a continued decline of Mexican-owned industrial manufacturing in the center of the country. Wages have fallen even while productivity has increased. And the flow of Mexicans out of the cornfields and out of the shuttered factories has allowed companies like the non-union meat packer Iowa Beef Packing (IBP) to staff its plants in Iowa and Nebraska with illegal Mexican workers it actively recruits in Mexico.[8] RMALC makes clear that NAFTA has undermined workers both north and south.

The FAT–UE Strategic Alliance

At a 1991 RMALC meeting held in Zacatecas, the seeds for a new level of international cooperation were planted when FAT leaders met the political action director of the US-based United Electrical Workers Union (UE). A friendship between the unions soon developed. The UE, like the FAT, is relatively small. Like the FAT, the UE has a history of political autonomy—it withdrew from the CIO in 1949 following increasingly bitter disputes over labor's direction. It also has demonstrated a genuine commitment to internal union democracy and to international labor solidarity.

The UE was concerned that a number of its union locals were faced with companies that were closing or threatening to close plants and move operations to Mexico. According to Robin Alexander, the UE's director of international labor affairs, "The union had the foresight to see that the only way to stop the downward pressure on US wages was to stand together with militant unions in other countries to take on the transnationals together."[9] Ultimately they hoped to find a way to bargain collectively with Mexican workers who were dealing with the same employer. A RMALC statement reflects the views of the FAT.

> The best way to defend jobs in the United States is to work together to elevate the level of salaries and workplace and environmental conditions in Mexico, so that our misery stops being the way we compete with our fellow workers to the north. We Mexican workers are not enemies but strategic allies for workers north of the Rio Grande.[10]

The UE and the FAT decided to establish a strategic organizing alliance whose task would be to organize independent unions in Mexican plants of corporations that also dealt with the UE in the United States. A UE flier publicizing the alliance urges the reader to "Take On the Global Economy." It declares:

> We must build an international labor movement focusing on cross-border organizing. If we fail, we face a future of common misery. If we succeed, workers will be able to unite in their demands for decent wages and working conditions on both sides of the border.

Taking on General Electric

The first target the FAT–UE alliance took on was the mammoth General Electric corporation. During a fall 1992 meeting of anti-NAFTA activists from Canada, the United States, and Mexico, organizers from the United Electrical Workers met organizers from the FAT and started to build a common strategy. UE represented workers at several GE plants in the United States, some of which had recently been shut down and the work moved to Mexico. At other US plants, management frequently used the threat of shutdown as a major device in renegotiating contracts. The FAT was eager to begin organizing workers in the maquiladoras. But organizing would be hard, and allies were needed.

The FAT and UE agreed to support each other in an effort to organize CASA, the GE motor plant, in Ciudad Juarez, just across from El Paso, Texas. The plant was similar to plants organized by UE in the United States, but the wages paid in Juarez were less than one tenth of those paid in the United States. It was easy to understand why GE wanted to move its plants to Mexico.

In 1994, just after NAFTA took effect, Benedicto Martinez of the FAT's metalworkers' union (STIMAHCS) began talking with GE's Mexican workers to see if they wanted a union. They were so eager to organize, in fact, that they told him they had organized a meeting of 80 of the plant's 950 workers. This was a problem, however. Martinez had told the workers to keep quiet and never to form groups of more than 10 workers. He had been right to worry.

GE discovered the plans to organize a union and responded by firing 120 workers. This was a huge setback in terms of the lost leaders, and it intimidated many of the remaining workers. In keeping with Mexican law, GE then offered to pay those workers a severance that would end all future claims against the company. Many workers initially refused to sign, preferring to fight their terminations. They were told if they didn't sign they would be charged with stealing company property or dealing drugs. Although the company had no evidence against them, workers knew they could spend a long time in jail waiting to be cleared, so most signed. Two workers, Roberto Valerio and Fernando Castro Hernandez, refused to sign and became full-time organizers. Valerio recalls: "I refused to take their trivial payoff. I preferred to give them a fight and see if we could win. That way, at least the people still organizing inside wouldn't feel alone."[11]

When the UE heard of the firings, they began pressuring from north of the border. GE insisted that all the fired workers had been bad workers and needed to be replaced. UE organized a visit by rank-and-file members from three of their GE plants. When these workers arrived in Juarez they were shocked at what they saw. For far less money, these

Mexican workers were doing the same work they did, but in worse conditions. Many of the Mexican workers lived in houses made of wooden pallets that were no larger than their living rooms. The dirt streets, outhouses, and miserable wages reminded them of tales they had heard of workers a century earlier in the United States, before unions were able to force conditions to improve. During the visit, workers from both countries met and formed bonds of real friendship, and pledged to support each other in their common struggle. However, when the tour group went home, six more of the Juarez workers found they had lost their jobs.

UE workers turned up the heat back home by contacting sympathetic congressional representatives and generating national news stories. GE pledged to mend its ways. It claimed it would rehire the six workers and fire no more. The company also began to feed free hamburgers to its workers and told them to ignore the troublemaking union agitators. We are your friends, GE assured them.

Union organizers responded with leaflets at the plant gates, one of which asked workers if their children at home got hamburgers, too. To block further contact, GE started busing the workers through the gates. Organizers then simply threw wads of leaflets through bus windows that eager workers then opened. Organizers also did the hard work of visiting workers one-by-one in their homes, tramping dirt streets in the hot August sun. When workers conquered their fear enough to give leaflets to the security guards and to post them on the plant walls, Martinez sensed they were ready for the next phase.

In keeping with Mexican labor law, the FAT filed a demand that GE sign a contract with STIMAHCS or face a strike. The demand was properly filed with the state labor board, and a catch-22 run-around began. The president of the board objected that the demand had been addressed to him; it needed to be addressed to the board instead, he claimed. While this is the opposite of normal procedure, after some objections the FAT resubmitted the forms addressed to the board directly. Now the president objected that the demand was inadequate because it lacked signatures of the workers. The FAT objected that a demand for a contract never requires workers' signatures and that, if it had them, all those workers would get fired. The president then told the FAT to appeal his ruling to a court. When the FAT objected to the likely delay of several months that would destroy their organizing drive, the president suggested that they appeal to the political authorities in the state government. Thus began run-around phase two.

After several rounds of visits to politicians, the state's second-highest political official, the secretary of government, seemed to level with Martinez. Since the state government had recently been taken over by the opposition National Action Party (PAN), Martinez was hopeful that treatment would be different from what the PRI would hand out: absolute refusal to deal with an independent union in a major corporate plant. However, as Martinez tells it, the secretary said:

> Look, this is not a legal question. It's a political question. We know who you are. We know your history of independence. There is no legal solution for you. We won't allow you to organize a maquila. We can't risk the jobs. If we did, the business might leave. Others wouldn't come. We can't allow it.

He then advised Martinez to go see the secretary of labor again.

The secretary of labor said that GE was willing to allow a vote of the workers to unionize or not. This was not what the FAT was seeking, but under the circumstances, it seemed the best they might get. The FAT negotiated conditions for the vote, including an end to firings, an end to company indoctrination meetings in the plant, and a vote by secret ballot to be held outside the plant. This would be the first secret ballot union election ever held in Mexico, so that seemed a significant procedural victory at least. It seemed almost too good to be true. It was.

By this time, Martinez and the other FAT organizers were well advanced in their organizing work: a process that had included visits to the homes of nearly all of the 1,200 workers. They felt confident that the vast majority of the workers supported the FAT's unionization drive.

The night before the election, though, they got bad news. In spite of its agreement, GE had called a series of in-plant meetings for each shift. They each began with a worker from another plant that did have a union (one associated with the government, not the FAT) who told of how corrupt the union was, how they had to pay dues and got nothing in return. The second speaker was the plant manager, a man who had previously been nearly invisible. He said he had the workers' interest at heart and was willing to meet nearly all the conditions of the contract STIMAHCS was asking for, as long as they didn't vote for the union. If they did vote for the union, it would cause such problems that they would probably have to close. The final speaker was a well-coached "worker" who said if unions were corrupt, and if a union would cause them to lose their jobs, and if they were going to get what they wanted from GE anyhow, then they should vote no.

The speakers were very effective, and to make matters worse for the FAT, GE also approached key individuals and offered them retroactive wage hikes. When the hour of voting came, known organizers were pulled off to "chat" with their bosses just before workers in their sections were led off to vote (inside the plant, not outside as called for in the agreement) by supervisors who reminded them how to think and how to vote. The FAT had been prepared for last-minute violence, but not for this US-style psychological warfare. The FAT lost 914 votes to 159.

Under those conditions it was surprising the union got as many votes as it did. Yes, GE had violated the conditions of the vote, but what could be done? The whole process had been improvised outside the boundaries of Mexican labor law. It was clear that there was no route of appeal through politicians or the courts. And GE now had the results of a secret ballot vote to support it. The trap had been set and sprung. While all were disappointed, the FAT–UE alliance was only strengthened by this shared experience of injustice.

Honeywell in Chihuahua

At the same time the FAT was organizing workers at GE's plant in Juarez, it began organizing workers from Honeywell's plant in the city of Chihuahua, 200 miles to the south. The Honeywell plant employed approximately 500 workers, mostly women, making thermostats, circuit boards, and other switches used in heating and cooling devices.

A small group of women, fed up with minimum-wage pay, unsafe conditions, and oppressive supervisors, began to meet at the home of Ofelia Medrano. In November 1993, Benedicto Martinez met with them to tell them about the FAT union STIMAHCS and to encourage their organizing efforts. Within days Honeywell began calling workers in to the personnel director's office to ask them why they were trying to form a union. They were asked to name names of others involved, and were told that Honeywell would close before it would allow the formation of a union at the plant. They were then told they were fired and they should sign certain forms to receive the severance pay required by law.

Most of them signed, unaware that they were giving up any legal right to appeal. They signed to get the money that they would desperately need, since Mexico has no unemployment insurance and their miserable wages had not allowed them to accumulate any savings.

The last to be fired was Ofelia Medrano, the main organizer within the plant. She was kept in the office for about four hours in an effort to intimidate her into informing on others. Finally, she was told that if she simply admitted to what she had done they would forgive her and allow her to go back to work. At this point she signed. They then gave her a severance check and asked her to sign for it. She refused, but they told her she had "screwed herself" by signing the paper. After talking to the local FAT organizer, Librado Tarrango, Medrano filed a complaint with the local labor board for being fired for trying to organize a union.[12]

Two weeks later, Honeywell announced that it had laid off twenty workers due to lack of work at the plant. Having fired all the workers initially involved in trying to form a union, Honeywell effectively ended this organizing effort.

But the fight wasn't over yet. In discussing the situation with the UE, the FAT discovered that the Teamsters had contracts with Honeywell plants in Minnesota that had been losing jobs to Mexico. Contacts were made, and the Teamsters agreed to add their muscle to the FAT–UE alliance.

Testing NAFTA's Labor Side Accords

In Chihuahua, Honeywell had killed off a union drive by firing all involved. In Ciudad Juarez, where the organizing effort had been too far advanced to kill off by firing workers, the state government had refused to follow its own laws, proposing instead an irregular election and then violating its conditions. Once again the FAT had run into determined resistance, but now its international allies created a new set of options. The FAT, along with the UE and the Teamsters, could try turning to the US government for justice.

The Clinton administration had negotiated a labor side agreement to NAFTA that insisted that governments had to at least follow their own labor laws, and, if they didn't, they could be brought before a hearing board in one of the other countries. The UE and Teamsters filed complaints that would become the first cases before the US Department of Labor's National Administrative Office (NAO).

On September 12, 1994, the NAO held hearings in Washington, DC, too far for any active workers from Juarez or Chihuahua to attend. And it did, eventually, make specific findings: that there are obstacles for independent unions' gaining legal recognition; that large numbers of workers had been fired at the time of organizing campaigns; that there is blacklisting of union activists; and that there is a practice of using economic hardship to force workers to accept severance pay rather than assert their rights when they are fired for union activities.[13] But the NAO also determined that these finding were not sufficient cause for the US secretary of labor to hold consultations with the Mexican secretary of labor. (When workers' rights to organize their own union are involved, consultations are the most serious hand-slap available under the side agreements.)

In the Honeywell case, the NAO ruled that there was no remaining conflict to worry about since all but one of the fired workers had signed voluntary severance agreements when they were dismissed. The NAO noted that even Ofelia Medrano eventually signed such an agreement, giving up her rights. They barely acknowledged her sworn affidavit in which she claimed that although she had to sign to pay medical bills for a family member, she had been unjustly fired.[14]

One of the problems that the NAO had with the GE case was that the FAT had not filed a case in the Mexican courts about the matter. (In this, it also ignored the sworn testimony of Benedicto Martinez about the government's refusal to follow its own laws.) To have the US NAO as a partner to the Mexican government's run-around was discouraging, to say the least. Workers on both sides of the border would have to do what they could to strengthen their own forces before they could hope for any support from legal mechanisms on either side of the border.

A third case filed with the NAO later in the year involved 50 workers fired for challenging a CTM union at a Sony plant in Nuevo Laredo. Workers who tried to run their own slate of officers were fired, and when they protested outside the plant, they were beaten by the local police force. The head of the CTM in Nuevo Laredo was praised in the

"Maquiladora Newsletter" of the American Chamber of Commerce of Mexico as "consistently cooperative and helpful." He "can get guys out of your hair without having to pay severance." His cooperation has led to "excellent conditions for the industry characterized by relatively low wages and long hours."[15]

The Sony case was brought with the support of four non-governmental organizations: Mexico's National Association of Democratic Lawyers (ANAD), the Coalition for Justice in the Maquiladoras (CJM), the International Labor Rights Fund, and the American Friends Service Committee. This complaint got further than the previous two, resulting in a consultation between the secretaries of labor for the United States and Mexico and an agreement to hold a series of public conferences exploring the legal process for registering unions in Mexico.[16] While these public relations disasters may have been embarrassing to the Mexican government, so far this punishment-by-seminar is the worst consequence it has suffered for its flagrant violations of the NAFTA side accords.

These initial defeats in efforts to organize maquila workers in the NAFTA era led the FAT to turn to a tactic that had worked well for it in earlier periods. Workers in Leon and Cuernavaca had first become educated and organized in workers' centers before they went on to storm their towns. Since opposition was fierce within the factories, and since education about workers' rights was extremely low among the maquila workers this was a logical next step. With the support of the UE and the Teamsters, the FAT opened its Workers Study Center, CETLAC, on September 28, 1996, in the heart of Ciudad Juarez. Its goal was to offer the maquila workers of Juarez a place to learn, to socialize, and to organize.

The Maquiladoras of Juarez

The maquiladora program began in 1965 to stimulate employment along the border in the wake of the 1964 termination of the *bracero* program that had legally supplied Mexican workers to US farmers. The maquiladora program allows the duty-free importation of goods to be assembled in Mexico, then re-exported. The United States also treats these goods favorably, taxing only the value added by Mexican manufacturers. Originally limited to the border area, these conditions now apply throughout the country.

Maquiladora production has grown at an incredible rate, and Ciudad Juarez, at the border's mid-point, has grown the fastest of all maquila areas. With the collapse of the peso and the advent of NAFTA, its maquila workforce grew from 140,000 workers in 1994 to 220,000 in 1999.[17] The city continues to grow at approximately 7% per year.

New wealth is apparent to anyone who explores Ciudad Juarez. The city boasts 15 industrial parks that, except for the blooming flowers in January, look as if they could be in any city in the United States. The concrete streets are clean, wide, and well lit. The global corporate logos are familiar: Alcoa, Sony, Mitsubishi, Sylvania, Phillips, and Siemens. Delphi electronics—now the largest private-sector employer in Mexico—has several plants here. One of Juarez's largest employers is Thomson, the French-owned transnational that in 1998 closed one of the last US factories to assemble televisions (sold as RCA or GE).

Yet a look in the parking lots of these plants reveals some details of where that new wealth is going. At many plants the parking lots are restricted for executives only, and half the cars have Texas or New Mexico license plates. Upper management, going home to the United States every night, is not much concerned with what it is like to live in Juarez. Very few workers can even afford cars.

Not far from some of these industrial parks, one sees new housing developments. The townhouses are pleasant, but small. The cars are recent models, but also small. These neighborhoods are pleasant, with small parks, and show a recent influx of money. These are the homes of the Mexican middle management.

If most of the time the industrial parks look as if they could be in the United States, at shift change they become very Mexican. As workers stream out of the plants, they scurry to get seats on modified school buses that quickly fill and then roar off to the workers' neighborhoods. The bus to the sprawling community of Anapra crosses town for more than half an hour, then leaves the crudely paved public streets and proceeds on dusty dirt tracks for another 15 minutes into the desert hills. Here growth is obviously occurring, too. New homes are springing up everywhere. Most are about the size of a one-car garage.

Shipping pallets are a favorite building material. Cast off or sold cheaply by the maquilas, they are gathered up and resold by local entrepreneurs lucky enough to own an aging pickup truck. The pallets are tacked together to form roofs and walls. The walls are then covered with tar paper. A new material that resembles egg cartons permeated with tar has replaced the tin roofs of a more prosperous past. Some of the homes have outhouses; others lack even these. None of the homes have running water.

Electric wires run overhead, recently extended here to power the refrigerators of the few small shops and to light an occasional street lamp. And electric wires also lie in the dirt streets, spliced together with tape at odd intervals. These bring power to some of the homes. Workers have simply tapped into the overhead lines at various points to steal the power. Occasionally someone dies in the attempt, like a mosquito caught in the grid of a black-light trap. One wonders about the safety of children kicking soccer balls through the live wires in these streets. It is risky for a worker to try to get power.

Two out of three workers in the maquilas of Juarez are women. Most are young. Most have recently arrived from other parts of the country, particularly from the countryside where education is quite limited. There is a labor shortage, so most of the plants have signs up saying they are seeking workers. Several have signs proclaiming, "*Se solicitan muchachas vivas*" (seeking lively girls). In the assembly plants, it is said that women are preferred for their smaller fingers, but also because they are assumed to be more submissive and less likely to have heard about unions or politics. Women must be at least 16 to get a job here, unless the employer doesn't check. While few employers check birth certificates, many have required pregnancy tests. Despite the illegality of this requirement, most workers comply. Beginning in 1995 a series of grizzly sexual assaults and murders gave workers another thing to worry about.

The maquilas were attractive to businesses even before NAFTA, when workers earned around $5 a day. The fall of the peso in 1995 meant that minimum wages—and that is what most maquilas pay—dropped to about $3 a day. Including benefits and overtime, paychecks for a 48-hour week in 1999 were generally between $30 and $40. The business press often says that total labor costs including wages, benefits, and payroll taxes come to about $2 per hour, compared to the more than $20 an hour that it costs to employ the average manufacturing worker in the United States.[18]

It is commonly thought that workers in Mexico can get by on lower wages because it costs less to live there. For some expenses this is true. What a US worker spends for a three-bedroom house on a tree-lined street is a lot more than it costs a worker to build a tar-paper shack in the hills of Juarez. And a Canadian worker spends vastly more on car payments and insurance than a maquila worker spends on the bus. But, thanks to the glorious efficiencies of the global free market, most commodities cost the same in Mexico as they do elsewhere.

An easy way to see the relative value of wages is through a market-basket survey, such as one conducted by the Coalition for Justice in the Maquiladoras. The chart below shows the cost of basic goods for a maquila worker who earns a relatively good wage of $5 per day and for a unionized US autoworker.

Figure 1: Time in minutes it takes a worker to earn enough to purchase the following goods.

Product	Amount	Mexico	US
Aspirin	100 ct	153.8 minutes	19.3 minutes
Cheese	1 lb.	125.0	13.2
Chicken	whole	87.0	4.5
Coffee	13 oz.	117.6	8.4
Coke™	6 pack	107.1	10.1
Eggs	12	69.8	4.1
Hamburger	1 lb.	88.2	7.0
Ice cream	half gallon	206.9	10.3
Milk	1 lb.	142.9	12.2
Onions	1 lb.	22.1	3.1
Rice	5 lbs.	69.0	13.5
Sugar	5 lbs.	96.8	8.4
Toilet paper	4 rolls	50.0	6.1
Tomatoes	1 lb.	20.4	5.7

Source: Coalition for Justice in the Maquiladoras (http://www.igc.apc.org/unitedelect/alert.html).

Another perspective on the life of workers in Juarez can be gained by spending a bit of time in the home of Alex and Veronica, a young couple who are doing relatively well. Alex earns four times the minimum salary and Veronica, who works the night shift assembling wiring harnesses, earns 1.2 times the minimum. Between the two of them they earn about $115 per week. They live in an established working-class neighborhood, one that has been around for over 20 years. They have managed to lay a cement floor on which they have built adobe walls made from dirt on the site. They have built their one-room, 18-by-25-foot house onto the side of the much smaller adobe house of Veronica's mother, the owner of the lot. All cooking is done in the mother's one-room house, essentially a small kitchen that includes a table, dresser, and double bed. The adjoining houses share a flush toilet, and they have recently been able to add a water heater for the shower. This comes in handy in a house with no heat on mornings that, for several months each year, start just a few degrees above freezing.

Alex manages to keep a beat-up car going because he uses it in his work. He must park it a few blocks away, in a relative's fenced yard with guard dogs, because several times when he has left it outside his window overnight, workers who are not so fortunate as he have climbed his fence and stolen the battery. Alex and Veronica have two kids, a boy and a girl, who consider a doll or a tablet and colored pencils incredible luxuries. The family supplements its diet by visiting the home of an uncle who makes his living selling cut fruit all day. When he arrives home in the evenings he shares what is left over with his family and with whichever visiting friends and relatives happen to be there. It takes the equivalent of over five minimum-wage salaries and a supportive extended family to live this well in Juarez.

For some, the maquiladora sector has been a tremendous success. Maquila exports are now as important to Mexico as its earnings from oil. A new maquiladora opens in Mexico every two days. Productivity improves each year. Many plants boast the latest international quality standards. Growth is rapid, yet the benefits filter down only to executives and middle management. Despite all the progress, wages that fell in early 1995 fell further in 1996. The good news is that they have almost managed to stay even with inflation since then.

Servando Sarabia is the executive director of the business-promoting Association of Maquiladoras of Juarez. Asked if the obvious shortage of labor didn't indicate that wages in the maquilas might rise, he said, "No, there is no danger of that." Given the government policy that limits wage increases and prevents effective unionization, he has no need to fear that the laws of supply and demand would ever benefit workers. "Workers don't want unions," he said, "because treatment is fair. We have no real problems."[19]

He did acknowledge, though, that the shortage of housing for workers, which he estimated at between 50,000 and 80,000 units, was a problem. Nonetheless, over a hundred maquiladoras have filed an injunction against the government requirement that they contribute to a fund to build worker housing. They claim that the requirement is unconstitutional.[20] Yet they, and the government, seem content to ignore the constitutional requirement that the minimum wage provide enough to cover food, clothing, shelter, education, and even a bit for entertainment, not just for an individual worker, but for the worker's family as well.

Despite the low wages, and despite the shortage of housing, an average day sees a hundred new families arriving in Juarez looking for work. Many of them are driven by the collapse of the rural economies caused by the cutbacks of subsidies to small farmers and the competition in basic grains brought on by NAFTA. Studies indicate that nearly half of Mexico's people live in "extreme poverty," meaning they subsist on no more than a dollar a day.[21] This would include nearly all campesinos.

The level of desperation in the countryside was made clear by a train robbery in May 1996. The train, carrying a shipment of corn, was stopped by the villagers of San Nicolas de las Garza in the northern state of Nuevo Leon. Nearly 400 villagers—men, women, and children—participated in carrying off nearly 40 tons of food. When 20 police showed up to stop the looting, villagers drove them off with stones. Eventually over a hundred police chased the villagers away from the train. The police chief said that hunger had driven the villagers to this extreme act, "to have tortillas at least."[22]

Due to NAFTA and other policies designed to increase Mexico's market efficiency, many Mexican peasants have slipped from poverty to desperation. Urban workers, formerly employed by small "inefficient" manufacturers, join the displaced peasants in the NAFTA-induced reserve army of labor. These hungry migrants supply a steady stream of new workers for the maquilas. They are drawn by the signs that always say "Workers Wanted" or "Now Hiring."

A security guard outside one of these maquilas points out that they aren't really hiring every day. But people quit often, or they fire some-one, and they always want a new worker ready to take their place.

> They have all these just-time contracts and they need to fill them without delay. They pay about $20 a week, almost nothing, no? And they work them very hard. They get all the production they can out of them. The supervisor is always watching, and if someone makes a mistake or slows up a little, they fire them, run them right out.

> It's like the time of black slavery in the United States, but now it's we Mexicans who are the slaves. People come from all over the coun-try to work in Juarez. They arrive every day. Better they should go back to their own towns.

"What?" I ask him. "Even if there is no work back home?"

"Yes," he replies. "Better to die of hunger than to work here as a slave."

Creating a Culture of Resistance: CETLAC

The task of the FAT in Juarez is to try to organize these workers. The grounds for dissatisfaction are plenty, but the obstacles to organizing are almost as numerous. The workforce—young, mostly female, mostly peasant raised, mostly undereducated—has a turnover rate of about 15% per month. If the workers have any experience with unions at all, it is al-most certain to have been with a corrupt organization that was seen as one more drain on their earnings, not as a source of support. Usually the workers hope to move to the United States or to save up enough to return to their villages. Each of these conditions makes it hard to form a union.

Despite these obstacles, workers from time to time decide to form a real union. Between 1986 and 1998 there were 20 attempts to register new unions at plants in Juarez. All have been rejected. Sometimes the workers have simply called wildcat strikes, as they did at the beginning of 1997 at the Thomson RCA plant. One of the strikers actually called the FAT's worker education center, CETLAC, for help, saying that they had completely shut down the 5,000-worker plant. But the plant man-ager's brother was the governor of the state, the same governor who had decided he would never allow the FAT to form a union there. By the time a CETLAC staff member got to the scene, anti-riot police were already breaking up the hastily organized strike.

Clearly CETLAC's project is a difficult one. Its organizers must establish contact with workers, most of whom are frightened or ignorant of unions, or simply not willing to get involved in any long-term project. So CETLAC works somewhat indirectly. The center has offered academic tutoring, workshops in nutrition and sewing-machine repair, and talks on healthcare rights, but those who came did so for very personal reasons. Few formed an attachment to the larger projects of the center. More recently organizers have developed a pocket-sized handout called "First Aid for Workers." Inside is basic information on workers' rights, as well as information on how to contact CETLAC for legal assistance with labor problems. The goal is to establish a long-term presence within the working-class culture of Juarez. Given the nature of that culture, this is an uphill battle. But that is nothing new. As of this writing, the FAT was engaged in clandestine talks with workers seeking to form unions at a number of plants. The strategy may yet pay off.

Linking Unions and Nations

On March 1, 1997, the FAT met with six other North American unions to form the Echlin Workers Alliance. At the time of the meeting, Echlin, an auto-parts company, employed 32,000 people in 100 locations on six continents, with earnings of $3.6 billion. Participating unions included the Teamsters, the United Electrical Workers, the United Steelworkers, the Paperworkers, the Canadian Autoworkers, and UNITE, as well as the FAT. The official statement of the meeting highlighted the perilous position of Mexican workers, and the importance of all North American unions, dedicating their efforts to lifting up the lowest:

> We are united in the belief that in this era of the global corporation and unrestrained corporate greed, we must seek new and concrete forms of solidarity between workers employed by the same multinational corporation.... As our bosses cross national boundaries in search of ever higher profits, our solidarity must also cross borders to build a strong international workers movement....
>
> We therefore pledge and agree to work to the following:

1. We will build rank-and-file solidarity between unionized Echlin facilities in North America and will offer each mutual aid and support to strengthen our hand at the bargaining table.

2. We will attempt to organize the thousands of unorganized Echlin workers throughout North America to bring justice to their workplaces and increase our collective strength in the chain.

3. We will make a special effort to support Echlin workers in Mexico, who suffer the lowest wages and worst conditions and who face the worst repression when they stand up for their rights.[23]

This degree of tri-national union cooperation—especially between unions in the same country who could potentially be seen as rivals competing for the same membership base—was unprecedented. Information was exchanged on the company's operations and apparent strategy. People from different unions discussed dealing with the same Echlin bargaining agent, comparing and contrasting the man's techniques under various scenarios. A comparison of wages and benefits at various plants showed a wide range in pay, from minimum wage to over $20 an hour. Discussion was aimed at moving the lower wages higher while avoiding divide-and-conquer strategies.

The gathering brought top-level and rank-and-file unionists together in the same conversation. Examples of the benefits of communication became evident. Members of UNITE who had organized the Friction Brake plant in Fredricksburg, Virginia, shared a flier they had produced to help workers at the Friction plant in Santa Ana, California, organize with UE. A Teamster from Dallas, Texas, told how he and his coworkers had received brake shoes shipped from Mexico in boxes that contained loose asbestos dust. Since complaining to the company through the union, they were now getting clean boxes.

A worker from the ITAPSA brake plant in Mexico City replied that he knew about the union brother's complaint because he packed the shoes that were sent up to Dallas. His plant was full of asbestos dust, so the boxes went out full of dust. When the complaint came in from Dallas, he was given a vacuum cleaner and told to be sure each box was clean before it was sealed up. The workers, however, were still given only one paper dust mask a month for their protection. For this they were paid between $5 and $10 per day. They were working with the FAT to get rid of the CTM union that held a protection contract with the company.

Support from the alliance was important to the organizing drive at Echlin's ITAPSA plant in 1997. Since the plant was within the sprawling valley of Mexico City, the FAT was able to devote three young organizers to conducting the effort full-time. The plant employed 300 workers, all very young. In fact, one of the organizers had applied for a job in the plant, but was turned down because, at 27, she was too old. Organizers met with workers in their homes, at soccer fields, wherever they could. The goal was to secretly build an organization of reliable people in all parts of the plant, on every shift, but to work only in small groups. This way, if someone were detected, he or she would not give away the whole organization. The decision was made to stay as quiet as possible until the day of an election that would determine which union had the most support.

One of the first workers to support the new union was Veronica, a slight woman with a huge presence. A worker with only a 30-day contract, she was one of the first to be fired when the company started to suspect an organizing drive. When asked to sign a voluntary resignation, she protested that she had done nothing wrong and would only sign a paper that said she was being fired against her will.

A supervisor in the plant approached another worker and told him, "Relax, you aren't doing anything illegal forming your own union." The worker, of course, denied any knowledge of the union effort. Another supervisor told him:

> We know all about the FAT. And we know they have a support network of unions at other Echlin plants, but we will never allow the FAT to organize ITAPSA. Be careful. They could even kill your family. It would be smart of you to back off.[24]

The FAT's efforts to get an election called were delayed several times on various pretenses, each time making it harder to maintain the confidence of the young workers, many quite eager to break the silence. Finally a firm date for the election was set. Workers celebrated election day by surrounding the plant with signs supporting the FAT union. This was meant to encourage workers as they entered, as most had never met more than two or three union supporters.

Management and the CTM union were not celebrating, however. They called their supporters at the labor board and got the election postponed. The CTM then used its exclusion clause to remove all the identified FAT supporters from its membership rolls and asked ITAPSA to fire them. ITAPSA gladly obliged, sacking 50 workers.

Many of these workers signed for severance pay and left the organizing effort, but others, like Veronica, worked more overtly now, handing out leaflets and talking to workers at the plant gates, showing those inside they should not be intimidated, that the FAT would support them.

A new date was set for the election: September 9. In the middle of the night two busloads of young men armed with pipes, clubs, knives, and several guns drove into the plant and unloaded. The night shift, which usually leaves at 6 a.m., was not allowed to go home. The day shift arrived to see banners hanging over the factory saying, "Get out foreign unions! Get out FAT!" The young thugs reminded them that if they valued their jobs—and their lives—they had better vote for the CTM. When Benedicto Martinez and a lawyer for the FAT arrived, the CTM immediately protested to the officials on-site to supervise the election. These officials called their superiors, who stalled an hour and then called back saying they could do nothing. It was "just an inter-union conflict." Nineteen fired workers who had come to exercise their legal right to vote in the election were not allowed to enter. One of the FAT's observers was beaten in front of other workers and in front of labor board officials, who refused to intervene.

Late in the day, when the night shift arrived, the election began. The third shift and the day shift were now being held against their will by armed guards. Workers proceeded to the voting table through a gauntlet of armed thugs, reminding them how to vote. They then had to declare their choice openly before management, union representatives, and labor board officials.

The final vote was 172 for the CTM union and 29 for STIMAHCS, the FAT's metalworkers' union. The "infernal trilogy" of corrupt union, government, and boss had once again carried the day.

But the fight did not end there. In addition to filing complaints with the Mexican labor board, the FAT was joined by its alliance partners in filing a compliant with the National Administrative Offices of both Canada and the United States. What proved most effective was a public protest at the corporation's annual shareholders meeting in Branford, Connecticut, on December 17. Attended by rank-and-file members and executives of the Echlin Alliance, the protest not only drew national US media attention to the abuses at ITAPSA, it forced Echlin to announce it would conduct its own investigation into the use of thugs to influence the union election. The company also agreed to consider adopting an alliance-proposed code of conduct.

"It's unusual for a company like Echlin to respond so quickly to protests from its workers, but its also rare for a company to face such strong opposition from workers in three countries," said Robert Kingsley, secretary for organization of the UE. Tom Gilmartin, Teamsters vice president, added:

> Strong cooperation among workers in the three NAFTA countries is putting a new level of pressure on companies that violate workers rights in North America. NAFTA's weak labor side agreement has left us no choice but to get in the face of the companies responsible for this kind of abuse.[25]

One of the more unusual projects taken on by the FAT-UE Alliance is the mural project. Mexicans are proud of their tradition of fiery political wall paintings, made world-famous by Diego Rivera. The Alliance has sponsored murals painted in Mexico by US artists and painted in the United States by Mexican artists. The new mural in the FAT's headquarters features men and women of all colors, from both countries, confronting the evils of greedy capitalists and boldly standing up for their own common dreams of dignity, freedom, and solidarity. Along with the frequent exchange of union members across borders, these murals are a testimony to the construction of a new culture of international solidarity that is rising to confront the misery that the forces of global business and their governing allies have been imposing on workers throughout the world. By finding new allies across the border, workers have managed to overcome the despair so often associated with increasing hunger, job loss, and community destruction. Together they have found new tactics to struggle in what is now a global arena of conflict.

Notes

1   Russell, Philip P. 1994. *Mexico Under Salinas*, 375. Austin, Texas: Mexico Resource Center.

2   Endnote Text

3   Ross, John. 1995. *Rebellion from the Roots: Indian Uprising in Chiapas*, 10, 21. Monroe, Maine: Common Courage Press.

4   Lustig, Nora. 1998. *Mexico: The Remaking of an Economy,* Second Edition, 159. Washington, DC: Brookings.

5   Velasco, Elizabeth. 1998. "Prevé Senado Mayor Deterioro Salarial en 1998." *La Jornada*, (August 24).

6   Arroyo, Alberto, and Mario B. Monroy. 1996. *Red Mexicana de Acción Frente al Libre Comercio: Cinco Años de Lucha (1991-1996)*, 32. Mexico, DF: RMALC.

7   Arroyo and Monroy.

8   Cason, Jim, and David Brooks. 1999. "Podrian Perder Sus Empleos en EU Unos 4 Mil 700 Inmigrantes." *La Jornada* (August 4).

9   Alexander, Robin. 2000. Correspondence with the author.

10   Arroyo and Monroy, 24.

11   Valerio, Roberto. 1997. Interview at his house in Zaragoza. Ciudad Juarez, Chihuahua.

12   Medrano Sanchez, Ofelia. 1994. Legal affadavit submitted to US NAO, (submission 940001) by Teamsters, El Paso,Texas, July 14.

13   U.S. National Administrative Office. 1994. *Public Report of Review: NAO Submission #940001, 940002*, 29. Washington, DC: United States Department of Labor.

14   U.S. National Administrative Office. 1994, 26–27.

15   Williams, Edward J., and John T. Passé-Smith. 1992. *The Unionization of the Maquiladora Industry: The Tamaulipan Case in National Context*, 56. San Diego: Institute for Regional Studies of the Californias, San Diego State University.

16   U.S. National Administrative Office. 1999. *Status of Submissions*, http://www2.dol.gov/dol/ilab/public/programs/nao/status.html.   US Department of Labor, 940003 (June 15, 1999). Despite efforts to keep these "public" forums secret and well controlled, ANAD lawyers heard of the first meeting and stormed in, demanding to be heard. For nearly three hours they contradicted the story that US and Canadian officials had just been given by Mexican officials, who had no response to ANAD. The same distorted story of Mexican labor relations was repeated at the hearings in San Antonio on November 8 and 9, 1995. "Labor Advocates

Turn Tables at Trinational Seminars," 1995. *Borderlines,* 3:19 (December).

17 "Maquila Scoreboard." 1999. *Twin Plant News: Mexico's Industrial Magazine* (El Paso, Texas) July, 70-71.

18 For example the maquiladora promoting magazine, *Twin Plant* puts total labor cost for an unskilled worker in Mexicali at $1.93/hour if employed for over 12 months. New workers cost only $1.58/hour. *Twin Plant.* 1999 (July): 34. US cost based on 1998 average manufacturing wage of $13.49/hr. *Economic Report of the President*, 1999, Table B-47.

19 Sarabia, Servando. 1997. Oral interview, Cuidad Juarez, November 26.

20 Villalpando, Rubén. 1998. "Explotación Intensiva en las Maquildoras de Ciudad Júarez." *La Jornada* (January 24).

21 Martínez, Cesar. 1997. "Alcanzan 75% los Niveles de Pobreza en México:Boltvinik." *La Jornada* (July 10): 20.

22 Carrizales, David. 1996. "Cientos de Colonos Saquean un Tren con Maíz." *La Jornada* (May 31).

23 Echlin Tri-National Alliance. 1997. "Statement of solidarity and Purpose"; adopted at founding meeting, Chicago, March 1.

24 Anonymous. 1997. Clandestine organizing meeting, Los Reyes, Mexico, June 5.

25 Alexander, Robin. 1997. E-mail.

8.

Signs of Change within Mexico

When a Mexican labor board official refuses to see a problem in armed thugs beating a worker during a union election, or when a government official insists that, regardless of the law, he will never allow the formation of an independent union in a maquiladora plant, or when the front man for maquiladoras in Juarez promises that wages will not rise despite a labor shortage, these are not just outrageous incidents. They are consistent manifestations of an economic policy that seeks to advance the interests of a few by selling Mexican labor cheaply in the global market.

A January 1997 report from the PRI-affiliated Labor Congress (CT) showed that for a worker to buy basic foodstuffs, he or she required more than two minimum-wage salaries, leaving nothing for housing, clothing, or transportation.[1] Little has changed since then. Since two-thirds of all Mexican workers earn less than two minimum-wage salaries, we know that this economic policy is destroying Mexican workers and their families. Because Mexican workers are sold in the global marketplace to attract jobs from countries like the United States and Canada, this constitutes an act of "dumping": selling goods—in this case, human labor—at below the cost of production. Industries have worked hard to preserve a right to slap tariffs on goods like steel or cheese if the producers are subsidized by their governments. Yet there are no penalties imposed on companies or governments that profit because workers produce goods at wages below what they need to live. Mexico, and many countries like it, sell exports at below the cost it takes to produce them. If the lives of workers mattered to those who write trade laws, wouldn't there be penalties for those who dump human labor, as there are for those who dump steel?

Policies that devastate a majority of the population can only be maintained through a non-democratic process. Since the 1930s, Mexican workers have been politically managed within a corporatist system that has kept union leaders and political representatives compliant through incentives and repression. Workers have been given noble words and occasional benefits. Yet the benefits have been so few since the early 1980s that the noble words have increasingly rung hollow. The system has been cracking.

During the presidential election of 1994 a feud between the tecnico and dinosaur wings of the PRI is widely believed to have led to the assassination of the PRI candidate, Donoldo Colosio, and the party's secretary-general, Francisco Ruiz Massieu. Ernesto Zedillo had no popular support, but his insertion into the race confirmed the tecnicos had won another round. Just months after his election, the economy collapsed, and former president Salinas fled to Ireland, a country with which Mexico had no extradition treaty.

By 1997 the economy had begun to recover, but few, if any, benefits had trickled down to the impoverished majority. At the age of 97, Fidel Velazquez, who had dominated the CTM since its founding in 1936, finally died. Trying to stave off any fundamental change, Zedillo appointed Leonardo Rodriguez Alcaine to take his place. Rodriguez Alcaine had risen to prominence when he took control of the electrical workers' union in the 1970s, helping to bring an end to the workers' insurgency. Congressional elections held just two weeks later produced a Congress no longer controlled by the PRI. Cuauhtemoc Cardenas and the PRD won control of the government of Mexico City. Several state governments threw off PRI control.

Finally, on July 2, 2000, Vicente Fox of the National Action Party (PAN) won the presidency and shattered the grip the PRI had held on the office since the 1920s. The elections also produced a Congress in which the PRI had a slight plurality in both chambers, but lacked a majority in either. While the PRI's ability to act unilaterally at the federal level has been destroyed, the party still controls the majority of state governments, and the PAN has previously demonstrated that it agrees with most of the economic policies of the PRI. So, it is far from clear what the future will bring. In this light it is useful to look in some detail at the political struggles from below that have occurred in recent years. What happens at the top of the system will have to respond to what has been happening at its base.

The Zapatistas: Peasants Strike Back

At the beginning of the 20th century, Emiliano Zapata emerged from the farming village of Anenecuilco in the southern state of Morelos to demand the return of lands seized by agribusiness interests. Of the major revolutionary leaders, Zapata alone remained true to his base in the common people. Because of this, the agribusiness magnates that took control of the Revolution had to kill him in order to consolidate a new government that honored peasants and workers in word more than deed. So in the 1990s, when President Salinas moved to end communal landholdings and implement free trade policies that would force peasants on mountainsides to compete with the mechanized corn growers of Iowa and Indiana, it was fitting that the name of Zapata should rise again.

Despite taking a namesake from the past, the Zapatista Army of National Liberation (EZLN) that rose up in arms on January 1, 1994, just minutes after NAFTA went into effect, has become known as the first post-modern revolutionary movement. Though they fought armed battles with the national army in the first days of their rebellion, they have survived since then by outflanking the Mexican political authorities through the media. Through creative use of the internet, they mobilized international opinion to their side. While pro-government Mexican television was preparing the nation for the obliteration of the rebels, the Zapatistas were mobilizing support not only among web-linked Mexicans, but also in Europe and the rest of North America. This support made a continuation of the military response impossible. Tales of brutal massacres and of the inhumane conditions that had led to the rebellion overwhelmed any government attempts to spin the news.

As investors from Europe and the United States pulled money from the Mexican stock exchange, Salinas quickly realized that a slaughter of Mayan peasants was not what a modern investor wanted to see. By January 12, he had halted the military operation. Subcomandante Marcos, the ski-masked, pipe-smoking spokesman and literary leader of the Zapatistas, was too much for the media to resist. His quips were readily quoted, and the fact that he was accountable to a democratic process rooted in the Mayan villages began to communicate the substance of the movement's goals.

Once the military situation had stabilized somewhat, the Zapatistas launched an offensive against the political process of Mexico. Since there was an election going on, they invited all presidential candidates to meet with them in the cathedral of San Cristobal de las Casas. Four minor parties sent delegations, as did the PRD. While nothing concrete was accomplished, aside from establishing friendly relations between the EZLN and the PRD, the event linked the Zapatistas to the broader political landscape of the country.

On April 10, 1994, the 75th anniversary of the assassination of Zapata, 75,000 peasants gathered in Mexico City's Zocolo and cheered the Mayan uprising. That summer the EZLN called for a National Convention for Democracy to be held shortly before the presidential elections in August. In their call, they used the words of a 1914 Zapatista to declare: "It is not just launching projectiles on the battlefield but launching new ideas and words of liberation that overthrows empires. The revolution is the wedding of the sword and the idea."[2]

While the Zapatistas were clearly no match for the Mexican government in terms of the sword, they had a huge advantage in the area of ideas. They spent $13,000 of scarce funds that had been raised for weapons and used it to build crude accommodations for the convention being held in the remote mountain village rechristened "Aguascalientes" after the site of the convention held by Zapata and Pancho Villa in 1914. Marcos wrote personal letters to Mexico's leading intellectuals, and got many of them to attend, along with another 4,000 supporters from various organizations of the left throughout Mexico and beyond.

By inviting people into their territory in the war zone, the EZLN broke the isolation imposed on them by the military's continuing encirclement. As they built support for their own movement, they also breathed new hope into many sectors of the Mexican left. Zapatista flags and curios became common throughout the country. The gathering in Aguascalientes occurred on Zapata's birthdate, and it also coincided with the 25th anniversary of Woodstock, an event that had given hope to Mexican students who had been so violently suppressed in 1968. The Zapatistas' gathering of stars and the improvised, communal aspects of the event—complete with torrential rains and the accompanying mudfest—helped to etch the rebellion deeply into the Mexican culture.

It was at this April 1994 meeting that the Zapatistas met leaders from the FAT and asked them to be their advisers on labor affairs. The FAT was eager to work with the Zapatistas, valuing in particular the EZLN's embrace of the Mayan ideal of participatory democracy, which closely paralleled the FAT's doctrine of autogestión. However, Alfredo Dominguez, named to be the FAT's liaison with the EZLN, pointed out that there were two serious complicating factors in the relationship: first, military organizations are structured hierarchically, and second, guns tend to inhibit dialogue. With those cautions in mind, the FAT embraced the Zapatista movement as part of the same struggle that they had been waging since 1960 and that workers and peasants had waged in Mexico since the conquest by the Spanish.

Support from throughout Mexico, Europe, the United States, and Canada was consolidated at the dramatically named "Forum for Humanity and Against Neoliberalism" held in June 1996. This international support—especially by human rights groups—has provided an important limit on the brutality of the government's continuing war of attrition. While this support has not prevented such atrocities as the massacre at Acteal of December 1997, it has forced the Mexican government to answer for its behavior at many international forums. The government must find these human rights visitors troubling because in the spring of 1997 it began expelling foreigners involved in monitoring the situation in Chiapas.

On March 21, 1999, the Zapatistas carried off another successful, and nonviolent, attack on the government's strategy to isolate them in a state of siege. They sent 5,000 masked but unarmed insurgents into city squares throughout the country to conduct a "consultation." They offered citizens a chance to respond to a series of loaded questions that, while bad social science, were great political theater. This event not only demonstrated support for the EZLN in all parts of the country and even in some Mexican communities in the United States, it also allowed the traveling Mayans to shore up political alliances wherever they went.

Despite strong support from the International Labor Organization and parliamentarians from Belgium and Germany, European labor unions were unsuccessful in their effort to force a social charter into the free trade agreement signed between the European Union and Mexico early in 2000. But they have repeatedly confronted the Mexican government on its human rights abuses whenever it sends dignitaries to Europe. The forces of the global market seem terribly ironic as they convince the Mexican government that its policy of oppressing and exploiting its peasants and workers is correct, but that it must be carried out in a way that does not upset the conscience of major investors or their happy consumers.

Labor's Approach to the Democratic Opening

The burgeoning civil society that embraced the Zapatistas and made life difficult for the neoliberal PRI also supported a more combative labor arena. The FAT and other labor formations have attempted to take advantage of this opening.

In 1995 the Foro—so called because it initially worked by holding forums on topics of great concern to workers—came into existence in response to two issues: the economic collapse of the nation and the government's policy of privatization. It brought together several service-sector unions that felt it was time to stand up to government policies that threatened their unions' interests. The unions' leaders complained that the government no longer considered workers when they made policy decisions. They harshly criticized the old leadership of the CT and the CTM, and they called for a renovation of the nation's labor unions.

Mexico City's electrical workers' federation, the SME, took the initiative to organize the Foro because they feared the government would soon privatize their utility, resulting in job losses and wage cuts. They had an insurgent style, inherited from the democratic tradition of the electrical workers of the 1970s, but their vulnerability led them to seek support from whoever they thought could help them the most at any moment. All within the Foro openly criticized the state of labor relations in Mexico, but while some, like the FAT, hoped to completely overthrow the charros, other groups often appeared most interested in restoring the privileges they had enjoyed when the state had more goodies to channel through them.

The leadership of the FAT responded to the Foro's call to other unions with cautious optimism. Within a year the FAT's metalworkers' union became part of the Foro's 25 affiliated unions. They joined to push forward the call to democratize unions and to reorient national economic policy, but they worried that many of the other unions had a long history of close ties to the PRI's power structure.

When the Foro attempted to define its goals and objectives, the larger unions—telephone workers, Social Security employees, and teachers—took the initiative, having better facilities to host meetings and more paid staff to draft and revise documents. Jorge Robles, an intellectual and organizer shaped by the student movement of 1968 and the FAT's 1974 strike at Spicer, was one of the FAT's representatives. Two examples from the drafting process show the difference between the FAT's vision, as proposed by Robles, and that of the major Foro unions.

> DRAFT: It is necessary to recover the capacity of unions to intervene forcefully in the tripartite organs of the state, [and] in the negotiation of pacts and agreements on social, economic, and labor policies.
>
> FAT: It is necessary to recover the organizational capacity of the workers, which begins in strengthening the structures of unions within the workplace, recovering the most fundamental principle of union democracy in which the workers themselves make decisions about their issues, converting their union representatives into spokespeople of grassroots organizations. Only when the workers themselves, through their delegates, speak, propose, reject, agree to, and finally carry into practice, said agreements can workers really recover their power of negotiation.

Here we see the contrast between unionists comfortable working at the top of a bureaucracy on behalf of workers and the FAT, which wants union delegates to be expressions of the wishes of empowered workers.

> DRAFT: We must build a unionism that places human needs above the demands of capital and the market.
>
> FAT: We must construct a unionism that places human needs above the demands of the state and capital.

Here the FAT makes clear the its distrust of the governing structures that the draft fails to question.

The FAT won most of the ideological battles, and the final adopted document was in keeping with the radically democratic values of the FAT. But unlike the FAT, the main complaint of most Foro union leaders was not the lack of democracy within their unions. For many, their vision was to become the new intermediaries of the working class in dialogues with the state. Although the Foro documents professed to condemn those old ways, the language was often flouted in practice.

While it is impossible to predict the future, it may be helpful to analyze some of the key dynamics that, to date, have shaped recent efforts to reform the shape of union politics in Mexico. The analysis that follows is contentious, especially in its close attention to two personalities whose role in the future is uncertain. It is, however, consistent with the ideas of several Mexican academics gracious enough to have long discussions with this author, with their writings, with the writings of many Mexican journalists, and the writings of several US-based academics.[3] This analysis does not rest on the goodness or evil of its protagonists, rather, it seeks to show the sorts of leadership styles that were rewarded under the PRI-dominated labor system, styles of leadership that will cause real problems in any sincere effort to democratize that system.

Caudillos or Coalitions: The Foro and the UNT

In October 1996, when President Zedillo was preparing to impose a new social pact setting limits on salary hikes and basic prices, he began his traditional consultations with official union leaders. At the last moment, four leaders of the Foro representing electricians, teachers, telephone workers and the Revolutionary Workers Confederation (COR)[4] entered into the negotiations. Acting in the name of the Foro, but with no permission to do so, they managed to increase the wage hikes from 15% to 17%.[5] This hike was not trivial—although inflation for the year did exceed 17%—but it did legitimate the structure of corporatist pacts that the Foro had officially condemned, and it did so in the old style of deal-making between individual leaders with no involvement of other members of the Foro, let alone the rank and file.

The key rival powers within the Foro were the teachers and the telephone workers. The teachers' union, SNTE, with 1.2 million members, is Mexico's largest union. Its members are better educated than most and they have a heritage of both teaching and actively promoting the nation's revolutionary values. The SNTE is partly an arm of its former secretary-general, Elba Esther Gordillo, who promotes herself as a progressive force in the labor movement. She also has been the leader of the Popular Sector of the PRI, an extremely important post within the party. Gordillo was made head of the SNTE by President Salinas when it became obvious that a corrupt leader needed to be replaced by a modernizing one in order to prevent the democratic dissidents from gaining control.[6] She seemed clearly willing to promote reform in order to maintain the power of the PRI. Through her the Institute of Education and Union Studies of America (whose source of funds is not entirely transparent), she promoted a lavish series of seminars in the summer of 1996 on the topic of modernizing the labor movement. While they burnished her image, they promoted no action. The SNTE has a huge number of dissidents within its ranks, including many who believe that Gordillo resorted to murder to secure her position of power.[7]

Rivaling Gordillo for leadership within the Foro was Francisco Hernandez Juarez, the head of the national telephone workers' union, STRM. Hernandez Juarez won the post of STRM secretary-general in 1976 as the head of an anti-charro coalition. In order to secure his tenuous position, he got his supporters to abolish the union's prohibition against reelection, and he has been in the post ever since. Although he initially kept some distance from the PRI, in 1984 he recommended that STRM members vote for the PRI, and in 1987 he was elected president of the CT. In 1989 President Salinas, seeking to promote a leader more interested in modernizing labor relations than Fidel Velazquez, supported Hernandez Juarez in the creation of a new federation in the service sector, FESEBS. (When Hernandez Juarez convinced the seven FESEBS unions to join the Foro, he came in with extra support.)

Hernandez Juarez negotiated new labor contracts with the national phone company, Telmex, when it was privatized. The new contract focused on increasing productivity of the company and preparing for competition with international telecommunications corporations. It also managed to preserve most jobs and to maintain salary levels. Salinas was so happy with him that he often took him abroad to display a new type of union leader "capable of understanding that we live in new times."[8] Throughout the '90s he sat in the top councils of the PRI.

Both Hernandez Juarez and Gordillo owe their advancement in large part to former president Salinas. These close party ties and their strong, personality-based leadership styles caused many to see them as *caudillos,* a combination of hero and ruthless boss. They both represent a wing of the PRI that sought to modernize labor relations, and politics in general, in the context of a new global economy. Their different strategies for renovating the PRI and their strong personal ambitions led to a major clash within the Foro.

Gordillo sought to use the Foro to stimulate reform of the CT and labor board system—a renovation of labor relations—while Hernandez Juarez sought to completely replace the labor dinosaurs who resisted any changes that might threaten the perquisites of power to which they had become accustomed. The difference came to a head in 1997 when the Foro moved to promote a national assembly of workers and to call for the founding of a new labor federation, the National Union of Workers (UNT).

Gordillo feared such a move could be seen as a call to workers to abandon the PRI. That would be unwise in a major election year in which control of the Congress and the capital city were at stake and the votes of workers were desperately needed. Although she was unable to prevent the formation of the UNT she was able to delay it until well after the July election. SME and the COR joined the teachers in refusing to join the new federation. Hernandez Juarez, apparently not content with the influence he had as first among equals in FESEBS, pushed aggressively for a new federation that could break the power of the dinosaurs in the CT. As both chief advocate and key celebrity, he assumed he would also be the dominant voice in the UNT. More power in the UNT might gain him more power within the PRI. However, the FAT joined the push for the UNT for its own reasons, eager to mobilize as many unions a possible in a movement that could potentially force the state to alter its labor policies.

The UNT, claiming a membership of 1.3 million workers and peasants, was officially born November 28, 1997, in a traditional *magno evento.* There were speeches, banners, and music. In a reminder that the dangers of clientelism and caudillos were not consigned to the past, most of the thousands of workers, paid to attend and hauled in on buses, seemed more interested in cheering for leaders of their own unions than anything else. Speeches condemned the CT as a useless, empty shell. The central principles approved at the event were quite distinct from those practiced by the old labor federation. They celebrated "democracy, autonomy, and independence for unions" from any political party.

The UNT's initial leadership structure reflected its stated desire to be "democratic, plural, and inclusive." It has three presidents and eight vice presidents to prevent its being captured as a tool of personal power and creating a new caudillo like Fidel Velazquez.

One of the eight named as vice presidents was Benedicto Martinez of the FAT. Another was Alejandra Barrales, head of the flight attendants' union. In her address to the founding gathering she stressed that those in attendance must be sure that their leaders follow the UNT's rules and insist on accountability to the base.[9]

The birth of the UNT attracted an impressive array of foreign unionists. Delegates arrived from Chile, Brazil, Italy, France, and the United States. They included leaders of federations, such as the AFL-CIO, that had previously restricted its Mexican contacts to official labor organizations like the CTM and the CT. It was obvious that these international unions were seeking alliances with what they hoped would be a new union movement within Mexico. Many of them stayed on to attend the National Congress of the FAT being held just south of Mexico City.

In the short time it has existed, the UNT has emerged as an alternative voice to the PRI-favored CT. While most UNT actions have taken place in the capital, its existence has encouraged organizing among affiliated unions throughout the country. In some cases, this has led to a new air of independence in local unions. On December 4, 1998, the UNT called all of its associated unions to hold a two-hour strike to protest the government's economic policies. This action was noticed throughout the country, but little disruption resulted and, despite threats of continuing actions, there has been no follow-up to date. Through the person of Hernandez Juarez, the UNT has intervened to arrange negotiations between government officials and strikers both in the case of Han Young in Tijuana and also in the Duro Bag strike that broke out in June 2000. In each case positive agreements were soon ignored by company and government officials. However, the UNT helped workers gain access to a national press audience and served to put additional pressure on the charro system. When that system fails to respond to such pressure, it accumulates one more straw upon its camel-like back, a back that some day may break.

Having a widely recognized voice of workers organized beyond the control of the PRI appears to be important. In the weeks following his election as president, Vicente Fox met with leaders of the UNT as well as with Rodriguez Alcaine of the CTM to hear their advice on labor matters.

On July 29, in a bid to increase its influence in the fluid post-electoral politics, the UNT called for the formation of the United Convergence Front. One of the three UNT co-presidents, Augustin Rodriguez declared, "The old wild beast [the CT and CTM] is dead. Now the UNT has a chance to convert itself into a great pole of attraction that can construct a real, transparent democratic labor unionism to defend and fight for workers' legitimate concerns."[10]

One of the first PRI activists to meet with Fox after the election was Elba Esther Gordillo. Speculation began circulating that she might serve as the new secretary of education. By mid-August—two weeks after the UNT's call for a new alliance—the unions with which she had proposed the Foro and boycotted the UNT—the SNTE, COR, and SME—now called for the formation of a National Workers Front and invited members of the CT to join them.[11] Gordillo's union, the SNTE, declared that all future leaders would be elected by direct universal vote.[12] Lopez Mayren of the COR declared that the old days of government-controlled unions were, "buried with the electoral defeat of the PRI."[13] We will have to wait and see about that, just as we will have to wait and see whether these recent changes are true democratic reforms on behalf of workers, as their proponents claim, or whether they are simply another round of political maneuvering by those who grew into leadership under the PRI's old system of control. It is possible that they are a mixture of both.

Freeing May Day from the Charros

May Day in Mexico, and most of the world, is celebrated as Labor Day. Specifically it recalls the US workers who, in 1886, called a general strike for the eight-hour day. It pays particular homage to the "martyrs of Chicago," the anarchist and socialist leaders framed for the bombing of police officers at Haymarket Square in Chicago. Business leaders and the press used the murder to discredit the entire labor movement and set back the cause of the eight-hour day for decades. But workers abroad have never forgotten these workers' bold example.

While most US workers are shocked to learn the degree to which Mexican workers have been cheated of their rights by their oppressive system of labor control, few realize the extent to which we in the United States have also been misled. The history of May Day has been obliterated from the popular memory due to the deliberate collusion of the reformist Samuel Gompers of the AFL and the interests of capital. Both sought to eliminate the more left-wing sector of the labor movement. Their efforts included sponsoring drives for a Labor Day celebration in September rather than May.

In Mexico, May Day was traditionally celebrated with a huge march of workers past the National Palace in Mexico City's Zocolo. There, the president, supposedly the embodiment of the Revolution, would stand on his balcony while hundreds of thousands of workers filed by in their official union contingents to give thanks to him for all he had done for them. This ritual became hard to sustain in the radical days of the '70s. It got harder when government policy began to reverse workers' gains in the '80s. With the economic collapse of early 1995 the ruling elites decided to avoid a potential disaster. They simply canceled the May Day celebrations.

With little time to organize, many independent unions and other social and political activists formed the May First Inter-Union Coordinator and issued a call for an independent workers' march and celebration. A huge contingent marched from Chapultepec Park to the Zocolo, about three miles away, and rejoiced at being able to express their outrage in space they had taken from the ruling party.

The marchers included large groups of workers laid off by various businesses. University unions and students joined with members of the radical soft drinks cooperative, Pascual, and members of the combative but defeated Ruta 100 bus drivers' union. The FAT showed up in large numbers. Dissident factions from several official unions, including the Social Security workers and the democratic faction of the teachers' union, contributed contingents. People carried posters of Zapata and of the Zapatistas' Marcos in his ski mask. The Asamblea de Barrios (assembly of neighborhoods) marched with their masked "wrestler of evil forces," Super Barrio.

Members of the middle-class debtors' organization, Barzon, arrived with their tractors or horses, broadening the May First march explicitly beyond labor and into a critique of PRI's neoliberal economic policies. *El Barzón*, the part of the harness that pulls the real weight, is the name chosen by the activist group of debtors that formed in the wake of the huge currency devaluation in the early weeks of 1995. Owners of many mid-size farms and small businesses, bankrupted when their dollar-denominated debts nearly doubled due to the deflation of the peso, rightly felt that they had been productive citizens and that their misfortunes were due to no fault of their own. They were outraged that government policy protected bankers more than debtors. The group made their demands for change known through a series of actions including shutting down the border crossings of El Paso-Ciudad Juarez and Tijuana-San Diego, occupying bank offices, surrounding the Congress with their tractors, and producing numerous policy statements, studies, and demands.

Another key group joining the 1995 May First march was the National Coordinator of the Education Workers (CNTE). A dissident, strongly left-wing, pro-democratic current within SNTE, the huge teachers' union, the CNTE began in 1979 and has been particularly strong in poor states with large indigenous populations, including Chiapas, Oaxaca, Guerrero, and Michoacan. Mobilization of teachers in reaction to the 1988 election fraud led to the consolidation of CNTE leadership in Section 7, representing Chiapas, Section 22 of Oaxaca, and Section 9, representing the elementary school teachers of Mexico City. In recent years, the CNTE has refused to go along with the pay raises negotiated by SNTE leaders, often holding marches of thousands of teachers for hundreds of miles from Oaxaca to Mexico City, then occupying several city blocks around the national education secretariat for weeks at a time.

The CNTE, a vital anti-government, anti-PRI force in many parts of the country, was seen as a real threat by the PRI elites. Many of its activists in rural parts of Oaxaca and Guerrero have been rounded up and accused of supporting the guerrilla factions there.[14] Leaders in Mexico City have been abducted, beaten, and threatened when emerging from political meetings.

Section 9, representing 58,000 primary school teachers of Mexico City, is the largest union local in the country. It has significant resources and, like all CNTE sections, its leaders are quite militant, sometimes referring to themselves as the heart of the revolutionary movement. In the summer of 1998 the SNTE's national leadership tried to impose new leadership on Section 9. Failing to overcome the electoral strength of CNTE, they refused to recognize the new elected leadership. When the CNTE members took their protest to the national legislature and got a bit rowdy, the government happily filed charges against the leaders and clapped them in jail. Nationwide and international protests led to the release of the leaders. However, SNTE and government leaders continued to wield the threat of new indictments. Not until late April 1999, after an all-night negotiating session between Esther Gordillo and Blanca Luna of Section 9, did SNTE agree to recognize the results of the local's elections and release funds it had been withholding for nine months. In return Luna agreed to allow Gordillo to appoint several additional members to the section's executive committee and to soften its criticism of SNTE's leadership.[15]

While the PRI made clear its determination to see that charros, not revolutionaries, controlled the resources of Section 9 in the run-up to the 2000 elections, Section 9 activists maintained their broad involvement on the left and received support from a nationwide CNTE that seemed to be active in more states than ever. The PRI's pressure did, however, succeed in splitting the CNTE. In December 1999, Blanca Luna opened new offices outside the Section 9 headquarters and, at the national CNTE convention later that month, she led a walkout by a third of the delegates.[16]

While some grumbling persists among dissident teachers, their more serious problem is the government's policy of superficially decentralizing decisions on education. In the late 1990s this forced teachers to negotiate in separate states despite their organization on a national level. In 2000 they ended their traditional weeks of sit-in demonstrations in the capital with a decision to reevaluate their tactics while maintaining their commitment to restoring the purchasing power their salaries lost in previous decades, increasing the resources available to their schools, and militantly supporting various struggles to democratize Mexico, beginning with their own union and including the May First coalition.

The May First Inter-Union Coordinator (CIPM) is an extremely diverse organization, but much of its most vocal leadership is firmly rooted within the left-wing labor tradition, the same tradition that nurtured the FAT since the '50s. A large majority of the CIPM's leadership were involved in the Insurgencia Obrera in the '70s. They see the world in terms of class conflict, with the state and the ruling party as servants of the capitalist class. Thus they seek complete autonomy from the state, the eventual elimination of capitalist oppression, and the establishment of some sort of democratic socialism.

This ideological clarity has certain advantages. Most CIPM members do not wish to waste time in dialogue with the CT, the CTM, or even the Foro. They see the Foro as neo-charros. In the October of 1997, before the Foro could form the UNT, the CIPM called into being its own "National Congress" of the working class. It resolved:

> We will not participate in the UNT. As currently planned, this organization will be born with very limited power to mobilize people and with corporatist tendencies. The continuation of the practices of the CT and the CTM can be seen in the UNT with the leading role played by Hernandez Juarez, who hopes to assume the position of the new voice of the union movement.[17]

The FAT has chosen to participate in both the CIPM and the Foro/UNT. While it feels at home with the sharper ideological critique of the CIPM, the FAT has a long history of trying to work with broad coalitions that may increase the possibility of change either by mobilizing popular pressure or through a more democratic governmental process.

May Day! May Day!: The PRI in Distress

Since 1995 Mexico's May Day demonstrations have signified the impending shipwreck of the PRI and the system that kept the party afloat for so long. For those in the opposition, the spontaneous filling of the Zocolo with well over a hundred thousand people was a marvelous chance to celebrate their growing strength.

The decision of the ancient Fidel Velazquez and President Zedillo not to hold their usual Labor Day March in 1995 broke a tradition established in 1925 and amounted to an admission that the PRI could no longer control a mobilized labor movement. At an official commemoration of the day held behind closed doors at the headquarters of the railworkers' union, Zedillo, addressing the small crowd of railworkers, urged the worker not to be led astray by noisy critics but to trust the neoliberal economic model that would soon lead to an economic recuperation. The heads of the CT and the railworkers' union both spoke as well, thanking the president for his support and for leading the economic restoration of the country. Neither even hinted at the abysmal conditions suffered by most of the working class.

In 1996 the CT also canceled its May Day parade, while both the Foro and the CIPM called marches. They agreed to have them at different times since they could not agree on a common message. Between the two of them they filled the Zocolo with over a quarter million workers over a space of seven hours. The FAT marched in both parades and was the only organization to do so.

Despite their inability to exist in the same time and space, the marches did agree on jointly publishing a Manifesto to the Nation, which urged President Zedillo "not to insist on imposing a neoliberal economic model, which has impoverished 40 million Mexicans and left 10 million young people without work while enriching only 37 families in the whole country."[18] In most of the states, official unions still held their official parades thanking the government for its good help, although several of these featured incidents of workers booing their leaders or distributing anti-government literature. The FAT held its own marches in some states. In Leon, Guanajuato, FAT marchers paraded with a huge, many-headed monster representing neoliberalism that was set on fire when they reached the central square.

In 1997 official unions held another indoor event in Mexico City's National Auditorium with President Zedillo. Admission was by invitation only and tightly controlled, yet critical messages slipped into the official celebration through the banners workers carried. The two-part messages must have been folded in half when they passed the censors. One read, "Oilworkers With Zedillo! We Want Real Wages!" Another proclaimed, " Mr. President, Tourist Guides Support Your Policies! We Struggle for Wages That Rise with Inflation!"

For the first time ever, CTM leader Fidel Velazquez (referred to in some press accounts as "not yet officially dead") was unable to attend. His second-in-command ended a long speech to an increasingly disorderly crowd with "For the workers organized in the Congress of Labor there is no doubt. Our political convictions place us on the side of the PRI!" Workers throughout the hall broke into loud choruses of "*Boo!*"

The crowd was more respectful for President Zedillo, who had been seen hastily amending his speech in the midst of the unruly crowd. He was interrupted only once with jeers, when he began to speak of his economic successes. Yet as he was leaving, a small group of workers took up the cheer, "*Hermano Zedillo, ya llena mi bosillo!*" (Brother Zedillo, fill my pockets now!).[19]

A long analytical piece in Mexico's equivalent to the *Wall Street Journal* was titled "CTM: Goodbye to the Streets." It found three possible conclusions to be drawn from the events: (1) While the CTM still had formal representation of the majority of Mexican workers, it had no control over them. Given this, it wondered how the PRI could keep awarding political positions to labor leaders. (2) There was no parade because there was nothing to give thanks for. However, the function of the CTM should not be to thank the president but to represent the workers. Failing to march meant giving up this role. Nonetheless, labor leaders shamelessly thanked the president. (3) PRI leaders simply didn't know what to do within the CTM or with the CTM.[20]

Dissident workers all over the country either held their own independent parades of protest or showed up in protest at the official celebrations. In Guerrero, workers booed the governor, who had many of them arrested, while others handed out literature encouraging support for anti-PRI guerrillas. In Veracruz a traditional parade was held to thank the PRI governor. When the vendors' union passed his balcony, instead of marching by, they stopped and stripped to the waist, to dramatize their state of impoverishment. Teachers throughout the country showed their disgust with the government. While many unions continued their traditional practice of threatening to dock workers three days' wages if they didn't march, in Nuevo Leon, workers were offered a three-day bonus if they did march.[21] Even in remote regions, the facade of a labor movement supportive of the PRI had been shattered.

May 1998 saw the PRI attempt to reassert itself with a public celebration of May Day, held in the Zocolo with shouts of "Viva Zedillo!" Slightly over 30,000 workers from official unions were hauled into the Zocolo by 9 a.m.—a faint echo of the two million that used to pass by in the heyday of official corporatist unions. Members of the teachers' union, SNTE, not only presented President Zedillo with a union hat, they also clamored—less respectfully—for real raises. Mostly, the workers listened in silence and the official rally broke up by 9:35, before the marches of the UNT and the CIPM began to arrive at 10. The CIPM and UNT marches were a replay of 1997—large, noisy, and critical.

In 1999, the PRI repeated the scenario of 1998 with an official rally, including the president and unionists hauled in early in the morning, before the huge independent marches could arrive. Many workers sported the new hats, shoes, or running pants their unions had given them for the event. The press noted that union members did not even pretend to cheer Zedillo or their leaders. Even when the president called out, "Viva Mexico!" no one joined in.

The independent marches were larger and more confident than ever, with three simultaneous marches with massive numbers of workers converging on the Zocolo for over five hours. There had not been such a massive display of workers' unity and defiance of the system since the combative days of the '70s. The 1999 march was swollen by two significant factors.

SME, the capital city's electrical workers, were protesting Zedillo's efforts to change the constitution to allow the sale of the electrical energy sector. SME had a history of militant activism. Unable to protect themselves by playing inside politics, SME workers were not shying away from the fight with the PRI. This was in contrast to the larger electrical workers' union, SUTERM, headed by the chief dinosaur, Leonardo Rodriguez Alcaine, the head of the CT and the CTM, and successor to Fidel Velazquez. The privatization of Mexico's electrical sector had been suggested by international bankers and supported by technocrats in the government, the chief of which was Zedillo. But the sale would require changing the constitution back to the way it was in the bad old days of Porfirio Diaz, when only the rich and the foreign had a say in Mexico's affairs. Putting the nation's energy supply in the hands of foreign capitalists was seen as a threat to the nation's sovereignty. And the opponents had studies available to show that in other countries privatization had led to rising energy costs for consumers.

Zedillo's plan was the perfect foil against which to rally the majority of the nation. Since Mexico City had already elected a PRD government in 1997, it was clear where the sentiments of its 20 million people lay. And Mexicans generally were outraged at the direction the country had taken since the early '80s, when the PRI had let the International Monetary Fund reorient their country. The SME created the National Resistance Front Against the Privatization of the Electrical Industry, gathering support from unions, social groups, and individuals—even PRI politicians—for months before May Day. SME led one of the three marches to converge on the Zocolo. It was huge and included 500 members of Alcaine's own SUTERM, none of them sporting new hats or shirts.

The other group that swelled the march was the students on strike at the enormous National Autonomous University of Mexico, UNAM. Their struggle resonated well with all the others. Mexico's constitution calls for free public education. Most universities had been charging modest tuition fees for some years, but UNAM, having imposed a fee decades earlier, had not adjusted it for inflation. Therefore it was so insignificant, it was not worth collecting. In the spring of 1999 the rector of the university imposed tuition fees over popular objections. In the words of one writer, he was "transforming rights into paid services ... subordinating rights to the market." And few were willing to believe that there was not enough money in the budget to pay for education when there were billions to bail out banks and the capitalists who had gone bankrupt trying to run the nation's highways "more efficiently" as privatized toll roads. Few could believe charging tuition was the only way the government could meet the needs of its people when it was "meeting the needs of the people" by stationing 40,000 troops in Chiapas.[22]

The participation of students, debtors, barrio organizations, and other social movements not only made for a larger march, they also demonstrated the growth and breadth of opposition forces intending to democratize the country and improve the lot of average citizens. Despite their differences, the labor organizations in the three 1999 marches published a unified call declaring:

> Our unity is based on struggle for a change of the neoliberal economic policy, for a real social and democratic reform of the state, and in the democratic transformation of the mechanisms and structures that define, decide, and apply the public policies of our country, especially in the areas of education, health, energy, telecommunications, political economy, etc.[23]

May Day 2000 saw the same three independent marches in Mexico City and the same quickie official event early in the morning. What was new was the steady growth of independent marches in the states, at least 20 of which had marches that criticized government policies and called for respecting workers' rights. Many of these were organized by local expressions of the UNT. The president's official rally in Mexico City had an air of utter unreality. While Alcaine had predicted the CT would mobilize 200,000 workers for the event, barely 20,000 showed up, and most of these refused to utter a word of support, even when President Zedillo called out to them. Alcaine did have a moment of lucidity when he declared that the government needed to address the issues of inadequate wages, unaffordable housing, and businesses' refusal to share profits with workers. But then he pledged that the CT would "maintain its total support of the political transformation of the country and the effort of President Zedillo to consolidate a strengthened economy ... rejecting the utopias of retrograde and denigrating oppositions."[24]

Zedillo responded that there would be "not even one step back in the conquests of the workers, but that, shoulder to shoulder, they would defend the right to dignified work, a just salary, and good benefits."[25]

If the official labor pep rally was full of hollow words, the three marches of the independents lacked spirit. And clearly, the fact that the three oppositional currents were, again, unable to agree on a common event indicated the fragmented nature of the movement. One sympathetic observer, Hector de la Cueva, remarked: "Right now, this struggle is frozen. Everyone is waiting for the political system to come apart in July. Maybe then vigor will return to the movement."[26]

The PRI had been committed to an economic policy that hurt the fortunes of the majority of Mexico's people for nearly two decades. Yet, forces beyond its control forced it to make Mexico's political process more democratic, to include the very people its policies had damaged. Those contradictory pressures resulted in the defeat of the PRI's presidential candidate and the election of Vicente Fox of the conservative PAN in the election of July 2000. But, contrary to the wishes of the May Day marchers, the PAN's policies are likely to leave those same, corporate-friendly economic policies in place. The issue of reforming Mexican labor law looms in the near future with no certain outcome. While the rejection of the worst aspects of the PRI's policies has now been made quite clear, many in Fox's party, for the sake of greater "efficiency," seek to dismantle the legal protections for workers that have often been ignored in practice. The workers organized in the CIPM, the UNT, and other independent movements are far from united. We have seen that the habits of thought and action of many in the UNT have been shaped by their years in the PRI's corporatist system. It is hard to imagine many within the CIPM supporting any compromise legislation that might come through the political process. At this point the FAT is committed to continuing what it has always done: work to educate and empower workers, democratize unions, and build the broadest coalitions possible to democratize Mexico.

Notes

1   Muñoz, Patricia, and Judith Calderón. 1997. "Aumentó 171% la Canasta Basica en Dos Años; los Salarios 71%." *La Jornada* (January 21).

2   Ross, John. 1995. *Rebellion from the Roots: Indian Uprising in Chiapas*, 361. Monroe, Maine: Common Courage Press.

3   While the analysis offered is solely the author's, it is encouraged by the thinking of academics and other writers cited frequently throughout this book including, but not limited to: Luis Hernandez Navarro, Elizabeth Velasco, Claudia Herrera Beltran, Andrea Becerril, Jose Orthon Quiroz Trejo, Luis H. Menez Berrueta, Graciela Bensusan, Enrique de la Garza, Luis Angel Gomez, Ignacio Medina, David Bacon, Philip Russell, Dan La Botz, and Tom Barry.

4   When the COR, a small federation, challenged the CTM at Ford's Cuautitlán plant in 1990, the CTM sent in 200 armed men, who killed one COR supporter while wounding 12. Yet the predominance of COR's ties to the PRI were emphasized in 1997 when COR head Joel Lopez Mayren agreed to accept the leadership of the entire Labor Congress, the CT, for a year. Account of COR at Cuatitlan from La Botz, Dan. 1992. *Mask of Democracy: Labor Suppression in Mexico Today*, 148-59. Boston: South End Press.

5   Becerril, Andrea, Roberto González A., and Roberto Garduño. 1996. "Alza en Tarifas Electricas; Se Evito en las Domesticas, Dicen Foristas." *La Jornada* (October 27).

6   Russell, Philip P. 1994. *Mexico Under Salinas*, 294-96. Austin, Texas: Mexico Resource Center.

7   The allegation comes from two active members of CNTE's Section 9 in Mexico City (oral interview July 10, 1996; Mexico City). One of them says his life was directly threatened by Manuel Camacho Solis, then head of Mexico City's government, who he believes was instructed by Gordillo. They also believe she was involved in ordering the murders of many CNTE activists in the state of Oaxaca. Phillip Russel puts the number of CNTE activists murdered at 150. Russel, 295.

8   *Proceso* 1992 (May 18): 22.

9   Union Nacional de Trabajadores: UNT. 1997. *Estatuto*, Working Draft of December, 11. Mexico, DF: UNT.

10   La Botz, Dan. 2000. " Mexican Labor Faces Greatest Crisis in 65 Years." *Mexican Labor News and Analysis,* 5: 5 (August).

11   Velasco, Elizabeth. 2000. "Convocaran a crear un frente nacional de trabajadores." *La Jornada*, August 17.

12   Herrera Beltran, Claudia. 2000. "Contra la extincion del SNTE, la reforma, propone Vazquez Vigil." *La Jornada*, July 27.

13   Velasco.

14   The Popular Revolutionary Army (EPR) emerged in the states of Guerrero and Oaxaca in 1996. Despite its name, it seems to lack the overt popular support that made it impossible for the PRI to treat the Zapatistas as solely a military threat. The government has used the appearance of the EPR as an excuse to attack politically active teachers and organizations of peasants.

15   La Botz, Dan. 1999. "Teachers Union 'Official' Leadership Reaches Agreement with Local 9 Exec." *Mexican Labor News and Analysis* (May 2).

16   Herrera Beltrán, Claudia. 1999. "Teme más ataques la líder magisterial Blanca Luna." *La Jornada* (December 2). "Abandonan 130 delegados el quinto congreso de la CNTE." *La Jornada* (December 20).

17   CIPM. 1997. "Primer Congreso Nacional Resolutivo de la CIPM." *La Jornada* (October 4).

18   CIPM y el Foro Sindicalismo ante la Nacion. 1996. "Manifiesto a la Nación." *Excelsior* (May 2).

19   Gallegos, Elena, and Antonio Vázquez. 1997. "En el Auditorio, Rechiflas y Traspiés a Intentos Proselistas." *La Jornada* (May 2): 1.

20   Fernadez Mendez, Jorge. 1997. "CTM: Adios a las Calles." *El Financiero* (May 2): 21.

21   "Mejor Nivel de Vida, Piden Miles de Trabajadores en Todo el País." 1997. *La Jornada* (May 2): 53.

22   In January 2000, a new rector was appointed to head UNAM and to end the strike. He called for a referendum to end the strike, return to the original 20 *centavo* fee, and to continue to work on other complaints. When the strike leaders insisted on negotiating those other complaints before ending the strike, he called 2,000 federal police onto the campus to arrest over 700 strikers at dawn on Sunday, February 6. Later that week prosecutors charged 10% of those with "terrorism" and released the rest. The conflict has not been resolved as of this writing.

23   UNT, Fesebes, SME. 1999. "Unified Call." *Mexican Labor News and Analysis* (May 2). *La Jornada* (April 26).

24   Soto, Orquida. 2000. "Respaldan Obreros al Gobierno para Lograr una Economia Fortalecida." *El Economista* (May 2).

25   Soto.

26   Martínez, Fabiola, Karina Avilés, and Carolina Gómez. 2000. "La marcha de los independientes no logró unir consignas en una sola voz."

9.

For Justice and Democracy

> On a personal level, it makes my heart bleed to see how Mexican workers are treated. On a professional level, we simply can't permit it. We need to find a way to bring Mexicans up to our level so we don't have to go down to theirs.
>
> —Ian Robinson, Southern Arizona Central Labor Council, Tucson, June 22, 1999[1]

> We are fighting an unequal war between those who have all the military power (the government) and those who have only reason, history, truth, and tomorrow on their side (us). It is obvious who is going to win: we are.
>
> —Subcomandante Marcos, Zapatista Army of National Liberation, July 19, 1999[2]

When protesters in Seattle shouted, "This is what democracy looks like," they joined a centuries-long list of people who had been gassed or beaten, jailed or shot, for insisting on their right to be heard.

Powerful leaders, confident that they know best, have long looked with disgust on those seeking a voice where they were not welcome. The consensus of the wealthy framers of the US Constitution was that democracy was to be avoided as much as possible. For one, it was "like giving the choice of colors to a blind man." Another urged, "Let the people be taught ... that they are not able to govern themselves." John Jay, soon to be the first chief justice of the Supreme Court, declared simply, "The people who own the country ought to govern it."[3] Similarly, for delegates attempting to attend the WTO in Seattle, the main problem was that the police had not been more effective in keeping the masses at a distance.

For years international leaders had been assuring people that free trade was the surest vehicle to extend democracy and justice throughout the world. Yet in Seattle, President Clinton and several ministers from Third World countries agreed: the WTO—the embodiment of the free-trade mentality—lacked democracy and would have to change. What could democracy look like in a global economy? Would it bring justice?

George Orwell wisely warned us that words like "justice" and "democracy" are useless at best, weapons to manipulate our thoughts and actions at worst, unless we know clearly what they mean.[4] We must define them before we can achieve them. If ordinary working people don't define them, transnational corporations will continue to define them in terms of free markets and economic policies that redistribute wealth and political power for their benefit.

Justice for All

The Mexican constitution sets a fine minimum standard of justice: anyone who works full-time is entitled to adequate food, shelter, and clothing for themselves and their family, as well as access to education, healthcare, and a bit of entertainment. Too bad the Mexican reality is no where near as rosy as this ideal. If each of our countries could achieve that standard, we would be more just societies. But justice is not just about individuals. It is also about relationships.

Before Thomson Electronics closed one of the last TV assembly plants in the United States, its workers in Indiana were earning $440 a week. Their wages represented 8-10% of the price of the $500 large-screen televisions they turned out. Now workers with equal or greater productivity in Juarez get about $33 a week, or less than 1% of the television's price.[5] Simply put, that means less money is going to workers while more is going to managers and owners. The same thing is happening throughout the world.

In 1960 in the United States, the share of total personal income derived from wages and salaries was 66%. By 1997, as the economy became more internationalized and corporations became larger, that had fallen to 57%. What wasn't going into workers' paychecks was going to non-workers; meanwhile hours worked per week increased by nearly

10%.[6] The difference between wages and salaries of those at the top and those at the bottom had also widened sharply. The Gini coefficient is a measure of inequality that ranges from 0.0 when all households receive the same income to 1.0 when all income in an economy goes to one household. Higher numbers indicate greater inequality. The Gini coefficient for the United States was .399 in 1967. By 1980 it had risen slightly to .403. From there it surged, reaching .459 by 1997, an increase of 13.9%.[7] In Mexico inequality also rose, moving from .456 in 1984 to .514 in 1994, a rise of 12.7% in a shorter time period.[8] In even more graphic terms, while the Mexican economy grew at an impressive 5% per year from 1996 through 1999, it began the year 2000 with 28% of its population in extreme poverty, almost twice the rate for 1992, the year that NAFTA was being negotiated, and three times as many hungry mouths as when Mexico joined the GATT in the mid-1980s.[9]

Let us define justice in a way that corresponds with most people's emotional response to statistics like those above. If one individual becomes richer by making another individual poorer we would call that person a thief. If a society's economic growth is the result of increasing inequality, then that society is increasingly unjust. It is also probably less healthy in physical terms.[10] Economic justice means that at least the basic needs of a full-time worker and his or her dependents are met, while the distance between those at the top and those at the bottom grows smaller.

Democracy and Self-Management

Technically speaking, NAFTA was passed in Canada, the United States, and Mexico in accord with those countries' democratic procedures. But we have already seen that in each country it was passed in spite of majority opinion, or, in the case of Mexico, in spite of a deliberately uninformed majority that was never consulted. There is something criminally wrong with applying the word "democracy" to such situations. Let us try to do better.

A minimum standard for democracy is the simple notion of "majority rules," along with protections of everyone's civil rights regardless of whether they are in the majority or the minority. In a democracy citizens must be able to express themselves freely, to communicate their thoughts with each other, and to gather together for common purposes, and they must be able to hold their political leaders reasonably accountable to the will of the majority.

If we think a bit about the above conditions, we realize that, in order to hold elected leaders accountable, we must also know what they are doing. NAFTA, the WTO, and most international economic agreements have been deliberately negotiated without public awareness. As such, they violate even our minimal definition of democracy. Activists like those who obtained the secret "Dallas Draft" of the NAFTA treaty and then made it available to the public were working for democracy.

A more ambitious definition of democracy would be what the FAT calls autogestión. Briefly restated, autogestión requires that decisions are made by consensus rather than simple majority vote, that each person is able to be involved in the decisions that directly affect them, and that they have the right and the responsibility for carrying those decisions into practice. Decisions are made within an ethic of solidarity, a concern for each other, and a realization that each is a part of a related whole. Autogestión is made possible by an educational process that gives each the capacity to participate and that fosters continued learning so that decisions may improve over time. We have a long way to go to realize this standard. Yet it allows us to judge policies that lead us in this direction as more democratic, and those that make autogestión harder as anti-democratic.

Autogestión radically expands the scope of democracy to include not just formal political structures like presidents and congresses, but all aspects of our society, including the economic sphere. Decisions about trade policy, wage policy, job relocation, and working conditions clearly affect large numbers of people who currently have little or no influence on the decisions being made. The policy of privatizing government operations may sometimes be motivated by a desire to increase efficiency or simply to transfer wealth to friends of politicians. What we must not ignore is that it also moves decisions out of the public sphere and thus reduces the scope for democratic influence. The shift to a more globalized economy puts many decisions beyond the scope of governments, and thus makes them harder, as the world is currently constituted, to promote democracy.

Since people's ability to meaningfully participate in decisions is dependent on basic and continuing education, policies that link educational opportunities to income in a society with increasing income inequality are anti-democratic. To the extent that one's ability to participate in decisions at all is linked to one's economic resources, as in the case of lobbying a government official or establishing corporate policy on job relocation, those decisions are anti-democratic. A worker's ability to form a labor union that is controlled by the workers increases his or her ability to influence corporate policy otherwise reserved to corporate elites. Authentic labor unions are a fundamental requirement for making our current societies more democratic.

The final basic requirement for democracy is the ethic of solidarity. Individuals must see their common interests if they are to form the organizations they need to gain a voice in shaping society. Then they need still more solidarity to find their common interests with other organizations—labor, environmental, human rights, or other groups—whether those organizations are across town or in other countries.

According to our definitions, a more democratic society can produce a more just society by giving workers a voice in decisions that directly affect their lives, decisions from which they are otherwise excluded. And a more just society—one in which the basic needs of workers are met and equality is increasing—can produce a more democratic society because it will be a society of people increasingly able to participate in making the decisions that shape their lives.

One of the most ironic aspects of the global economy is that while it seems to be producing greater injustice, its chief promoters insist they are promoting more democracy. In Mexico, this has meant that as the government implemented economic policies required by international bank loans and neoliberal principles, it also became more involved in an international environment that required at least the facade of more democracy. As Mexico internationalized its economy, its people not only had more to be angry about, the government also had fewer carrots and sticks with which to control them. Greater injustice combined with greater democracy meant that the PRI, after holding power for so long, finally lost its grip.

This book has been primarily about the Mexican people's struggles for justice and democracy, but now we must ask, how can we build justice and democracy throughout North America, and throughout the global economy? What are some of the factors that need to be changed in Mexico and the United States, and what are the prospects for those changes? How can North American workers act as allies across their national borders? Strengthening the relationships between these very different but very interconnected nations will go a long way toward addressing the problems of the global economy.

Changing Conditions within Mexico

In the days of the Aztecs, the emperor and his priests could command warriors to bring sacrificial captives to the top of the pyramid. There the victims' hearts were torn out. The people were told this was necessary to keep the sun in the sky. In the late 20th century the priests have been economists and the emperor-president has been chosen from their ranks. The warriors they have sent to gather the sacrifice have been the government officials and cooperating union leaders who have offered workers at ever lower prices to the hungry, transnational gods of industry. The people have been told this is necessary.

The tiny Spanish invasion force that conquered the mighty Aztecs had several advantages, but they could have done nothing if those who had provided the steady source of sacrificial victims had not joined their side against the Aztec rulers. When the base of the social pyramid rose up against those at the top, their downfall was inevitable. Unfortunately, the Spaniards constructed a new pyramid of power, and the current system is just the most recent structure of it.

It is clear that the majority of Mexicans have not benefited from the policies handed down from on high. The Aztec warriors did not live as well as the priests, but they had their reasons to fight in defense of the system. The PRI's long chains of supporters, people who lived their lives dependent on the corporatist system of privileges and punishments, included the strike breakers and thugs who did the bidding of those above them in the hierarchy, not because they were evil, but because the system allowed them to see few alternatives. They could not imagine how they would live if they did not get the few benefits the charro system allotted to them.

Well above these people in the hierarchy of the PRI decades were the leaders of the official union. They have lived adequately within the system and many are pragmatic operators who will continue to do what they can to assure their access to the perquisites of power. At the top they are people like Hernandez Juarez of the telephone workers. He has one foot in the PRI and another one feeling for a foothold in the post-PRI power pyramid. Even Leonardo Rodriguez Alcaine, head of the CTM, is having problems with his executive committee. He has accused them of treating the union's resources like "economic plunder ... the spoils of war" and of introducing an "awful corruption." A member of the executive committee reveals that the main complaint Alcaine has is that there is "a river of money in dispute that is not reaching the union's national coffers."[11] The system of control is shaken and even old corrupt union bosses are no longer marching in lock-step. Further down the chain of command are other officials who are watching their options. Their loyalty to the old system is also highly uncertain. Their ability to make a meaningful contribution to the construction of a more just and democratic system is equally unclear.

The Election of 2000

The PRI's neoliberal economic policies steadily eroded both its public support and its ability to control dissent. Even the PRI politicians campaigning in their party's first-ever primary election for president found it necessary to criticize "an economic model that benefits only a few while the great majority not only don't gain, they get poorer every day."[12]

The pessimism about change that had resulted from the fraudulent election of Carlos Salinas in 1988 was largely reversed in 1997 when, for the first time since the Revolution, the PRI lost control of the Chamber of Deputies, the equivalent of the US House of Representatives. The PRD and the PAN, together with the smaller Labor Party (PT) and the Greens, formed an opposition alliance in the Congress, thus checking the president's hitherto unlimited power. The change was important, but the alliance was not always united. In the crucial vote over whether or not to bail out banks that had failed or found themselves in trouble due to poor business practices and corruption, the pro-business PAN joined with the PRI.

Many progressives, NGOs, and intellectuals whose desire for change was greater than their attachment to any political party pushed for a grand alliance of the opposition to endorse a common candidate for the presidential contest of 2000. Such a candidate, they felt, would almost certainly win. Putting an end to the PRI's control was essential for ending the corruption and impunity that had so long perverted the nation's politics. Only after breaking the stranglehold of the PRI could real reform begin. But the alliance was not to be. Neither the PAN nor the PRD was willing to yield, nor could they agree on rules for a national primary to let the people decide on a common candidate. In the ensuing three-way contest between the PRD's Cardenas, the PAN's Fox, and the PRI's Labastida, Fox led in most opinion polls as the mostly likely to unseat the hated PRI.

As it turns out, many on the left decided to cast their vote for Fox in what they described as "the pragamatic vote (*el voto útil*)." Given that he commands no majority in the Congress and has an uncertain relationship with his own party, Fox began reaching out to all parties and social movements soon after the election to put together a workable plan for governing. Alcaine, speaking for the CTM, asked Fox to preserve the corporatist structure of labor relations that has served it so well. The UNT, however, called for serious changes in the federal labor law, including the elimination of the federal commission on minimum salaries; the elimination of the "*requisa*," the ability of the government to seize the operations of an "essential" service when its workers are on strike; the elimination of the right of one union to have a monopoly on unionizing employees of a given government agency; the elimination of protection contracts and phantom unions; the promotion of the right to organize unions and conduct collective bargaining; and the internal democratization of unions.[13]

In the wake of the election there has been a new burst of activity responding to the possibility of greater democracy. At the top we have seen both the UNT and the Gordillo-SNTE-COR-SME group call for new federations to replace the dinosaur-led CT and CTM. To shore up the SNTE's legitimacy, its leadership called for direct elections of all future leaders. The head of the miners' union has been blocked from naming his own son to succeed him. From within the petroleum workers' union there is a demand for direct election of its leaders by means of secret ballot, and chief dinosaur Leonardo Rodriguez Alcaine faces a challenge for reelection within SUTERM, the first challenge in 28 years. His opponent declared, "With the democratization of the country, workers can no longer tolerate these dictators who perpetuate themselves in office [with] terrorist methods, intimidation and threats."

In Ciudad Juarez workers braved those methods to assert their rights. Five hundred workers from states who had been brought to the border by a contractor to build a government hospital stormed off the job, blocked streets and fought police sent to control them. "We didn't want to be treated like slaves," they declared, explaining that they had been paid half the wage promised them and forced to live in crude barracks locked within the construction site. Also in Juarez, 200 workers who had been fired in February by the Lear plant for organizing for better wages and working conditions surrounded the plant, declaring they would stop all shipments until they were at least paid their legal severance pay. Police beat and jailed several of the workers, and the company called in helicopters to fly out their products. But the bold new mood amongst the workers will not be so easily contained. The country's recent steps towards democracy in the electoral arena has led them to want the day to be soon when democracy can put food on their tables and remove naked exploitation from their daily lives.[14]

Between 1996 and 2000, Mexico's Volkswagen plant had increased production by a third while doubling its income from sales. At the same time, it had cut its labor costs from 10% to 3.7% of its total production costs. Yet when workers demanded a wage increase superior to the cost of inflation, government officials supported management's refusal to share the wealth by declaring the union's strike illegal. In a new sign of militant solidarity in the post election era, the UNT declared it would call its unions out in strike. The UNT declared it would "take to the streets and highways" to put pressure on the government and the businesses, and it would "battle with imagination" to protect workers' right to strike. As this book goes to press negotiations are on-going, marches have clogged highways, and several unions have filed notice that they would soon be going out on strike.[15] While the old system continues to protect the interests of international business against its own workers, workers are insisting that it is time for a new day to dawn.

Mexican workers have suffered in recent decades, not merely because they have lived under an oppressive political system, but also because their country has had to adapt to a new global economic system. Replacing the PRI will not change that global context. In August 1999 John Reed, president of the enormous US conglomerate Citigroup, was in Mexico to advise President Zedillo on the banking crisis. In a meeting with the press, he suggested that the international financial community would look very favorably on an opposition candidate as long as his party "demonstrates that it can change governments without changing economic course." Business does not care which party wins as long as its candidate "presents himself as a centrist."[16]

Reed was making clear the constraints of what was acceptable within the global economy. In Germany in 1998 voters chose a left-wing chancellor, Gerhardt Schroder, to lead them out of their declining position in the global economy. Within a year he had accepted the discipline of the global market and veered sharply to the right.[17] If the new Mexican government were to allow workers to raise their wages too close to the value of what they produce, it might find corporations drifting off to Guatemala or China to find workers sufficiently hungry and repressed to accept wages of a dollar or two a day.

Electoral change in Mexico is a necessary ingredient in building a more just and democratic society. But in this integrated world, it is not sufficient. It may no longer be possible to build democracy in one country.

Bearing in mind all the problems that face workers in Mexico, labor organizer Manuel Mondragon of Matamoros has a recurring complaint. He hates it when groups arrive to see the conditions of the "poor Mexicans" and then ask, "How can we help you?" He asks back, "Is everything wonderful where you work? Are labor rights respected in your country? Are your jobs secure?" He prefers the question, "How can we help each other?"

Changing Conditions within the United States

Workers in Mexico want stronger unions in the United States so US workers can work more effectively in the struggle to improve the global economy. While acknowledging horrendous abuses of workers rights in Mexico, we can't forget the miserable state of labor rights north of the

Rio Grande. A key indicator of the weakness of organized labor in the United States is that the percent of the workforce that belongs to unions is below 14%, less than half the level it was in 1960, far below its high mark of 35% in the mid-1940s. US workers lack an effective right to strike. Unlike their Mexican neighbors, they cannot legally shut down activities at a struck facility. Furthermore, since the early '80s, workers on strike are frequently fired and "permanently replaced."

A report prepared for the World Trade Organization lists a long series of problems facing US workers. Although the right to organize unions is protected by law, penalties for breaking labor laws are so limited and ineffective that corporations routinely flout them. At least 1 in 10 union supporters campaigning to form a union is illegally fired.

Employers also frequently engage in illegal surveillance and harassment of union supporters and hold illegal "captive meetings" at which employees are taught why they should not unionize. National Labor Relations Board procedures "do not provide workers with effective redress." The report also criticized the extensive use of child labor in agriculture and the expansion of the commercial exploitation of prison labor.[18]

Problems for US workers are often exacerbated by the ability of businesses to exploit Mexican workers. From 1993 to 1995, half of all US employers who faced a union organizing drive threatened to move their plant to Mexico. Where unions won organizing drives, 15% actually closed and moved to Mexico within two years. The actual shutdown rate within two years of unionization is triple the rate found in the late 1980s before NAFTA went into effect.[19] Meat packing used to be a highly paid, heavily unionized industry. Now the jobs pay $6 to $8 an hour, and, due to repetitive motion and rapid work with knives, is the most dangerous industrial occupation in the country.[20] Many of the workers are recruited in Mexico and bused to plants in the Plains states. They are needed to replace other Mexican workers who have been injured, decided to find better work, or been run off by the INS. Few local residents will take these jobs.

When the meat packers' unions were broken in the '70s and '80s and new businesses opened without unions, the plants were staffed by uprooted farmers and industrial workers suffering through years of high unemployment. Once US-born workers had other options in the expanding economy of the '90s, the low-quality jobs came to require the services of immigrants. The fact that many immigrant laborers have limited English or lack legal work status makes it less likely they will complain of the abuses they suffer. It will take unionization and/or serious health and safety inspections to bring these jobs up to a level consistent with human dignity, or even with current US law.

These problems are all tied to labor's lack of political power. Unions in the United States are tied to the Democratic Party much as the CTM has been tied to the PRI. Both complain about workers' problems, but both urge their members to support the party on election day. After decades of disappointment, Mexican workers and many union officials have deserted the PRI. Most US labor leaders still find pragmatic reasons to work with the Democratic Party. John Sweeney, head of the AFL-CIO since 1995, has decided on a three-pronged strategy to rebuild labor influence: spend heavily in elections and in lobbying Congress, increase efforts to organize workers, and educate workers whether they are unionized or not. At least in the Congress, the political fortunes of labor have improved since he took office as we can see by examining the cases of NAFTA and fast-track authority. Seeking further improvements, both the United Autoworkers and the Teamsters put the Democrats on notice by refusing to join Sweeney in an early endorsement of Democratic candidate Al Gore for president in 2000, and talked instead about the merits of Ralph Nader, the only candidate to support labor's positions on the global economy and corporate political influence.

NAFTA's Bastards

It is often said that politics produces strange bedfellows. The strange bedfellows that created NAFTA produced unwanted offspring known as the National Administrative Offices (NAOs) of Mexico, the United States, and Canada. Empowered to hear complaints that one of the three countries is failing to enforce its labor or environmental laws, the NAOs, so far, have pleased no one.

The NAOs and the side agreements that describe them came into existence only because enough people in the United States were upset by NAFTA. Clinton couldn't get the treaty through Congress without offering workers at least some fig leaf of democracy to cover the shameless corporate bonanzas embodied in the treaty. It is worth noting that the la-

bor and environmental side agreements to NAFTA are called such because the negotiators had entirely avoided those topics in the body of the
treaty. However, the fact that something was added also shows the needs
of elites to respond to workers' mobilization. The democratic process is
not entirely dead, even if it is unwanted. One analyst aptly called the side
accords "an unwanted bastard, ... one of the strangest institutional ex-
periments the neoliberal era has yet produced."[21]

As of June 1999, the three NAOs had received a total of 20 cases.[22]
Of these, eleven concerned Mexico, seven concerned the United States,
and two dealt with Canada. Of the cases dealt with so far, none has ended
any of the abuses detailed in the hearings.

Several cases have resulted in ministerial consultations. Some of
these have led to agreements to hold seminars addressing the underlying
issues involved in the complaint. Some have led to commissioned studies. Three cases so far have led to ministerial consultations[23] and "a series of programs designed to publicly address these concerns in all three
countries." These programs did nothing to resolve the issue that workers
were unable to choose their union leadership or to respond to abuses on
the job; therefore the complainants requested a follow-up review. "The
NAO conducted the follow-up review as directed and a report was issued on December 4, 1996."[24] That is the most serious consequence yet
imposed for violating NAFTA's labor side accords.

In the public seminar held in Tijuana designed to inform workers of
their freedom to organize unions, both the PAN (state) and PRI (federal)
demonstrated the depth of their cynicism about the process. Most available space was occupied, an hour before the meeting, by a large group of
students that had been used repeatedly to break up strikes and demonstrations in the city. Moctezuma Barragan, Mexico's undersecretary of
labor, began the seminar with a recitation of the progress made for workers under his government. When workers from Han Young and other
maquiladoras replied by raising signs demanding their rights be respected, they were attacked by the young thugs until they were driven
from the hall. Barragan explained to the press that evidently there had
been a lack of space in the hall. The seminar on workers' freedoms continued as planned.[25]

The best result of the side agreement is that it has encouraged labor
unions to work with each other across borders to publicize often outra-

geous abuses of labor law. The violations have been well substantiated by testimony and reports that are publicly available. The proceedings and reports have generated some publicity about labor abuses. While the side accords are structurally powerless to cause important changes in labor policy, making these cases more widely known may help create a political climate that could lead to significant change. At this point, no one can seriously argue that NAFTA protects workers' rights.

Stopping Fast Track

While the side accords were sufficient to win the passage of NAFTA in 1993, disillusionment with free trade has made it a harder sell since then. Many congressional representatives who bought the Clinton administration's argument that NAFTA would lead to more jobs have been disappointed to see the loss of jobs in their districts that have resulted from NAFTA. By the end of 1997, the US Labor Department had certified over 200,000 workers for retraining because their job losses were directly attributed to NAFTA.[26]

In an economy that has created 10 million new jobs since NAFTA, many feel this is trivial. Yet if a few thousand industrial jobs are lost in any given congressional district, the representative will probably have cause to notice. Nationwide, since NAFTA came into effect, while the economy has grown and overall jobs have increased, jobs in manufacturing have barely held their own.

Structural changes in the nature of jobs may prove at least as important as the total number of jobs. In 1970, 27% of all US jobs were in manufacturing. By 1998, this had dropped to less than 15%.[27] While some of this change is due to increased productivity, much is due to increased international trade. In absolute numbers, industrial employment in the United States peaked in 1979. Unions had forced a more equal distribution of income through raised industrial wages, but the decline in industrial jobs has reversed those gains.

Since Canada signed its Free Trade Agreement with the United States in 1989, its industrial sector has also declined sharply, and the gap between its rich and poor widened sharply. In 1989, its top 10% took home 50 times as much income as those in the bottom 10%. By 1996, the top 10% took home 314 times as much. At the same time workers' safety net shrank. In 1989, 87% of Canadian workers were covered by unemployment insurance. By 1997, only 37% qualified.[28]

In Mexico, the percent covered by unemployment insurance remained unchanged at zero. The good news in Mexico is that, since NAFTA came into effect, both productivity and jobs in manufacturing—mostly in maquiladoras—have risen steadily. Exports and export earnings also rose briskly, as hoped for by Mexican economists. The bad news is that wages for those workers fell just as rapidly as their productivity rose, and the national debt continued to increase. NAFTA has not served Mexican workers, nor has it met the goal of reducing Mexico's debt that was supposed to justify the workers' sacrifice. In all three countries, the productivity of industrial workers increased under NAFTA while their real wages fell. Workers in each country lost out.

Many Democrats voted for NAFTA because they believed strongly in the argument that more trade would be good for the country. Others had their doubts about that argument but were persuaded to support their president in 1993. Since that time the doubters have had their doubts confirmed, and some of the free-traders have either left the Congress or changed their minds. In September 1998, when the House of Representatives considered renewing the president's fast-track authority to negotiate more trade treaties, only 29 Democrats voted "aye." Democrats opposed to fast track were joined by 71 Republicans. Many of the Republicans were from districts in southern states that had lost jobs in the textile and garment industries. Still others simply didn't want to give President Clinton more authority of any kind. Together this coalition of the left and right out-numbered the free-traders 243 to 180.[29]

Those active in the defeat of fast track would like to be able to promote a positive alternative. Thea Lee, trade lobbyist for the AFL-CIO, would urge representatives to support fast-track authorization if it met two conditions: (1) that it require any negotiated trade treaty to have enforceable labor and environmental standards at it core, and (2) that it require consultation with Congress during the negotiations.[30] Both Lee and George Wilson, legislative assistant for trade matters for Marcy Kaptur (D-Ohio), agree that such a bill would not easily pass the House, as most Republicans opposed to fast track are also opposed to expanding workers' right to organize effective labor unions.[31]

It is precisely the establishment of such rights at an international level that is required to put a brake on the increasing inequality of income and power in the world, and to make it possible for the will of the majority to be respected. And the United States Congress is one of the few places in the world where a decision to establish those rights could have international influence. While any country could vote to trade only with other countries that respect labor rights, only the United States and the European Union have enough economic clout in world markets to make such a decision count. If either of these governments included labor rights as a prerequisite for trade, it could put global economic development on a very different path than the one it has been following for the past 20 years.

Prospects for such a policy advance are uncertain, but popular mobilization in Seattle forced President Clinton to call for just such a change in WTO policy. European trade ministers in Seattle refused to endorse Clinton's call for enforceable labor rights within the WTO, preferring to side with Third World officials who feared that protectionist use of such labor rights would hurt their economies. To the extent that Third World ministers represent governments with policies like Mexico's, we must realize that they probably do not speak for the interests of their working people. In February 2000, presidential candidate Al Gore quietly broke with Clinton, insisting that if he were president, he would include the labor rights that Clinton had left out of the November 1999 trade deal with China. While Gore did this to shore up labor's political support, he was silent during the congressional debate that led to approval of Clinton's pro-business deal.

Thea Lee says that removing workers' wages and rights from global competition would allow workers to reverse the downward spiral they've been in. If NAFTA had protected labor rights the way it protected investor rights, the FAT would have won its organizing campaign at GE, and GE would be paying higher wages and improving working conditions because it can easily afford to. The same would be true throughout Mexico. GE, Sony, Thomson, GM, Levi's, and hundreds of other highly profitable transnational corporations don't pay good wages now, simply because they don't have to.

What explains the difference in wages in Mexico, the United States, and Canada is no longer productivity; it is power. Workers in all three countries lost power to a globalizing capitalist class beginning in the mid-1970s.

Since at least 1919, when the International Labor Organization (ILO) was formed, workers have recognized problems arising from the competition among nations to sell their products. The ILO preamble noted that competition by undercutting a nation's workers might be "an obstacle in the way of other nations to improve the conditions in their own countries."[32] That is why the ILO has always maintained that there must be global minimum standards for the treatment of workers. Otherwise nations like Mexico must compete against nations like Guatemala and China to sell its goods and its workers cheaply to countries like the United States and Canada.

Thea Lee believes that if we could establish global labor rights we could start an upward spiral to a better global economy. We would have more unions that could assure that workers earned enough to support their families. With a better distribution of income, the world would have a larger middle class that could buy more goods and services. This would lead to more trade. But this would be a more reciprocal trade than we now have. "Now we buy and they sell," she says, "because we are too rich to make and they are too poor to buy. But this system is unsustainable." It is a system that is held together by repression in low-wage countries and trade deficits in high-wage countries. Who could hope to build a future on this basis?

Cananea and Cross-Border Solidarity

A strike at the Cananea copper mine from November 1998 to February 1999 provoked one of the finest examples of cross-border labor solidarity ever seen. But the strike ended in defeat for the miners—due to collusion between their union, their government, and the interests of multinational capital—and disillusionment for many of their supporters north of the border. A better understanding of cross-border solidarity can help turn that defeat and disillusionment into future victories for workers on both sides of the border.

Cananea is located in the Mexican border state of Sonora, just a two-hour drive from Tucson, Arizona. The mine was the site of a 1906 strike that, along with the strike at the Rio Blanco textile mill, became the Mexican equivalent of the revolutionary Battle of Concord and Lexington. The 1906 strikers were threatened by the Arizona Rangers and crushed by the Mexican Army of Porfirio Diaz, leaving a total of 21 dead miners and a broken union. The Revolution came just four years later.

In the early 1970s, the historic mine was nationalized in a flourish of nationalist and revolutionary rhetoric. Then in 1989, President Salinas sold the mine to a friend who was on his way to becoming one of Mexico's 11 billionaires. In preparation for the sale to Jorge Larrea and his Grupo Mexico, the government provoked a strike that it ended forcefully. Miners noted that Salinas was only the second president to send troops to Cananea. In 1999, President Zedillo would become the third.

Grupo Mexico is a huge conglomerate. In collaboration with Pennsylvania-based Union Pacific, it owns all the railroads of northwestern Mexico, and has fired half the workers since buying it from the government in 1997. With Cananea and its three other mines, Grupo Mexico controls over 90% of Mexico's copper. With its enormous Mexican profits Grupo has gone global. Now located in the United States for better access to Wall Street, it is the world's third-largest copper producer, fourth-largest silver producer, and fifth-largest zinc producer, with mines in the United States, Canada, and Peru, as well as Mexico. It is also planning to expand its transport holdings globally.[33]

When Larrea bought the Cananea mine in 1991, it employed 3,300 workers. Over the next six years, he cut the unionized workforce by 1,300, replacing many of the miners with indigenous peasants from southern Mexico, formally hired by two US contractors as "temporary" help. The 1998 strike was provoked by the announcement that Larrea would eliminate another 435 jobs, over 20% of the 2,000 union jobs remaining at the time. Included in those planned cutbacks were the workers who maintained the mine's tailings pond. If the pond were to start leaking, its toxic wastewater would soon contaminate the Sonora River, water source for much of the dry state of Sonora.

In January 1999, the government declared the strike illegal on a technicality. In mid-February, acting through the national miners' union—the same union that had broken the Spicer strike in 1975—the government forced the local union to accept the loss of nearly a thousand jobs. When workers heard the terms of the final settlement, many moved to occupy the mine. On February 15, judicial police rousted workers from some of the buildings. Manuel Romero, secretary-general of the miners' local, along with the town's mayor, also a former miner, walked through the mine begging remaining workers to leave before they would be shot by the 600 army troops camped on the outskirts of town. The strike was over.[34]

Local union officials soon closed ranks and tried to cover up or downplay their role in the defeat. In June 1999, when this writer first tried to contact two union members who had worked hard to arrange international support in Tucson, he was told curtly, "They don't work here anymore," and later, simply, "Voluntary retirement." A well-dressed official from the miners' national office firmly pointed out that, "The government supported us fully as always."

The union's leader, Manuel Romero, when asked if the new temporary workers in the mine who didn't even speak Spanish were being exploited, replied that they were not his concern. They were not in the union. When asked if he were free to act on his own would he not be concerned about losing nearly half of his union's jobs to workers getting less than half what his men had earned, his eyes flickered in recognition. Then he turned his head away. He was very grateful for the international support, he explained, but their strike had been illegal, and he had saved the source of employment. He did not mention that the labor board had asked him to choose between job losses and the end of the miners' contract. These miners had also preserved their own jobs within the official union bureaucracy.

Mariano Fragoso is the town of Cananea's top financial officer. He calls the town progressive because, "We want progress here." Full employment at the mine was around 3,000 workers, he explained; with only 1,000 miners now, the town needs to diversify. It is trying to attract investors to build maquilas. He says the town is full of well-trained, experienced workers. It's very tranquil, the small border crossing nearby has almost no waiting, and, he adds, it also offers incentives—a fine industrial park with all infrastructure provided. When asked about the difference between the miners' wage of $8-$16 a day and a maquila wage of $4, he seemed either naive or willfully ignorant. "Our workers are very skilled. Perhaps with competition the wages will rise."[35]

Francisco Mendez, who lost his mine job in the 1989 strike, seems somewhat more realistic about the town's future. "A maquila," he says, "needs a manager, a couple supervisors, a secretary, and one mechanic. The rest of the jobs pay nothing." He now makes his living selling roasted chicken in a small shop just down the street from Fragoso's office. Sales are slower since the strike. The minimum wage is 37 pesos a day, and he has to charge 50 for a chicken. As we talk, a man stops in to see if we would like to buy any knives. Francisco says that never used to happen, but without jobs people are looking for any way to stay alive. He is angry at the government for its handling of the strike, and for the economy in general. "Those government officials went to Harvard to become economists," he says in derision. "The real Mexican economist is the mother of three kids who tries to feed them with 30 pesos a day."[36]

When the strike first broke out in 1998 the miners' Local 65 sent a small delegation to Tucson to seek support that would allow them to endure a difficult strike. There they found refugees from the 1989 strike and from the 1978 strike at the Narcoseri Mine. They also found a man who had cousins working at the Cananea mine, Jerry Acosta, Arizona's director of mobilization for the AFL-CIO. Along with the tiny but effective American Friends Service Committee of Tucson, they began to assemble a support coalition. Donations of food, clothing, and money began pouring in.

In December Eduardo Quintana, a machinist active in the Southern Arizona Labor Council, took part in the first caravan of 15 cars and trucks to bring relief to the now hungry townspeople. Cheering miners led them into town, where streets were lined with "thousands of shouting and waving people, welcoming us with tears and smiles. We felt like war heroes. None of us will ever forget it."[37]

The outpouring of support continued with a rally in January bringing in another two tons of food. Environmentalists from Earth First!, the Sierra Club, and the Southwest Center for Biodiversity also joined the campaign, alarmed by environmental damages from the mine that had mounted over the years and now threatened to get worse. Nineteen different unions had people there, and checks came in from as far away as Alaska. At the rally Quintana explained: "No local can win a strike by itself anymore. It takes all of the labor movement and all the allies we can get."[38]

But Quintana was soon worried. On January 30 he attended a meeting in Hermosillo, the capital of Sonora, to coordinate Arizona's campaign with the solidarity being mobilized in Mexico. In addition to the miners Local 65, there were representatives from the railworkers' union who had recently lost a strike to Larrea, the UNT, the teachers' union, as well as the CTM. Would these unions reflect the interests of their local rank and file or their elitist national leaders? Tim Beaty, then representing the AFL-CIO's new office in Mexico City, was there and offered to mobilize a campaign that would put pressure on Grupo Mexico through its shareholders and financiers. He was rebuffed along with an activist who criticized holding the meeting of only 45 people in such a small place, rather than planning an event for 4,000, and a woman who suggested that the May First Coalition hold mass rallies in Hermosillo and Mexico City to build support. The meeting's chairperson said no, they would take their direction from the national leadership of the Miners union. At that point Quintana realized, "We are not all in this together."[39]

In mid-January, police broke into the Cananea homes of Rene Enriquez and Reynaldo Palomino, two of the three miners who had traveled to Tucson to rally support. They terrorized their families. This came after several days of death threats from state police and company guards. Then the food shipments, which previously had all been waved through by smiling Mexican border officials, were stopped. Officials now wanted to charge a steep duty. Eduardo Quintana, who led the last caravan recalls, "Manuel Romero, secretary-general of the miners' local, was there at the border. But he did nothing." Months later there was still $4,500 worth of food waiting at the border for the hungry town.[40]

Months after the strike, people in Tucson were still trying to sort out what they had learned. Ian Robinson, president of the Southern Arizona Central Labor Council, is a miner himself. He says, "On a personal level, it makes my heart bleed to see how Mexican workers are treated. On a professional level, we simply can't permit it. We need to find a way to bring Mexicans up to our level so we don't have to go down to theirs."[41]

Jimbo Watson, head of community services for the AFL-CIO in Tucson, helped coordinate the logistics of the food drive. He was amazed at the rights Mexican workers have during a strike to totally shut down a workplace until a strike is settled, a right workers lack in the United States. "The only problem with workers' rights in Mexico," he concludes, "is that the government administers those rights. We can offer lots of support, but until they change the way they govern their labor movement we are blocked."[42]

Miguel Guzman, who was an organizer for the Communications Workers of America at the time of the strike, seems to agree with Watson. "We can't get much accomplished from here," he said, "unless we work to change things in Mexico and try to influence the local union."[43] But he also thinks there is much to do in the United States. He feels there is a need to educate workers here on how they fit into the global economy. Without education, the passions of one movement die as it fades. The huge outpouring around the Cananea strike needs to be continued to address the issue of worker exploitation that unites us all.

Guzman gives the example of a meeting of the Tucson city council where two businessmen from Sonora asked for support to stimulate cross-border business connections. The council approved, saying it would be good for the economy. Moments later it was Guzman's turn to address the council. He asked them to set a policy against giving tax breaks to local corporations if they don't pay a decent wage and was told the council didn't get involved in private business. When one of his allies on the council suggested they provide a space for business and labor to come together to discuss their problems and joint concerns, the council again refused, saying even discussing the issue would set a bad precedent for attracting jobs. Guzman sees many similarities in how labor is treated on both sides of the border. And the problem is complicated in the Southwest, where he feels many Spanish-speaking citizens are used to accepting discrimination.

Ian Robinson is excited about the new program in Common Sense Economics that the AFL-CIO and the American Friends Service Committee are beginning to offer together in Tucson, based partly on the contacts with area churches that supported the mobilization around Cananea. They hope to educate 4,000 people by the end of the year 2000, and he hopes their *formación*—as the FAT would call it—will lead them each to commit themselves to mobilize around economic justice issues for four hours, two times a year. That would build a force of 400 people 20 times a year, he says with a strategic gleam in his eye. With that they could address a future strike at Cananea, force the city council to deal with a living-wage campaign, and work to end the discrimination against Mexican immigrants that hurts all workers in the area.[44] By February 2000 they had already reached several hundred people and found how to tailor their approach to different groups. Already new faces were beginning to show up on picket lines and at social justice meetings.[45]

Eduardo Quintana is also excited that there are now "unlimited opportunities for people who want to work for social justice in labor unions." With the arrival of young children in his family he was inactive for several years, but says coming back to a newly politicized labor movement "was like waking up from the Cold War ... which it was." When he imagines a union shop closing up in Arizona to exploit the unemployed miners of Cananea, he looks forward to working together with the people he has met there to see that they get a good contract. Reflecting on the Miners' union betrayal, he says the labor movement in Arizona is committed to continuing to work with Mexican workers, but he is now unsure who to trust. "It's hard to help people when you don't get the whole story." He wonders how to help workers when their national union is always prepared to sell them out.

Tim Beaty of the AFL-CIO's Mexico City office says he tried to help the miners, and he was frustrated at their defeat, but he continued to work closely with government-affiliated union leadership. He says the AFL-CIO is seeking to improve the lives of Mexican workers and that to do so they must build ties to workers throughout the country. "The fact is that the CTM and other big unions have contracts for most of the organized workers in the country." [46]While he admires groups like the FAT he feels it would be foolish for major US unions to have relations only with independent unions.

He was proud that the AFL-CIO and the CTM have signed a collaboration agreement that, among other things, calls for the end to protection contracts. He explains that the national CTM is opposed to protection contracts because most of them are set up not as craft or industry unions, but as company-specific unions. They are set up through lawyers friendly with local labor boards. The end result that upsets CTM leaders is that little or no dues ever get to the national level. By finding these supposedly shared concerns, he hopes they can work together to improve the lives of workers. He feels there are decent local unions within the CTM and the CROC and hopes these can be encouraged.

Gerry Barr of the United Steel Workers of Canada is in complete disagreement with Tim Beaty's strategy. He was not involved in the Cananea strike, but the Steel Workers Humanity Fund did channel support to workers at the Custom Trim plant near Matamoros when it was in open rebellion against its CTM leadership. (See chapter one.) The steelworkers continue to support Manuel Mondragon and the local independent organizing group in their efforts to help workers in spite of, rather than through, their local union leadership.

Barr likens the decision of the AFL-CIO to work with the CTM and other PRI-linked unions like the miners to the decision of the United States to maintain close relations with the government of China despite many apparent disagreements. The policy is justified by the theory of "constructive engagement," the belief that simply maintaining contact will eventually bring good results. But he is unable to think of anything positive that has come out of the CTM in recent years, and he knows of much harm. While he does agree with Beaty that there are some good local unions within the official unions, he finds they all work in an environment of profound impediments. "We have to decide what is most useful and what moves the workers' interests forward. To us that means building links with unions that are unimpeded. Our most effective links are with independent unions like those of the May First Coalition and the FAT."[47]

Independents certainly agree with Barr. Manuel Mondragon was shocked that the AFL-CIO had contracted with the CTM to provide data on workers in his state of Tamaulipas. He knows their tiny organization could do a lot with a bit of money from the AFL-CIO, and they would provide very different data.[48]

Independent labor organizers in Mexico all agree on the desirability of establishing international relationships, and all insist that the relationship be one of mutual respect. Many recall distasteful experiences of organizations arriving from the north with money and telling them how to operate. The long-standing FAT–UE Strategic Organizing Alliance operates by focusing on establishing mutual goals and then deciding how each union can help the other. But the understanding is clear that the FAT will make the decisions about what is done within Mexico, and the UE will decide what it does in the United States. That is the sort of relationship called for by organizations throughout Mexico.

One simple way that Mexican workers can help people from the United States and Canada is by educating them about the true nature of the corporations that operate in their own communities. There have also been very concrete examples of interventions by Mexican organizers in the United States. The FAT sent an organizer to help the Teamsters and the United Farm Workers in their effort to organize apple workers in Washington state. Earlier, the FAT helped the UE organize a largely Mexican workforce in Milwaukee. And in 1995, the Mexican telephone workers filed a complaint with the Mexican NAO when a subsidiary of Sprint Corporation fired 240 Spanish-speakers at its San Francisco office shortly before a union representation election.[49]

The Cananea strike raised questions of how or when it makes sense to work with members of Mexico's official unions. When the miners' union betrayed its members, Tucson attorney Jesus Romo Vejar chose to support one of the key Cananea activists, Martin Sanchez, by helping him apply for political asylum in the United States. Sanchez was one of the three miners in charge of mobilizing support from Arizona. But he went further than his two colleagues. He was one of the last to leave the mine when the troops threatened to drive them out. And he spoke out publicly against the settlement as "disastrous," "forced upon us," and a "betrayal."[50] Romo helped the miners with legal advice throughout the strike, and having encouraged some to push the limits, he stood by Sanchez when he could no longer return to his homeland.

The FAT–Teamster collaboration in Washington State raises complications for the policy of decisions being made by the "home" union. The FAT's organizer, Jorge Robles, a major proponent of autogestión, was disquieted by the Teamsters' more vertical style of decision-making. But while he disagreed about organizing strategy, the principles at the core of the FAT–UE Alliance dictated that in the country of the Teamsters, the Teamsters should decide. Yet in a campaign to organize Mexican workers within the United States the idea of borders becomes quite fuzzy. US laws apply, but the workers—raised in a culture of repression and fearful of deportation—were thinking in a context that Robles felt the US-born organizers could not fully appreciate.

Are the orchards and packing sheds of Washington State more within the purview of the United States or Mexico? For corporations, the reality of borders has been fading for decades. The same is now happening for workers.

Crossing Borders

Driving south from Bisbee, Arizona, one sees the border as an ugly black scar on the landscape. Almost before one can make out the small border town of Naco, one sees the dark line snaking its way across the barren hills. The 10-foot rusting black steel wall ends a mile or so out of town, in the desert. At several points on the Mexican side of the wall, in Naco and in most towns along the border, some new incarnation of Diego Rivera has painted a mural, holding up an icon of cultural pride or simply a moment of relief from the wall's ugly message: "We don't want you unless you have money. Stay out!"

As a response to anti-immigrant politics in the United States, the wall began going up shortly after the Berlin Wall was torn down. The wall does not stop illegal border crossings; it just makes it more likely that people will have to cross farther out of town, away from the roads, often in the desert, where they are prey to the heat of summer, the cold of winter, and criminals who rob, rape, or kill. The harsh climate and criminals thus become allies of the US Immigration and Nationalization Service, better known as the INS or *la migra*.

Since NAFTA and the peso crash of 1994 the flow of immigrants has increased. As the United States has built walls and beefed up its patrols, the number of arrests has remained fairly steady. For California they average 450,000 per year. But the number of those dying in the attempt to cross rose sharply when the walls went up. In California deaths rose from 21 in 1994 to 145 in 1998.[51] In 1997 alone, the United States spent $2.2 billion trying to stop the flow of Mexicans seeking jobs in the United States.[52]

Border controls slow the immigrant flow, but they do not stop it. The Mexican Electoral Commission estimates that there are 7 million adult Mexicans living in the United States. If they were allowed to vote in Mexican elections they would constitute nearly 14% of all voters.[53] The INS estimates that about half of those are in the United States illegally. The most widely repeated indicator of Mexican influence on US culture is the fact that salsa now out-sells catsup. What few people in the

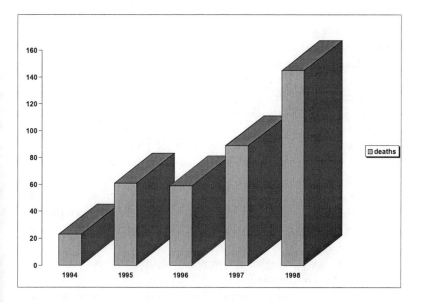

Figure 2: Confirmed deaths of California border crossers

Source: Centro de Apoyo al Migrante (CAM). 1998. Situación General de los Trabajadores Migratorios en la Frontera de California y Baja California, Study of Human Rights Abuses in Migrant Stream, chart 11. Tijuana, Baja California, Mexico: Partido de la Revolucion Democratica.

United States realize is that whether they put catsup or salsa on their meat, that meat was probably packed by a Mexican worker. And probably that worker, somewhere in Iowa or Nebraska, has no legal document to protect himself or herself from abuse on the job.

We know a fair amount about those who cross illegally. One study of nearly 700 Mexicans waiting to enter California found that 75% were male; 62% were between 18 and 35 years old; 80% had not entered high school; 90% said their reason for crossing was to find work; and 53% claimed they made less than $35 per month before they left home. Most were from quite rural states, with one of five being a farmer.[54]

Raul Ramirez of the Migrant Assistance Center of Tijuana helped coordinate the study. He says that both NAFTA's free trade in corn and the end of the ejidos are pushing people out of the countryside. With the lack of decent unions to defend urban workers, these young people with limited education face a series of unattractive options. They can enter the huge informal sector of the economy and join millions trying to sell something on the streets; commit robbery or join the drug trade; take a low-wage job in a maquiladora; join an armed uprising like the Zapatistas; or leave the country.[55]

Ramirez suggests that instead of spending billions of dollars on border control, the United States would be better served by investing some of that money in development projects in the Mexican states with the highest rate of "expulsion," as it is called in Mexico. On top of that the United States should encourage decent unions and be willing to pay prices based on decent wages. "Given a reasonable choice," he said, "most Mexicans would prefer to stay Mexicans." If the US government followed his suggestions, it would reduce the migrant flow, reduce the drug trade, create more markets for US goods, and reduce human misery. He finds his plan logical and wonders why it hasn't occurred to anyone in the US government.

The US government refused to even discuss the issue of human migration during the NAFTA talks. NAFTA allowed goods, agricultural produce, investment capital, technology, business executives, and business organizations to flow across borders, but it refused to allow workers or their organizations to join in the flow. But the flow goes on.

Emigration is vital to those who can't find acceptable alternatives within Mexico. It is also vitally important to the relatives they leave behind and to the Mexican economy as a whole. In 1998 the Bank of Mexico registered $6.4 billion in wire transfers from Mexicans in the United States to their relatives. That figure leaves out cash or transfers by minor wire services—an omission that could represent a third to half of the flow. Even this low estimate makes the exportation of workers the third-biggest source of foreign exchange for Mexico, just slightly behind tourism, which brings in $7.9 billion, and oil, which earns $7.2 billion.[56]

Thirty thousand people who live in El Paso, Texas, make their living as managers or technicians in Ciudad Juarez.[57] No one knows the size of the daily flow in the other direction since much of it is illegal. One of these workers, a woman who preferred to stay anonymous, lives in the shantytown of Anapra, just west of Juarez and less than 100 feet from the border. When we talked in 1997 the wall along that section of the border was still being built. One could walk around it easily, but doing so in bright daylight drew the attention of the Border Patrol just a hundred yards to the west. She crosses three or four times a week and walks into El Paso, where she does domestic work. "When the wall is finished," she assured me, "I will still find my way into town. I can't afford to work in a maquila."

On February 10, 1997, members of the Binational Indigenous Oaxacan Front held simultaneous demonstrations in the southern Mexican state of Oaxaca, in Tijuana, and in Fresno, California. They are a tightly organized community occupying what they now call Oaxacalifornia. As indigenous people they don't recognize the border or the governments that erect them as legitimate. They have brought their culture with them as they've moved north. In central California one can now attend Sunday competitions of the old Mixteca ball game. There is also a Mixteca farmworkers' organization that is negotiating with both strawberry growers and the largely Chicano United Farm Workers Union.[58]

The INS recently began its new "application in the interior" program. It has clamped down on meat packers as well as the apple industry in Washington state. Incredible as it may seem, a spokesperson for the American Meat Institute, which represents 400 packing companies, actually declared, "We feel victimized." When INS inspections scared off 500 Mexican apple packers, the state legislature voted 97 to 0 to condemn the policy. An apple grower reasoned:

> If the government promotes a policy that actually ends the practice of hiring undocumented workers, the agricultural industry will be in serious trouble. People don't want us to hire illegals, but at the same time they want to find cheap food in their stores.[59]

The global economy is erasing borders, but workers have long been encouraged to see workers of other nations as enemies. Seeing Mexican immigrants as "illegals" or as job threats or cultural invaders simply makes discrimination easier. But it is not the Mexican workers on either side of the border that pose a threat to US workers. The threat is from employers and policy makers of any country who seek ways to "reduce labor costs" while ignoring their impact on human lives.

At its annual meeting in February 2000, the AFL-CIO recognized this reality by reversing its previous policy and calling for a new amnesty program with full workplace rights and freedoms for all workers—immigrant and native-born, documented and undocumented.[60] They realize that if immigrants don't have rights, all workers in the country can be more easily exploited. National borders have lost their meaning. The conflict between classes has not.

The FAT has demonstrated what it means to work for the dignity of workers, for more justice and more democracy. From its birth it has been engaged in international solidarity. It has worked always in a climate of harsh opposition. The FAT is not a large organization but, due to its integrity and persistence, its influence in Mexico is far greater than its size. Gerry Barr of the Canadian Steelworkers says, "The FAT was really meant to be a giant redwood tree, but because it has been growing on the side of a cliff in a sub-arctic environment it is only ten inches high."

Its task at the moment is to maintain and expand its unions in the central part of the country, several of which are enduring long strikes, while organizing maquilas in the north, advancing the rights of Mexican women, expanding work in its other sectors, advancing two Mexican union alliances, making sense of the evolving but uncertain Mexican political context, strengthening the capacity of international workers in solidarity throughout the Americas, and educating workers in their legal and human right to live lives of dignity.

In a meeting in El Paso in the summer of 1999, Benedicto Martinez, the Mige Indian from a small peasant village who is one of the three national coordinators of the FAT, spoke to 15 unionists from three different countries. He summed up some accomplishments of the last two years. The UNT had been formed. "It is diverse, and it has some problems, but we hope it will be a real alternative." Ties between unions in Mexico, the United States, and Canada had grown and developed. The Echlin Alliance had become the Dana Alliance due to a corporate buyout and had grown larger. The cases filed with the NAO had made some progress, if not all they had desired. The People's Summit in Chile had been a chance to begin strengthening alliances throughout the Americas. These alliances would soon bear fruit in Seattle.

The system the FAT and its allies struggle against is morally unacceptable in the present, and economically unsustainable in the long run.

More and more activists across North America are realizing this. Every union struggle or worker training session in Mexico helps spread the consciousness needed to build a stronger, more democratic union movement there. And whenever unions from the United States or Canada are involved in those struggles, they come to better understand the true nature of the global economy.

Business leaders know how to compete, and competition has brought us enormous technological improvements and constructed a world communications infrastructure that allows us to find friends and allies around the world. But competition has also brought us the contradiction of a hugely expanded global food supply and increasing hunger. What business elites lack is the ethic of solidarity that is at the heart of the labor, human rights, and environmental movements. These movements have developed the ability to block some of the competitive corporate agenda. They must soon find ways to advance our common human needs on a global level. This book has detailed many victories of elites over workers, but it has also shown initial advances of workers both within Mexico and on a global level. This is not a book about defeats. It is a book about daring to make a difference.

In December 1999 the FAT began organizing workers who pump gas throughout Mexico City and who, despite the law, receive only tips, rather than wages, for their efforts. In January workers from several gas stations filed to create a new broadly defined union of service sector workers. The labor bureaucracy took no action on their petition until July 3, the day after the PRI's historic defeat. While the workers won legal recognition as a union, they face a difficult struggle to win contracts. Encouraged by the timing of this small victory, the FAT sees potential for organizing the unorganized in many parts of the capital's diverse service sector. The FAT senses a new feeling of hope and rebelliousness exhibited by workers they support—directly and indirectly—throughout the country. Their work will be strengthened, as always, by the alliances they form with other unions and NGOs both within Mexico and beyond. Their work will be in workplaces, in homes, in the streets, and in Mexico's hopeful but uncertain political process.

For four decades the FAT has taken on nearly impossible struggles, partly out of faith and partly out of the simple feeling that there is nothing else people with self-respect can do. Their faith in and devotion

to the struggle have been strengthened each time they meet other workers equally committed to what they mean by justice and democracy. In
his travels throughout North America, Benedicto Martinez now often
acclaims the power of this solidarity: "The best thing we have gotten out
of NAFTA is the alliances of workers in our three countries. The best
thing is that we have found each other."

Daring to Make a Difference

Workers have been finding each other and discovering their common interests both within countries and across borders. For decades the
FAT has encouraged workers to believe that they could bring an end to
the oppressive labor system run by the PRI and its charros. It seems now
that they may have been right. Yet they are clear that they now confront
a global system of oppression that requires them to find allies across borders. By daring to kindle RMALC, they have helped to spark a new
wave of labor solidarity that is just beginning to sweep throughout the
Americas. Daring to make a difference, workers, students, environmentalists, and all who converged on Seattle made the first real stand against
global governance of, by, and for the corporations. Daring to make a difference, the brown-clad workers of UPS pulled off a militant na-
tion-wide strike that succeeded, in large part, because it inspired feelings
of respect and support from people throughout the United States. That
strike in turn, inspired other workers to stand up and win as well in the
years that have followed.

The FAT refused to work with the PRI, even when it appeared to be
the only game in town. In the summer of 2000, both the UAW and the
Teamsters held out for months before joining the rest of the AFL-CIO in
backing the Democratic party's presidential candidate, supposedly labor's only choice even though he had opposed many of their top policy
priorities. Bucking the trend of labor's traditional allegiance to the Democrats, the FAT's ally, the United Electrical Workers joined the California Nurses Association and one brave AFSCME local, number 1108, in
endorsing Ralph Nader, the Green Party's candidate for president. They
are aware that political change may be even harder in the United States
than it has been in Mexico (where at least it's easier for new parties to
gains seats in the legislature), but they declared, "the wasted vote in this

election would be for the pro-business Democrats and Republicans." Instead they endorsed a candidate they felt would "bring us closer to real labor law reform, national health care and a challenge to—if not controls on—the power of multinational corporations."[61] This political endorsement may seem like empty symbolism, but opposition to the PRI also used to seem hopeless. Creation of the FAT and RMALC must have seemed futile to most observers at the time. What the FAT has always believed is that what is futile is to support a system that is sapping one's lifeblood.

Workers have often been separated by international borders. That is beginning to change. Yet some of the greatest borders are those constructed within our minds, borders that make an undesirable present seem the only possible model for the future. The FAT's work of *formación* has always confronted those borders by nurturing a worker's belief that they deserve justice and democracy in their lifetime. The FAT has reached across borders to find new allies out of both necessity and hope. Its history, and the new history of international labor that is just beginning, show that those who dare to make a difference can make all the difference.

Notes

1   Robinson, Ian. 1999. Telephone interview. Tucson, Arizona.
2   Communigue from the EZLN to Asma Jahangir, UN Special Releator for Extrajudicial, Summary and Arbitrary Executions, "From the mountains of the Mexican southeast," translation by Irlandesa.
3   George Mason as cited in Wright, Eric. 1976. "Revolution and the Constitution: Models of What and for Whom?" *American Academy of Political and Social Science Annual*, 428 (November):1–21. Jeremy Belknap and John Jay, as cited in Greenberg, Edward. 1986. *The American Political System: A Radical Approach,* 56–57. Boston: Little, Brown.
4   Orwell, George. 1968. "Politics and the English Language." In *The Collected Essays, Journalism, and Letters of George Orwell*. Harcourt, Brace, Jovanovich.
5   O'Malley, Chris. 1997. "Set on Mexico." *Indianapolis Star* (March): A1, 6–7.

6   Council of Economic Advisors. 1999. *Economic Report of the President*, B-29. Washington, DC: GPO.

7   US Census Bureau. 1999. "Historical Income Tables - Households," data table, http://www.census.gov/hhes/income/histinc/ho4.html.

8   Boltvinik, Julio. 1997. "Los Ciudadanos Dijeron No." *La Jornada* (July 18): 16.

9   Gonzalez Amador, Roberto. 2000. "Pobres extremos, 28% de Mexicanos; el mayor numero en tres lustros." *La Jornada* (February 13).

10   Wilkinson, Richard G. 1996. *Unhealthy Societies: The Afflictions of Inequality*. New York: Routledge.

11   Velasco, Elizabeth. 1999. "Se Requebraja la CTM por Pugnas Internas y Falta de Liderazgo de Rodriguez Alcaine." *La Jornada* (July 26).

12   Ramirez de Aguilar, Fernando. 1999. "Madrazo, 'Ciudadano de Clase Media.' " *El Financiero* (June 27): 4.

13   Velasco, Elizabeth C. 2000. "Lideres sindicales presentarán hoy a Fox propuestas en materia laboral." *La Jornada* (August 1).

14   Mexican Labor News and Analysis. 2000. 5:5 (August).

15   Fabiola Martinez. 2000. "Integrantes de la UNT, a huelga solidaria con obreros de la VW." *La Jornada*. (August 31).

16   Martínez Aznárez, César. 1999. "Citigroup Augura Éxito a la Alianza si se Presenta Como Opción de Centro." *La Jornada* (August 4), http://unam.netgate.net/jornada.

17   Cohen, Roger. 1999. "German Laborers Challenge Social Democrats' Right Turn." *New York Times* (August 2), www.nytimes.com.

18   International Confederation of Free Trade Unions (ICFTU). July 12–14, 1999. "Internationally Recognised Core Labour Standards In The United States," http://www.icftu.org/english/els/escl99wtousa.html.

19   Bronfenbrenner, Kate. 1997. "We'll Close! Plant Closing Threats, Union Organizing, and NAFTA." *Multinational Monitor* (March), http://www.essential.org/monitor/hyper/mm0397.04.html.

20   Cason, Jim, and David Brooks. 1999. "Podrían Perder Sus Empleos en EU Unos 4 Mil 700 Inmigrantes." *La Jornada* (April 24).

21   Damgaard, Bodil. 1998. "Cinco Años con el Acuerdo Laboral Paralelo." Paper presented at the XXI Congreso Internacional de la Latin American Studies Association, 2, Chicago, Illinois.

22   U.S. National Administrative Office. 1999. *Status of Submissions*, http://www2.dol.gov/dol/ilab/public/programs/nao/status.html.

23   Consultations have been held regarding the cases of Sony in Nuevo Laredo, Han Young in Tijuana, and Itapsa in the state of Mexico (US NAO 940003).

24 U.S. National Administrative Office.

25 Union de Defensa Laboral Comunitaria. 2000. "Maquila Workers Attacked at Forum on Freedom to Organize." E-mail correspondence from June 24.

26 Anderson, Sarah. 1999. "Five Years Under NAFTA." Paper presented at the Annual Meeting Coalition for Justice in the Maquiladoras, Institute for Policy Studies, Ciudad Juarez, México.

27 Council of Economic Advisors. 1999. *Economic Report of the President*, B-46. Washington DC: GPO.

28 Anderson.

29 "Issue: Fast-Track Authority." 1998. *CQ Weekly* (November 14): 3130–31.

30 Lee, Thea. 1999. Telephone interview, AFL-CIO, Washington, DC, June 28.

31 Wilson, George. 1999. Telephone interview, June 28. House of Representatives; Lee interview.

32 International Labor Organization. 1999. *Humane Conditions of Labor*, http://www.ilo.org/public/english/50normes/whyneed/lbrcomp.htm.

33 "Grupo Mexico S.A. De C.V. Will Adapt Its Corporate Structure for the Globalization of Its Operations." *Business Wire* (July 25, 2000).

34 Bacon, David. 1999. "Miners' Strike Broken in Revolutionary Cananea." *Mexican Labor News and Analysis* (March 16); Rubio Landers, Antonio. 1999. Oral interview. Cananea, Sonora, June 24.

35 Fragoso Rodriguez, Mariano. 1999. Oral interview. Cananea, Sonora, June 24.

36 Mendez, Francisco. 1999. Oral interview. Cananea, Sonora, June 24.

37 Quintana, Eduardo. 1999. Oral interview. Tucson, Arizona, June 23.

38 Shriver, George. 1999. "Arizona Labor Holds Rally and Food Drive for Striking Miners in Cananea Mexico." *Mexico Labor News and Analysis*, (February 2): part II.

39 Quintana interview.

40 Quintana interview.

41 Robinson interview.

42 Watson, James (Jimbo). 1999. Oral interview. Tucson, Arizona, June 22.

43 Guzman, Miguel. 1999. Telephone interview, Tucson, Arizona, June 23.

44 Robinson interview.

45 Paula Arnquist. 2000. Telephone interview. Tucson Arizona (February 25). For more information on "Common Sense Economics," go to http://www.aflcio.org/front/cse.htm

46 Beaty Tim. 1999. Oral interview, Ciudad Juarez, Chihuahua, June 19.

47 Barr, Gerry. 1999. Telephone interview, Steelworkers headquaters, Toronto, Ontario, July 16.

48 Martinez Aznárez interview.

49 U.S. National Administrative Office. 1999. *Status of Submissions*, http://www2.dol.gov/dol/ilab/public/programs/nao/status.html.

50 Vanderwood, Tim, and Darrin Mortenson. 1999. "Cheap Labor…Cheap Lives: What Big Business Has Been Doing in the Mexican Mining Town of Cananea." *Tucson (AZ) Weekly* (April 8): http://www.tucsonweekly. com/tw/04-08-99/feat.htm.

51 Centro de Apoyo al Migrante (CAM). 1998. *Situación General de los Trabajadores Migratorios en la Frontera de California y Baja California*, Study of Human Rights Abuses in Migrant Stream, g11, g13. Tijuana, Baja California, Mexico: Partido de la Revolucion Democratica.

52 Anderson.

53 Associated Press. 1999. "Breakdown of Mexican Living in US." *New York Times* (May 22).

54 Centro de Apoyo al Migrante.

55 Ramirez, Raul. 1999. Oral interview, Centro de Apoyo al Migrante, Tijuana, Baja California.

56 Cano, Araceli. 1999. "Creciente, la Transferencia de Dinero de EU a México." *El Financiero* (June 30): 25.

57 La Franchi, Howard. 1999. "Making a Hole in the Mexican Border." *Christian Science Monitor* (June 9): 6.

58 Rivera-Salgado, Gaspar. 1999. "Mixtec Activism in Oaxacalifornia." *American Behavioral Scientist* (June–July): 1439–59.

59 Cason and Brooks.

60 AFL-CIO. 2000. "Union Leaders Stand With Immigrants Workers." (February 17): http://www.aflcio.org/publ/estatements/feb2000/ec_immigr.htm.

61 "United Electrical Workers Vote to Endorse Ralph Nader" (August 30, 2000).

Index

N

About the Author

Dale Hathaway is Associate Professor of Political Science at Butler University in Indianapolis. A former Teamster and Boilermaker, he is the author of *Can Workers Have a Voice: The Politics of Deindustrialization in Pittsburgh* and the co-author, with Ignacio Medina, of *El Sindicalismo Mexicano al Fin del Siglo XX.* In his activist life, Hathaway is Chair of Our Party, a local electoral party formed to inject progressive ideas into politics in Indianapolis. Hathaway is also a trained mediator, having worked with juvenile courts and adult conflicts in the community, and is the former President of the Indianapolis Peace and Justice Center.

About South End Press

South End Press is a nonprofit, collectively run publisher with over 200 titles in print. Since its founding in 1977, South End Press has tried to meet the needs of readers who are exploring, or are already committed to, the politics of radical social change. Our goal is to publish books that encourage critical thinking and constructive action on the key political, cultural, social, economic, and ecological issues shaping life in the United States and in the world. In this way, we hope to give expression to a wide diversity of democratic social movements and to provide an alternative to the products of corporate publishing.

Through the Institute for Social and Cultural Change, South End Press works with other political media projects—*Z Magazine*; Speakout, a speakers' bureau; and Alternative Radio—to expand access to information and critical analysis. For current and updated information on our books, please visit our website, at www.southendpress.org

Related South End Press Titles

Powers and Prospects:
Reflections on Human Nature and the Social Order
by Noam Chomsky $16

Year 501: The Conquest Continues
by Noam Chomsky $19
Also available in Spanish as *Año 501* $18

Necessary Illusions: Thought Control in Democratic Societies
by Noam Chomsky $20

Chaos or Community?:
Seeking Solutions, Not Scapegoats for Bad Economics
by Holly Sklar $15

Triumph of the Market: Essays on Economics, Politics, and the Media
by Edward Herman $16

Women in the Global Factory
by Annette Fuentes and Barbara Ehrenreich $6

War at Home:
Covert Action against U.S. Activists and What We Can Do About It
by Brian Glick $5

Freedom Under Fire: U.S. Civil Liberties in Times of War
by Michael Linfield $14

Break-ins, Death Threats, and the FBI:
The Covert War Against the Central America Movement
by Ross Gelbspan $14

Write to South End Press, 7 Brookline Street, Cambridge, MA 02139 for a free catalog or visit our web site, http://www.southendpress.org. To order by credit card, call 1-800-533-8478. Please include $3.50 for postage and handling for the first book and 50 cents for each additional book.